TAKE TEN II

TAKE TEN II

MORE TEN-MINUTE PLAYS

EDITED BY *Eric Lane*
AND *Nina Shengold*

VINTAGE BOOKS

A DIVISION OF RANDOM HOUSE, INC.   NEW YORK

A VINTAGE ORIGINAL, NOVEMBER 2003

Library of Congress Cataloging-in-Publication Data
    Take ten II : more ten-minute plays / edited by Eric Lane and Nina
Shengold.
        p. cm.
    Includes index.
    ISBN 1-4000-3217-2 (trade paper)
        1. One-act plays, American.   I. Title: Take ten two.   II. Lane,
Eric.   III. Shengold, Nina.
    PS627.O53T353 2003
    812'.04108—dc21
    2003052542

Book design by Mia Risberg

www.vintagebooks.com

Printed in the United States of America
10   9   8   7   6   5   4

CONTENTS

INTRODUCTION

A ten-minute play is a jolt of theatrical energy. It can move you to tears, shock you to the marrow, or send you into uncontrollable spasms of laughter.

It's just over twenty-five years since the Actors Theatre of Louisville announced its first Ten-Minute Play Contest. In its second generation, the ten-minute play has evolved from a novelty item—often derided as "short-attention-span theatre," "theatrical sound bites," and the like—to a vital new force in American theatre.

Why ten-minute plays?

Theatres love them. A ten-minute play festival is a great way to forge relationships with many playwrights at once, to cast actors in new combinations, and last but not least, to attract a huge audience. It introduces theatregoers to fascinating stories, diverse worlds, and exciting theatrical voices, in record time.

Actors love them. An evening of ten-minute plays is often cross-cast, giving each actor a smorgasbord of juicy roles (and a welcome relief from typecasting). Ten-minute plays are marvelously portable, at home on stages, in cabaret spaces, cafes, student unions, and classrooms. Since they tell complete stories with richly detailed characters, they're perfect for scene work and showcases.

Playwrights love them. While writing a full-length play is a feat of endurance, akin to climbing a small Himalaya, a ten-minute play is a breathless, exuberant sprint. The form's very compactness allows writers the freedom to try things they might not take on in a longer work. It's hard to think of a major contemporary playwright who hasn't assayed the ten-minute play form. In this

book you'll find brilliant short plays by award-winning dramatists Warren Leight, Donald Margulies, and Dael Orlandersmith,
comic treasures by Laura Shaine Cunningham, Christopher
Durang, David Ives, and Mark O'Donnell, and dozens of equally
wonderful scripts by both established and emerging playwrights.
Many are published here for the first time.

The plays in this book premiered all over the country: Minneapolis, Louisville, Phoenix, Los Angeles, New York City, and
more, with voices that reach out to Ireland, the Middle East—
even (in Susan Miller's astounding *The Grand Design*) outer space.
They are comedies and dramas, monologues, two-handers, and
ensemble pieces, with a fresh diversity of voices that speaks to a
new multiculturalism in the American theatre.

You'll find roles here for Asian Americans (*Antigone's Red,
Table 5 at Empire Szechwan*), Latinos (*El Santo Americano, Virginia
Street*), Middle Easterners (*The Sniper*), African Americans and
Native Americans (*Classyass; My Red Hand, My Black Hand*).
Some plays, like *The Grand Design* and Craig Pospisil's *It's Not You*,
specifically encourage multiethnic casting. Others, like Warren
Leight's *Nine Ten* and Diana Son's *The Moon Please* take this so
much for granted that their characters use such phrases as "racial
profiling" and "woman of color" without indicating *what* race
or color they might be. There are plum roles for teenagers (*Rosie
in the Shadow of the Melrose, Men's Intuition, A Whole House Full of
Babies*) and seniors (*Deer Play, The Find*) and everyone in between.
There are plays about gay men and lesbians, Mexican wrestlers,
Appalachian midwives, Oscar winners, and seductive French cats.

There seems to be nothing beyond the range of the ten-minute
play. In swift, bold strokes, playwrights grapple with issues ripped
from the headlines, spin wild comic riffs, and create wondrous
myths with the logic of dreams. As editors of two anthologies of
ten-minute plays, and participants in several annual ten-minute
play festivals, we have read or seen over a thousand of these
remarkable works. Like snowflakes, no two are alike. The best
are like snowflakes in other respects: crystalline and astonishing,
miniature worlds.

The thirty-five plays in this book are gems. Whether you're a theatre professional looking for scripts to produce, an acting student who needs a new project, a writer in search of inspiring new voices, or a reader who wants a crash course in the depth and diversity of the American theatre, you'll find it between these two covers. Enjoy!

NINA SHENGOLD AND ERIC LANE
March 2003

ACKNOWLEDGMENTS

Many individuals generously contributed to the creation of this book. We'd like to thank the literary managers, agents, and publishers who helped us find such a wealth of material and secure the rights for this collection. In particular, we'd like to acknowledge Toni Amicarella at New York Theatre Workshop, Elizabeth Bennet at Manhattan Theatre Club, Pam Berlin at HB Playwrights Unit, Bill Craver and Chris Till at Writers & Artists, Gloria Falzer at Turnip Theatre, Sarah Jane Leigh and Kent Eiler at I.C.M., Bruce Ostler and Melissa Hardy at Bret Adams, Ltd., Tom Rowan at Ensemble Studio Theatre, Steve Supeck at Helen Merrill, Ltd., Jean Wagner at Voice & Vision, Stephen Willems at MCC Theater, Samantha K. Wyer at Arizona Theatre Company, and the folks at New Dramatists. Many thanks to Sarah Bisman and Warren Leight for their gracious help with the cover photo.

Grateful thanks also to Steven Corsano, Tina Howe, José Rivera, David Robinson, Paula Vogel, Shelley Wyant, Maya Shengold, and Werner Schnackenburger. And the Corporation of Yaddo, where work on this book began.

The number of theatres around the country producing annual ten-minute play festivals continues to grow. We'd especially like to thank Actors & Writers, as well as Tanya Palmer and Amy Wegener at Actors Theatre of Louisville—both theatres have been constant sources of material for our collections. And the Berrilla Kerr Foundation, which has generously supported so many of the playwrights in this collection.

Our sincere gratitude to Michael Bigelow Dixon at the Guthrie Theater and John McCormack at All Seasons Theatre Group and the Zipper Theatre—we truly appreciate their vast knowledge and continued generosity. Both Michael and John have brought to our attention countless terrific new playwrights and plays.

Many thanks to Phyllis Lane, whose love, support, and mandel bread are truly missed.

As always, we'd like to thank our agents, Phyllis Wender and Susie Cohen, whose invaluable guidance made this collection possible. Also our wonderful editor at Vintage Books, Diana Secker Larson, for all her support and the opportunity to publish this book. And most of all, to the playwrights who sent us their amazing scripts—many more than we could include in this book—and to the actors and directors who bring their work to life.

TAKE TEN II

ANTIGONE'S RED

Chiori Miyagawa

CHARACTERS

ANTIGONE: Japanese American woman in her early thirties.
ISMENE: Antigone's younger sister.
TADASHI: Japanese American man in his early thirties.
BRIAN: Caucasian man, Ismene's husband.
GUARD: Caucasian man.

TIME: 1942.

PLACE: Manzanar, California.

PROLOGUE

ANTIGONE: With my bare hands I dug the dry earth and covered my lover's corpse with dirt and tears. The desert land is cruel to those who want to bury loved ones. My nails ripped from my fingers. I made an offering of my blood. Antigone's lover's grave is red. That was my last red.

(ANTIGONE *takes a long red ribbon out of her pocket. She holds the ribbon up vertically, and with a pair of scissors, cuts the ribbon in half. The bottom half falls to the floor. Lights down.*)

SCENE 1

(*Manzanar, California. One of the sites of the relocation camps for Japanese Americans during World War II. 1942.*)

ANTIGONE: Manzanar, California. The dust storms consume our days. We breathe and eat the sand which fills our lungs, leaving a gritty, bitter taste on our tongue. The air is murky coarse white. Ten thousand Japanese and Japanese Americans are here, imprisoned in the barracks at the foot of the magnificent Sierra Nevada Mountains. In the middle of the ground stands a tall pole with a large American flag violently fluttering in the wind. We were allowed to bring what we could carry of beddings, linens, clothes, and eating utensils. We had forty-eight hours to pack. Forty-eight hours to leave our lives behind. I left my dog with the neighbor who looked at me

with blue eyes full of tears and said that she would keep my
dog until I return. I said no, he is yours now. I had a piano at
home. I made the last payment on it two weeks ago. It took
me five years to pay for it. Well. Anyway.

(*Lights change.*)

SCENE 2

(ANTIGONE *is sitting outside the barracks with* TADASHI.)

TADASHI: I'm going to answer no/no to the loyalty oath questions.

ANTIGONE: What will happen?

TADASHI: I don't know. I may get deported.

ANTIGONE: But you were born here. On this land. You've never
been anyone other than who you are.

TADASHI: My father was a Japanese veteran, so he was one of the
first people arrested after Pearl Harbor. He had been a gardener for twenty years. He was distraught to leave my mother
and sister. I heard he tried to commit suicide by biting off his
own tongue while being transported. I received a telegram
today that he was shot to death in the Enemy Alien Intern-
ment Camp in Oklahoma. I am no longer who I was once.
(*Pause.*) I will not go to war to fight for this country from a
prison camp. I will not swear allegiance to the country that
robbed and humiliated my family. I have to answer no to both
questions, even if it means that you and I will not be together.

ANTIGONE: But why allow them to take away your future? If you
get stripped of your citizenship for two checkmarks on no and
deported to Japan, how will you survive? You don't speak the
language. You've never even been to Japan.

TADASHI: They've taken away my past. My life up until the
moment of reading the evacuation order was a lie. Thirty

years of my life was an illusion. You can't build a future on illusion.

ANTIGONE: They want us to give up. They want to crush us and make us surrender the life we are entitled to. We have to fight them.

TADASHI: I'm not giving up. I'm refusing to compromise the fundamental nature of my being—What I will lose is nothing; it's tarnished forever. Antigone, what we must fight for is the courage to believe in what is right, not what is possible. (*Pause.*) If something happens to me, would you try to find my mother and sister? I think they are in the camp in Heart Mountain.

ANTIGONE: What shall I say to them?

TADASHI: You'll know then. That part of my history is not written yet. You will tell them either that you are the last person I loved in this country, or the last person I loved in this life. (*Pause.*)

ANTIGONE: It's suppertime. I have to report to the mess hall duty.

TADASHI: Stay for five more minutes.

ANTIGONE: I can't. The tension there is already high because of the rumor that the guards have been stealing meat and sugar from the kitchen. And we found out while we work for eighteen dollars a month, the white commuting workers get paid fifty dollars a week. We're planning a walkout.

TADASHI: Listen, Antigone, be careful. Stay away from all that. There have been shootings of inmates in different camps. The guards are murdering people claiming that they tried to escape. But all the bodies have been found inside the fences, shot in the front. They were not running away. They were all facing the guards.

ANTIGONE: You just told me to act on what is right. The only thing I can do is to fight small, insignificant injustices, since

I'm unable to fight the big crime, the betrayal of our dreams and violation of our beings.

TADASHI: Stay for five more minutes.

ANTIGONE: Nothing will happen to me. Don't worry. Our time together isn't over yet.

TADASHI: Just stay and hold my hand.

ANTIGONE: Later. I'll hold your hand later, my love.

(ANTIGONE *exits.* TADASHI *is left alone.*)

SCENE 3

(*The same evening. Late night.* ANTIGONE *is asleep. Her sister* ISMENE *comes in quietly and approaches* ANTIGONE.)

ISMENE: Antigone, wake up.

ANTIGONE: What?

ISMENE: Are you awake?

ANTIGONE: Did something happen to my lover?

ISMENE: Oh, my sister. I'm so sorry.

ANTIGONE: Stop crying, Ismene. Is he dead?

ISMENE: Yes.

ANTIGONE: (*desperate and angry*) How can I live then? What is life for?

(*Lights change. Back to the beginning of the moment.*)

ISMENE: Antigone, wake up.

ANTIGONE: What?

ISMENE: Are you awake?

ANTIGONE: Did something happen to my lover?

ISMENE: Oh, my sister. I'm so sorry.

ANTIGONE: Stop crying, Ismene. Is he dead?

ISMENE: Yes.

ANTIGONE: (*hysterical*) No, it can't be! Not yet, not yet! I didn't say good-bye to him! I didn't stay and hold his hand!

(*Lights change. Back to the beginning of the moment.*)

ISMENE: Antigone, wake up.

ANTIGONE: What?

ISMENE: Are you awake?

ANTIGONE: Did something happen to my lover?

ISMENE: Oh, my sister. I'm so sorry.

ANTIGONE: Stop crying, Ismene. Is he dead?

ISMENE: Yes.

ANTIGONE: (*calmly*) Then he is free.

(*Lights down.*)

SCENE 4

(*Lights up immediately on* ANTIGONE *and* ISMENE *in the exact same positions, but it is two days later.*)

ANTIGONE: Tadashi's body has been exposed for forty-eight hours now. An order forbids a burial for him. His corpse is to be left out in the middle of the camp for the dust storm to swirl around until it is rotten to the core of his disappointment.

ISMENE: Oh, my sister, I'm so sorry.

ANTIGONE: Stop crying Ismene. I'm going out there to bury him. Will you help me?

ISMENE: That is insane. We will be killed for it.

ANTIGONE: Tadashi exposed the meat and sugar scandal and orga-
nized last night's demonstration with twelve men who were
willing to die in order to gain justice. He never even told me
about his plans. After the tear gas bombs were thrown at the
demonstrators, they stormed the guards. The guards opened
fire. Tadashi was at the front. (*Pause.*) If not for the sacrifice he
made, we still owe him a burial for being a human being and
having lived among us.

ISMENE: We will be killed for it.

ANTIGONE: Possibly.

ISMENE: I have a husband. I want to have children.

ANTIGONE: If we don't bury him, then we are allowing them to
disgrace a soul, to condemn it to wander eternally. We are
allowing them to commit even a greater crime than our
imprisonment, our deaths.

ISMENE: Antigone, there are certain things that are beyond our
power to correct. We had no choice but to give up everything that our parents worked so hard to make possible—
our houses, our cars, our jobs, our rights, our dignity. All we
can do now is to hold onto the little that is under our power
to preserve. Identity. Survival. I want a future.

ANTIGONE: What does your future look like, Ismene? Like an
American dream? Like "give me your tired, your poor, your
huddled masses yearning to breathe free"?

ISMENE: I will not be victimized anymore. If it means that I'd be
accepted, I would cut off my flesh, go along with the system, and lose my name. I want to live.

ANTIGONE: I understand. It's not fair to ask you to give up what's
left of your life to allow my lover a noble entrance to the
next life. He had no family, so it's my responsibility.

ISMENE: I know you loved Tadashi and that he was brave. But you must let his body disintegrate out there. You cannot fight them. We are too small. Please promise me . . .

ANTIGONE: Don't ask me that. I will hate you for it.

ISMENE: Antigone, you are crazy. You will not survive this.

ANTIGONE: And you will?

ISMENE: Don't worry about my soul.

ANTIGONE: Report my crime to the guards. Take the opportunity. Oppress someone, Ismene, if you want to move up.

ISMENE: You're my sister.

ANTIGONE: I hate you.

SCENE 5

(*In* ISMENE's *room. Spare. A bed and a window.* ISMENE *sits with her husband,* BRIAN. *Her back is erect; she is listening intently for sounds outside.*)

BRIAN: You have been awfully quiet. What are you thinking?

ISMENE: Do you feel the pressure in the air? It's so heavy. Condensed. I can't breathe.

BRIAN: It's a strange night.

ISMENE: There will be a riot.

BRIAN: Just don't go outside. Stay in the room.

ISMENE: Antigone is out there.

BRIAN: She'll run straight into her own doom.

ISMENE: She is my sister.

BRIAN: Unfortunately.

ISMENE: What do you know about it?

BRIAN: You know she is dangerous. Stay out of her way, Ismene. Your sympathy for her will harm you in the end.

ISMENE: You don't know what you're talking about. You don't know anything about her.

BRIAN: If you go out there tonight and join her, I will leave tomorrow and never visit you again.

ISMENE: That's a toss-up.

BRIAN: I know you are upset. These are not normal times. You'll be all right once the war is over. You can come back and live with me, and no one will harm you.

ISMENE: Because you, my husband, my knight, are white.

BRIAN: Do you think I enjoy visiting my wife in a little room that you share with two other families separated by hanging sheets? Fair or not, this is not my fate. This is yours. I'm willing to share it because I love you.

ISMENE: Thank you.

BRIAN: I'm really sorry this is happening, but I'm not the enemy.

ISMENE: Who is the enemy?

BRIAN: The war.

ISMENE: Oh, I thought I was in this predicament because of the Civilian Exclusion Order 33 that stripped my constitutional rights and made it possible to detain me indefinitely against my will, without charge, without representation, in a bleak condition in this dump. I guess I was wrong. The war is the enemy.

BRIAN: They had to do something.

ISMENE: They?

BRIAN: There are close to one hundred thousand aliens and non-aliens who could possibly threaten the safety of the country. My heart is torn. I hate my country for what it has done to you. But the second attack must be prevented.

ISMENE: What's a non-alien?

BRIAN: You are, Ismene. You're not an alien. You are my wife.

ISMENE: Brian, who else is non-alien? Citizens! It means citizen if your last name is not Japanese. I am a citizen because I was born in this country. Not because I married you.

BRIAN: Ismene, I'm sorry for all the injustices of the world. I'd fix them for you if I could.

ISMENE: But you can't, can you?

BRIAN: What do you want me to do?

ISMENE: Be brave.

BRIAN: How can I show you my bravery other than by continuing to love you? Life is about the happiness that you and I will find when this is all over. You'll come home and we'll have children and forget about these difficult times. We'll go back to our life and try to live it the best we can. That's my bravery.

ISMENE: That's not good enough anymore. (*Pause.*) I'm going out there.

BRIAN: I'm warning you.

ISMENE: What are you warning me? That you will leave and take your white privilege with you?

BRIAN: What have I done to you?

ISMENE: You pampered, arrogant man. You have done exactly nothing, yet you expect everything. You did nothing to prevent my demise, but you expect me to recover and serve your concept of happiness. Nothing will ever be the same. Don't you understand that? I have been disgraced and deprived. We cannot go back to the life we had before I was broken.

BRIAN: Ismene, I can't believe you really think that. That is something Antigone might say. Don't let her poison you. Please. I can't imagine a life without you.

ISMENE: Brian, try this. When you walk out of here, see if you can take me with you. See if your wife wouldn't be ordered to stop at gunpoint. (*Pause.*) Antigone is out there. Fearless. Stupid. The color of her blood is the same as mine.

(ISMENE *exits.* BRIAN *remains motionless.*)

EPILOGUE

(*Lights up on the* GUARD.)

GUARD: These people don't understand the difference between good and evil. It's not in their culture. I had no choice. She was howling over the dead body like a witch, and on her hands and knees, she was throwing dirt over him. She looked like some wild animal with her black hair whirling in the dust storm. It was an ugly sight, this yellow creature spitting and crying, snot hanging from her nose. I have to admit that I was scared. She looked so crazy I thought she could attack me if I tried to stop her illegal act. Anyway, it was my job, so I called out a warning. She turned around and looked at me with red eyes, and stood up with all the threats of murder. I didn't have a choice.

(*Enormous sound of explosion. Black. A moment of silence and stillness. Lights up on* ANTIGONE *alone.*)

ANTIGONE: With my bare hands I dug the dry earth and covered my lover's corpse with dirt and tears. The desert land is cruel to those who want to bury loved ones. My nails ripped from my fingers. I made an offering of my blood. Tadashi's grave is red. That was my last red. Shortly after two enormous explosions over Japan killed 200,000 people who shared my ancestors, Japanese Americans were released from their imprisonment in America—nowhere to go, nothing to return to, their freedom owed to the bloody results of those two bombs. But I was already gone by then. I died without seeing the other red. It belonged to a young girl in Hiroshima. Her skin was hanging from her skinny body in strips of red ribbons. She was trying to hold onto her red.

(*She takes a long red ribbon out of her pocket. She holds the ribbon up vertically, and with a pair of scissors, cuts the ribbon in half. The bottom half falls to the floor. Lights down.*)

ARABIAN NIGHTS

David Ives

Arabian Nights was commissioned by and premiered in the 2000 Humana Festival of New American Plays at Actors Theatre of Louisville (Jon Jory, Artistic Director). It was directed by Jon Jory; the set design was by Paul Owen; the lighting design was by Paul Werner; the sound design was by Martin R. Desjardins; and the costume design was by Kevin McLeod. The cast was as follows:

NORMAN	Will Bond
INTERPRETER	Ellen Lauren
FLORA	Gretchen Lee Krich

(*Up right, a freestanding open doorway with a multicolored bead curtain. Center, a small, plain wooden table with a white cloth. On it: an ornament, a stone, a gold ring, and a figure of a frog.*)

(*At lights up,* FLORA—*very ordinary*—*is at the table, dusting the objects with a feather duster.*)

(*Through the bead curtain comes the* INTERPRETER, *in loose colorful robes and sandals. The* INTERPRETER *may be played by a woman wearing a dark beard.*)

(*Bowing deeply and repeatedly, the* INTERPRETER *leads in* NORMAN— *utterly normal—who carries a suitcase.*)

INTERPRETER: Right this way, sir, this way. The most beautiful shop in the world. All the wonders of the kingdom. For nothing! Nothing!

NORMAN: (*to* FLORA) Hello.

INTERPRETER: Hail, fair maid! says he.

FLORA: (*to* NORMAN, *putting the feather duster away*) Good morning.

INTERPRETER: All praise to the highest, says she.

NORMAN: Do you . . . speak any English?

INTERPRETER: Do you . . . speak any English?

FLORA: (*She speaks perfect, unaccented English.*) Yes, I speak some English.

INTERPRETER: Indeed, sir, I can stammer out a broken song of pitiful, insufficient words.

NORMAN: Ah-ha.

INTERPRETER: Ah-ha.

NORMAN: Well . . .

INTERPRETER: A deep hole in the ground.

NORMAN: I . . .

INTERPRETER: (*Points to his eye.*) The organ of vision.

NORMAN: Ummm . . .

INTERPRETER: Ummm . . .

NORMAN: Listen.

INTERPRETER: Do you hear something?

(INTERPRETER *and* FLORA *listen for something.*)

NORMAN: I'm sorry to rush in so late like this.

INTERPRETER: I'm sorry to rush in so late like this.

FLORA: No, please.

INTERPRETER: No, please.

NORMAN: But you see . . .

INTERPRETER: (*Points to his butt.*) But—(*Points to* FLORA.)—you—(*Does binoculars with his hands.*)—see . . .

NORMAN: (*Looks at his watch.*) Damn . . .

INTERPRETER: (*Produces an hourglass from among his robes.*) How swiftly flow the sands of time!

NORMAN: I know this sounds crazy—

INTERPRETER: I know this sounds crazy—

NORMAN: I only have about ten minutes.

INTERPRETER: Soon the golden orb of heaven will cleave the house of the hedgehog.

NORMAN: I have a plane to catch.

INTERPRETER: I must clamber upon the flying corporate carpet and flap away from your kingdom.

NORMAN: Anyway, I want to find . . .

INTERPRETER: Anyway, I want to find . . .

FLORA: Yes?

INTERPRETER: Yes?

NORMAN: I guess you'd call it . . .

INTERPRETER: Something unparalleled! Something sublime!

NORMAN: A souvenir.

INTERPRETER: (*You're kidding.*) A *souvenir* . . . ?!

NORMAN: Something to take with me.

INTERPRETER: A treasure!

FLORA: Any particular kind of thing?

INTERPRETER: Can the funicular hide the spring?

NORMAN: Excuse me?

INTERPRETER: Accuse me?

FLORA: How much did you want to spend?

INTERPRETER: How much did you want to spend?

NORMAN: It doesn't matter.

INTERPRETER: Let's haggle. I'm loaded!

FLORA: Is this for yourself?

INTERPRETER: Have you a mistress, a wife, a *hareem*?

NORMAN: No, this is for me.

INTERPRETER: Alas, a lad alone in all the world am I.

FLORA: Well . . .

INTERPRETER: A deep hole in the ground.

FLORA: I think I can help you.

INTERPRETER: Solitary sir, the maiden says, I look in your eyes and I see your soul shining there like a golden carp in an azure pool.

NORMAN: Really . . . ?

INTERPRETER: Really. Now, in this brief moment, in the midst of this mirage called life, here on this tiny square of soil on the whirling earth, I feel the two of us joined by a crystal thread, your soul to my soul to yours.

NORMAN: You do?

INTERPRETER: You do?

FLORA: I do.

INTERPRETER: She does.

NORMAN: You know, I've been up and down this street every day. . . .

INTERPRETER: Day and night I have walked the bazaar. . . .

NORMAN: I sure wish I'd seen this place sooner.

INTERPRETER: Only so that I might see *you*.

FLORA: I've noticed you walking by.

INTERPRETER: How I pined for you to enter as you passed.

NORMAN: You did?

INTERPRETER: She did. She asks your name.

NORMAN: My name is Norman.

INTERPRETER: My name is Sinbad!

NORMAN: I'm here on some business.

INTERPRETER: I am the merchant son of a great prince, exiled from my land.

FLORA: Is that so.

INTERPRETER: Her name is Izthatso.

FLORA: People call me Flora.

INTERPRETER: But people call me Flora.

FLORA: With an "F."

INTERPRETER: With an "F."

NORMAN: I . . .

INTERPRETER: The organ of vision.

NORMAN: (*Looks at watch.*) *Damn* it . . .

INTERPRETER: (*Produces hourglass.*) *Damn* it . . .

NORMAN: Y'know, Flora . . .

INTERPRETER: Y'know, Flora . . .

NORMAN: You shop and you shop . . .

INTERPRETER: We live our brief lives . . .

NORMAN: You never seem to find that special thing you're shopping for.

INTERPRETER: . . . each day awaiting the dawn that will give us purpose, bring us happiness.

FLORA: That's so true.

INTERPRETER: That's so true.

NORMAN: Maybe what I'm looking for is right here.

INTERPRETER: Perhaps my dawn has come.

FLORA: Shhh!

INTERPRETER: Shhh!

FLORA: I thought I heard my father.

INTERPRETER: My father may be listening!

FLORA: It's almost time for his tea.

INTERPRETER: If he sees me talking to you, he'll cut your throat!

NORMAN & INTERPRETER: (*Simultaneous—as they pick up the suitcase together.*) Maybe I should be going . . .

FLORA: No—

INTERPRETER: No—

FLORA: He won't bother us.

INTERPRETER: Have mercy, good sir!

NORMAN: (*Hefts suitcase.*) I do have a plane to catch.

INTERPRETER: Take my suitcase.

(FLORA *takes the suitcase from him and sets it down.*)

FLORA: There's plenty of time.

INTERPRETER: Keep your voice low.

FLORA: Shhh!

INTERPRETER: Shhh!

FLORA: I thought I heard him calling.

INTERPRETER: He's sharpening the blade.

(*We hear the sound of a blade being sharpened.*)

NORMAN: (*cry of surprise*)

INTERPRETER: (*cry of surprise*)

FLORA: He's watching old movies.

INTERPRETER: The old man is *mad*.

FLORA: Anyway, I'm sure I'll have something you'll like.

INTERPRETER: Act as if you're buying something.

NORMAN: What about these things right here?

INTERPRETER: What about these things right here?

FLORA: Maybe an ornament?

INTERPRETER: Can you conceive, prince, how lonely my life is?

FLORA: Or a stone?

INTERPRETER: It's as hard—and as cheap—as this stone.

FLORA: (*Gestures left.*) I have more in the back.

INTERPRETER: (*Gestures left.*) He keeps me locked in a tiny cell.

NORMAN: No. No.

INTERPRETER: Stay with me.

FLORA: Maybe . . .

INTERPRETER: What I long for . . .

FLORA: . . . a golden ring?

INTERPRETER: . . . is love.

FLORA: A figurine?

INTERPRETER: But my father has betrothed me to a man as ugly as this frog.

FLORA: Interested?

INTERPRETER: Would *you* marry this?

NORMAN: Not really.

INTERPRETER: Not really.

FLORA: I don't know what else I can show you.

INTERPRETER: I have nothing, sir. Nothing! Zip zero nada zilch!

NORMAN: My God, you're beautiful.

INTERPRETER: My God, you're beautiful.

FLORA: Excuse me?

INTERPRETER: Excuse me?

NORMAN: I'm sorry.

INTERPRETER: I'm sorry.

NORMAN: I don't usually say things like that.

INTERPRETER: I know I sound like a jerk.

NORMAN: Sometimes it's something so simple.

INTERPRETER: So complicated are the ways of kismet.

NORMAN: You walk into a shop. . . .

INTERPRETER: I look at you. . . .

NORMAN: . . . and everything's suddenly different, somehow.

INTERPRETER: . . . and my heart flutters inside me like a leaf of the
    perfumed gum tree at the scented bounce of bedspring.

FLORA: Really?

INTERPRETER: Really.

NORMAN: Now in this brief moment . . .

INTERPRETER: Now in this brief moment . . .

NORMAN: On this tiny patch of ground on the whirling earth . . .

INTERPRETER: In the midst of this mirage called life . . .

NORMAN: I feel us joined by a crystal thread, your soul to my soul
    to yours.

INTERPRETER: Etcetera.

FLORA: You do?

INTERPRETER: You do?

NORMAN: I . . .

INTERPRETER: The organ of vision.

NORMAN: . . . do.

INTERPRETER: He does.

NORMAN: How can I leave, now that I've seen you, met you, heard you?

INTERPRETER: How can I get on a plane?

NORMAN: Now that fate has brought me to this bazaar?

INTERPRETER: It's so bizarre. But fate has decreed that we must part.

NORMAN: (*Takes out an hourglass.*) O cruel fate! How swiftly flow the sands of time!

INTERPRETER: (*Looks at a watch.*) Shit . . . !

NORMAN: The stars have decreed we must part.

INTERPRETER: Look, I really gotta go.

NORMAN: (*Kisses* FLORA's *hand.*) But I will return, O my florid queen!

INTERPRETER: Maybe I'll get back here sometime.

FLORA: I will wait for you, my Norman prince!

NORMAN: Izthatso.

FLORA: It *is* so. I will be yours and you will be mine and we will be each other's.

INTERPRETER: Maybe I'll have something you like.

NORMAN: Well . . .

INTERPRETER: A deep hole in the ground.

FLORA: Well . . .

INTERPRETER: With purest water at the bottom.

NORMAN: Salaam!

INTERPRETER: So long!

FLORA: Salaam!

INTERPRETER: So long! So long! So long!

NORMAN: Open, sesame!

(NORMAN *whirls out, followed by the* INTERPRETER.)

FLORA: (*Sighs.*) Oh, well. (*She takes out the feather duster—and it's been changed into a large red rose.*) Shazam!

(*She starts to dust the objects with it. Blackout.*)

CLASSYASS

Caleen Sinnette Jennings

Classyass premiered in Actors Theatre of Louisville's 26th Annual Humana Festival of New American Plays, March 3–April 7, 2002.

Timothy Douglas was dramaturg. Rajendra Ramoon Maharaj directed the following cast:

AMA	Jason Cornwell
BIGB	Nikki E. Walker
MILES	Robert Beitzel

CHARACTERS

AMA: Or Amadeus. Black college freshman.
BIGB: Or Belinda. Black woman, twenty, dressed like a street person.
MILES: White college senior and radio station manager.

SETTING: A small room that serves as a modest campus radio studio at Bellmore College. Ama speaks into the mic with a suave broadcaster's voice.

AMA: Okay you Bellmore boneheads, that was Tchaikovsky's "1812 Overture." Bet those cannons busted a couple of you dozers. Perfect for 3:47 A.M. on a cold, rainy Thursday in finals week. It's the end of time at the end of the line. Study on, people. Bang out papers. Cram the facts. Justify that exorbitant tuition and make Bellmore College proud. I'M FEELING Y'ALL! Especially those of you studying for Calc 801 with Professor Cobb. Call me if you have a clue about question #3 on page 551. You're listening to Casual Classics, because you don't have to be uptight and white to love classical music. This is WBMR, the radio station of Bellmore College. Miles Morgan is your station manager. I'm Ama— Amadeus Waddlington, with you til 6 A.M. Guzzle that warm Red Bull and cold Maxwell House. Here's music to squeeze your brains by. It's Dvořák's "New World Symphony" comin' atcha. (*He puts on the CD, grabs a beer and a huge textbook, and sprawls out on the floor. A bold knock interrupts him. He shouts.*) Go to hell, Miles. I like "New World"! (*Another knock.*) Okay, okay. I'll play Beethoven's Symphony #1 next. Lots of strings, okay? (*Persistent knocking.*) Damn! (AMA *strides to the door and opens it.* BIGB *strides in, carrying shopping bags and waving several faxes.*)

BIGB: You messed up, boy!

AMA: Excuse me?

BIGB: And your smart-assed faxes made it worse!

AMA: Do I know you?

BIGB: (*examining the mic and CDs*) I want a public apology.

AMA: Don't touch that! Listen, whoever you are . . .

BIGB: Whomever!

AMA: Whatever!

BIGB: You ain't got a clue who I am.

AMA: A fabulous person, no doubt, but you've got to go. This is a classical music show and I've got a killer calculus final tomorrow.

BIGB: Color me compassionate. You're shorter than I thought. But I figured right about you being a dumb ass. I told you right here. . . .

(BIGB *shows* AMA *the faxes and he realizes who she is.*)

AMA: Oh my God . . . you're . . . BigB! I thought you were . . .

BIGB: . . . a brother, I know, 'cause I ain't hearing none of your bullshit. Well, I thought you was a white boy, and I was right.

AMA: Look, I don't know what you want. . . .

BIGB: How long I been faxing you, moron? You said the "Gloria" was by Fauré. . . .

AMA: . . . As I told you one thousand faxes ago, "Gloria" is by Poulenc and when I played it, I said Poulenc. . . .

BIGB: . . . Fauré!

AMA: . . . Poulenc!

BIGB: I know what I heard, you arrogant shithead.

AMA: Does that BigB stand for "bitch" or "borderline psychotic"?

BIGB: I ain't even 'pressed by you trottin' out them tired SAT joints. I'm down at the Palmer Street Shelter, which you knew by the headin' on the fax, and you just figured I didn't know shit about classical music.

AMA: BigB, I'm truly flattered that you even listen, but you don't . . .

BIGB: My crew at the shelter want to come up here and kick yo ass.

AMA: Whoa, whoa there. I'm sorry about our misunderstanding, okay?

BIGB: And that s'posed to float my boat?

AMA: Let's be calm, okay, B?

BIGB: BigB to you, and I know you ain't s'posed to be drinkin' beer up in here.

AMA: You never saw that.

BIGB: Now I got two things on ya. This gonna be what they call an interesting evening. (*Thumbing through his calculus book.*) This the shit probably got your brain too messed up to know your Poulenc from your Fauré. (*She sips* AMA's *beer.*)

AMA: Don't do that. Suppose I have a social disease?

BIGB: Ha! Bet you still a cherry.

AMA: Suppose YOU have a social disease?

BIGB: I'll just call your dean and tell him I caught it sippin' outta your freshman-ass beer bottle.

AMA: What do you want from me?

BIGB: You made me look stupid in front of my crew.

AMA: Look, I'm just a nerd playing dead white men's music. Why do you even listen to my show?

BIGB: So a sister like me ain't s'posed to be a classical music affectionado.

AMA: The word's "aficionado." . . .

BIGB: Boy, I'm feelin better 'n' better about bustin' yo ass.

AMA: This is like something out of Scorsese. If I apologize for the thing I DID NOT DO, will you go?

BIGB: Maybe. Or maybe I'll stay and watch you work awhile.

AMA: It's against the rules.

BIGB: Lots of things against the rules, freshman boy. Don't mean they ain't delicious to do.

AMA: If my station manager comes in . . .

BIGB: Tell him I'm studyin' witcha, that we putting the "us" in calculus.

AMA: Well, you don't exactly look like a student.

BIGB: Well, you don't exactly look like a asshole, but you the poster boy. Where you get "Ama" from anyway?

AMA: Wolfgang **Amadeus** Mozart. My dad's a classical musician.

BIGB: Oh yeah? Where he play at?

AMA: He sells insurance. No major symphony'll hire him.

BIGB: I know that's right. Oughta be called "sym-phoney"—like phoney baloney, right?

AMA: (*patronizingly*) That's very clever, BigB, but I've got a lot of work to do. How about I give you and your people at the shelter a, what do you call it, a "shout out." Right in the middle of Dvořák. How would you like that? (AMA *goes to the mic, but* BIGB *stops him.*)

BIGB: How you gonna interrupt "New World Symphony" and mess up everybody's flow? You crazy, Amadeus Waddlington. You also a lucky bastard. BigB like you. She gonna take it easy on you.

AMA: Why does your use of the third person chill my blood?

BIGB: Take me to dinner and we cool.

AMA: What?

BIGB: Over there to the Purple Pheasant, where the president of Bellmore College eat at!

AMA: . . . Are you crazy? I don't have that kind of . . .

BIGB: . . . an' buy me a present . . .

AMA: . . . a present? I'm broke!

BIGB: . . . somethin', how they say it, "droll." Yeah, "droll" and "ironic"! Like a CD of "Dialogues of the Carmelites" by POULENC. I can see you 'n' me sittin' up in the Purple Pheasant, chucklin' over our little in joke, sippin' a half-ass California pinot grigio.

AMA: Who the hell writes your material?

BIGB: And pick me up in a shiny new car.

AMA: Hello? Freshmen aren't allowed to have cars.

BIGB: Beg, borrow, or steal, my brother, but you better have yo ass waiting for me at the shelter tomorrow night at 7:30. And don't shit in your khakis. My boys'll watch your back in the 'hood.

AMA: You're delusional.

BIGB: Oh, you insultin' BigB, now? You don't wanna be seen with her?

AMA: I'd love to be seen with her . . . you! I'd give my right arm to have the whole town and the president of Bellmore see me escort you into the Purple Pheasant. Hell, I'd even invite my parents. But I'm a scholarship student with five bucks to my name.

BIGB: (*sniffing him*) Ya wearing cashmere and ya reek of Hugo Boss. Don't even try to play me, boy.

AMA: Maxed out credit cards, BigB. I'm just a half-ass, wannabe, freshman with a little gig, trying to make some headway with Mr. Mastercard. I'll apologize on air. I'll stamp your name on my forehead, I'll run naked down the quad and bark like a dog. . . .

BIGB: . . . anything but take me out. You're a snob, Amadeus Waddlington. You a broke-ass, cashmere-wearin' shit-talkin' loser who don't know his Poulenc from his Fauré. . . . (BIGB *finishes off* AMA's *beer*.) . . . and drinks Lite beer! My crew was right. Ya need a beat down.

AMA: BigB, please . . .

BIGB: See, I be down at the shelter, diggin' on ya voice early in the mornin'. People say you ain't shit, but you gotta way a soundin' all mellow an' sexy. And when you spank that Rachmaninoff, oh yeah, baby! So when you screw up the Poulenc I send a friendly fax to point out yo error and help yo ass out. . . .

AMA: And I appreciate . . .

BIGB: But you had to get up in my grill wit that, "what-do-you-know-about-classical-music-you-stupid-ass-homeless-crack-head" kind of attitude. (*She starts to leave.*) Well, Palmer Street crew will be very happy to whup yo behind.

AMA: (*stopping her*) I didn't mean to give you attitude. I'm sorry. I'm broke, I swear! I'll show you my bills, I'll show you my bank statements. Isn't there anything else I can do, BigB? Please!

(*Pause.* BIGB *looks* AMA *up and down, to his great discomfort.*)

BIGB: Kiss me.

AMA: What did you say?

BIGB: I'm gettin' somethin' outta this deal. Kiss me.

AMA: But . . .

BIGB: Not one a' them air flybys, neither. Gimme some tongue!

AMA: Oh God.

BIGB: (*She advances on him.*) Lay it on me, Amadeus Waddlington. Kiss me or kiss yo ass good-bye.

AMA: (*backing away, near tears*) This isn't Scorsese, it's John Woo.

BIGB: Come on classyass, pucker up! (BIGB *tackles* AMA *and plants
a long, deep kiss on him. When she lets him go,* AMA *steps back, looks
at her, touches his mouth, and faints.* BIGB *kneels calmly beside him.
Her entire demeanor changes. Her voice is rich, cultured, her gram-
mar impeccable. She sits him up and gives him a few light slaps.*)
Hey! Hey! Ama? Damn it, Amadeus Waddlington, wake up!

(MILES MORGAN *enters drinking a beer.*)

MILES: Who are you, and what the hell did you do to Waddlington?

BIGB: He just fainted. Get something cold.

(MILES *pours cold beer on* AMA*'s head.* AMA *comes to.*)

BIGB: Have you sufficiently recuperated Mr. Waddlington?

MILES: (*to* BIGB) Hey, you look familiar. . . . Where do I know
you from? . . . In the paper . . . from the shelter. You're. . . .
Man you sure look . . . different! Oh my God. . . . You're not
going to tell your father about the beer, are you? I'm a fifth-
year senior trying to graduate. . . .

BIGB: Just make sure he's okay.

(MILES *bends down to* AMA *who grabs him by the collar. They whisper
urgently, while* BIGB *thumbs through the CDs and eavesdrops, greatly
amused.*)

AMA: Oh God. Oh God! I kissed her!

MILES: Way to go, man!

AMA: I'm gonna die!

MILES: She's that good, huh? Bet she's a knockout under all that stuff she's wearing. You all going to a costume party or something?

AMA: Don't you get it, Miles? I kissed her!

MILES: Lucky bastard! Kickin' it with Dean Stafford's daughter.

AMA: (*after a beat*) What did you say?

MILES: That's Belinda Stafford, Dean Stafford's youngest daughter! She dropped out of Bellmore to work at the shelter. It was all in the papers and everything.

BELINDA: (*handing him money*) Thanks for the beer and the amusement, Mr. Waddlington.

AMA: Is this true? Are you really . . . ?

BELINDA: (*removing her dirty garments and putting them in a bag*) I work night shifts at the Palmer Street Shelter. You can imagine that some of the women find it hard to sleep. Your music and your incredibly boring commentary usually do the trick. Everything was fine until you responded so rudely to my fax. You assumed because it came from the shelter . . .

AMA: No . . . I just . . . I didn't. . . .

BELINDA: You're an arrogant, ill-informed elitist, Amadeus Waddlington. I've known guys like you all my life. It broke Daddy's heart when I dropped out of Bellmore, but your faxes reminded me exactly why I did it. So, I decided to teach you a lesson. You're not going to die from my kiss, but I hope you won't forget what it felt like to think that you were. (*She scatters the faxes over his head and starts to exit.*)

MILES: Now, uh, Ms. Stafford, you wouldn't mention this to your father . . .

BELINDA: I've got people without winter coats on my mind.

AMA: (*Rushes to her.*) BigB, I mean Belinda, I mean, Ms. Stafford, please wait. I get a lot of shit from people about this show and I thought you were just another brother hassling me. I don't have an attitude about the shelter because I've got too many poor folks in my own family. I'm sorry about the vibe. Can I make it up to you? Maybe put in some hours at the shelter.

BELINDA: If you think you can hack it. I picked out some CDs for you to play. My people sleep well to Debussy. I'll be checkin' you! (*She puts on her headphones as she exits.*)

MILES: And you won't mention this to . . .

(MILES *exits calling after* BELINDA. AMA *suddenly remembers he's on air. He runs to the mic.*)

AMA: Yo, my people, was that dope? Bet the "New World Symphony" woke yo asses up! Hey, I'm still waiting to speak to anybody with a clue to #3 on page 551 in Cobb's calculus class. Anybody? It's 3:59 on WBMR the voice of Bellmore College. I'm Amadeus Waddlington and this is Casual Classics, because you don't have to be uptight and white to love classical music. You don't have to be a snob either. I wanna give a shout out to my girl BigB. I think I'm in love, people. Yo, B, I apologize. "Gloria" was, is, and always will be Poulenc. I dig the lesson. . . . (*He touches his lips.*) . . . and I dig the way you taught it. I'll be down to lend a hand, you better believe that. And for the folks listening at the Palmer Street Shelter, here's a little Debussy to soothe you to sleep. Better times ahead, my people. Better times ahead.

(*Lights dim as sounds of Debussy come up. Blackout.*)

THE CURE

Romulus Linney

CHARACTER

A midwife.

TIME: 1800–2000.

PLACE: Appalachia.

(*Appalachia.*)

(*A wooden porch. Before it sits a very very large green frog. On it sits a woman in late middle age, with white hair. She is rocking quietly in a slat-backed rocking chair. There is a leather pouch at her side.*)

MIDWIFE: Green frog tea is good for women moon-bleeding. Watermelon seeds make tea for kidney stones. Dew off a straw can rub away freckles. If you break your bed, a relative's coming to visit. Dream about catching a fish, you'll get pregnant. You keep bees? If a body dies, tell them bees. Jest say it to the hive and don't fergit. Otherwise, at the funeral, they'll plain rise up and go. I'm daft?

(*She chuckles at us, smiles, and rocks.*)

Three ways in the Smoky Mountains fer a woman to live her own life. Midwifing is best, since no strong man hereabouts will abide a foot first baby ripping out his woman's guts. Strong men run away from that. So if you know how to turn that baby in the womb, they will call you ma'am, and leave you alone. Otherwise, they'll marry you and work you to death, or leave you an old maid so your mother can work you to death. Nother way, just kill a man. Any man. Hide behind a tree and shoot the son of a bitch. Act wild, drink your likker by yourself, and play like you enjoy it. They respect that. Number three, eat roots for supper, frogs for breakfast, and chew yourself to salvation.

(*She reaches into the leather pouch, pulls out a root shaped like a tiny man.*)

Gin sang. Means root of life, bottom of everthang. Grows wild in the mountains, once ever seven year, and I know where. Looks like a little man. See, his head, arms and his legs and his little horn hanging right yonder. Relish that. I'm alone now but I married. Lots. Would again.

(*Points to her white hair.*)

Snow on the roof don't mean there ain't fire in the house. Five men. One died a decent farmer. Second, half man, half buzzard. We went together like cheese and chalk, but not onct did I lower my eyes to him, not in field, church, porch, or bed. He died, mortified, he said, by a witch. I'd been called that for a long time, so almost everbody believed I kilt him, but such is the onery fascination of men, I turned around and married again, three times. Good men too, one even bettern that. Fifteen grandchildren, and thirty-eight great grandchildren, and an eleven-year-old great-great-grandchild I am trying to keep from running off with a scoundrel. Maybe she will, maybe she won't, since the children who loved me when they was young change their minds growing up, and look at me slant-wise now.

(*She leans forward.*)

I don't purpose to frighten young women. Men are all right, if you know where sang grows, chew it, be patient, let every soul see the root of life you are eating up looks like a man.

(*She smiles and rocks.*)

I knowed I had "second sight" when I was just a girl. The Company had come into the cove where we lived and started the mine. They opened the mountain, built the houses all alike up the one hill, commenced the company store where we had to trade. The men went off to the mines, my Daddy with them. A coal mine, it's just a big road underground. With rooms off of it. Men go into them rooms and pull out the coal, sometimes standing up and breathing all right, sometimes on their knees ten hours a day gulping black dust and dirt. Whichever, they git the coal out of the mine. And when they do, they move backwards, pulling out ribs of coal past old four by fours left to hold everything up. They can't leave nothing. Not one piece. They have to what's call "retreat," pulling out with them ever last rib of the mine.

(*She looks off into the distance, seeing the past.*)

My Daddy walked off to his work that morning. I yelled when I seen him walking right toward her. A woman dressed in snow white rainment, a-smiling at him, who kept smiling while he walked to her, then past her and through her, then on down into the mine. When they pulled out the coal ribs that day, the mountain fell in on them. One hundred and twenty-three men died, my father with them, leaving a hundred and two widows, a hundred sixty-five fatherless chilluns, me amongst them, with second sight. Everbody had heard me that morning when I cried out: "Daddy! She's waiting fer ye! Don't ye see her? There, at the mouth of the mine! You'll die in there!" It commenced then, calling me witch.

(*She closes her eyes.*)

Sperits. Beautiful death-wimmen, always in white amongst the black dust which never touches 'em. I seen they wasn't no wimmen at all but great beasts protecting their mountain home with the dire destruction of tunneling fools. I could see them, second sight. I still can. I can't see Daddy, though. But I remember him. Pulled my ear. Take his knuckle, like this one here, to the top of my head. Spin it around and say, buzzzz. Just another man, going into the mine, the pieces of him dug out later. The Company gave my mother a check for twenty-five dollar and said we could stay in the house, until the end of the month. I don't know the cure for that.

(*She opens her eyes, rocks.*)

For years I wasn't allowed in town. No sluts, said the church ladies. No witches, said the police. No midwives, said the doctors. Then not long ago this man come all the way from Paris, France, to see people like me and nobody else. He said for a hundred years babies been birthed all wrong. Under blinding bright light, washed in cold alcohol water in steel basins, stinging in their eyes, their hearts beating hard enough to kill a grown man. Plain terrified scared, and sometimes never given to no mother at all, until days later. He asked if he could watch me. I said, "Shore if you stay out of my way." He did. I keep the lights low, the woman breathing deep and the husband quiet. Afterwards, I use my Lysol, and chase them germs away. I treat the eyes and wash the baby clean and proper, but I wash it in a sweetwood basin in warm water and I quick put that baby back to its mother's flesh, soon as I mortally can. The little hearts, I almost touch, a-beating in panic, slow down, get calm, and commence to feel some better about life we must endure. Sometimes look like they smile. The Frenchman said, "You are right and the doctors here are wrong. This baby will be a happy child." The doctors throwed him out of town. But I know this. When you come into the world under blinding light, in a tile cold room, washed off by alcohol in steel basins, and such, then finally, you get to your Momma, oh, what relief, and what do you expect the rest of life to be, but crazy madness for other bodies, whiskey, drugs and what all, to take away your screaming? It's a wonder we ain't all worse than we are.

(*She smiles, rocks, chews.*)

I live chalk line straight with men. I love my Daddy dead in the mine. My Momma at thirty looking seventy. For a cure at night I chew gin sang, and in the morning pleasure the legs of a green mountain frog hopping for breakfast in my skillet. And that child I delivered to this life, running down that mountain yonder, is as pleasant to me as the flowers are made.

(*Lights fade on her.*)

DANIEL ON A THURSDAY

Garth Wingfield

Daniel on a Thursday was originally produced by All Seasons Theatre Group (John McCormack, Artistic Director) at New York Performance Works in New York City on July 17, 2000. It was directed by Christopher Gorman. The cast was as follows:

DANIEL   Steve Roman
KEVIN   Tom O'Brien

The play was later produced by Urban Empire & Francis Ford Coppola's *Zoetrope: All-Story* at Show World in New York City. AnnaCatherine Rutledge directed the following cast:

DANIEL   Matthew Del Negro
KEVIN   Jack Merrill

Subsequently, the play was produced, again by Urban Empire and *Zoetrope: All-Story,* at the Tiffany Theatre in Los Angeles. It was directed by Bjorn Johnson, and the cast was as follows:

DANIEL   Scott Paetty
KEVIN   Jack Merrill

The play was developed at the Harbor Theatre, New York City (Stuart Warmflash, Artistic Director).

CHARACTERS

DANIEL: Early thirties. Very neatly dressed.
KEVIN: Early thirties. Not so pulled together.

A slash in the text (/) is a cue for the next actor to begin speaking, creating overlapping dialogue.

> *"Oh, life is a glorious cycle of song;*
> *A medley of extemporanea;*
> *And love is a thing that can never go wrong;*
> *And I am Marie of Roumania."*
> —Dorothy Parker

(*A crowded bar. Two guys leaning against a wall, facing out, nursing beers.* KEVIN *eyes* DANIEL *for a moment. Then* DANIEL, *sensing he's being cruised, turns, gives him a once-over.*)

KEVIN: Hey.

DANIEL: (*weakly, not encouraging*) Hey.

KEVIN: I like your beer.

DANIEL: What?

KEVIN: God, that was an incredibly stupid thing / to say.

DANIEL: Did you just say you liked my beer?

KEVIN: I, um . . . yes . . . it's a very attractive . . . Beck's. It looks good on you.

DANIEL: Thanks? (*He gazes out again. Little beat.*)

KEVIN: (*Extends his hand.*) It's Kevin.

DANIEL: Look . . .

KEVIN: I'm Kevin.

DANIEL: Right . . . Kevin . . . I don't mean to be rude. I'm sure you're a nice guy and all. It's just, I really don't feel like talking tonight.

KEVIN: Oh. That's fair. (*Beat.*) So that was my one chance with you, and I just blew it, right?

DANIEL: Excuse me?

KEVIN: I compliment your beer for some reason I can't fathom, and that's that.

DANIEL: Look . . .

KEVIN: Is it my body?

DANIEL: What?

KEVIN: Is my body this major turnoff? Or my hair?

DANIEL: Of course not! You're a perfectly nice-looking guy—not my type, as it turns out—but perfectly nice-looking . . .

KEVIN: Huh.

DANIEL: Anyway. Good talking with you. (*Beat. They both face out again.*)

KEVIN: So let me get this straight. Even though I don't disgust you outright—and I don't actually disgust you, do I?

DANIEL: You don't disgust me!

KEVIN: Even so, you wouldn't shake my hand.

DANIEL: What are you talking about?

KEVIN: I held out my hand to introduce myself, and you wouldn't take it or tell me your name even.

DANIEL: You're reading way too much into this.

KEVIN: (*getting really pissed*) I don't think so. I don't think so at all. See, what I think is that actually—on the inside—you see me as this leper-person who's not even worthy of being TOUCHED! And that is just righteously shitty, okay? It's a handshake! A HANDSHAKE! FOR THE LOVE OF FUCK, WHAT KIND OF SUPERIOR *ASSWIPE* DO YOU THINK YOU ARE?!

DANIEL: Oh my God, no—NO! I didn't mean to / insult you, believe me.

KEVIN: (*cracking up*) Daniel! Take it easy, man! It's Kevin . . . Kevin Carpenter. From high school. I'm just screwing with you, buddy.

DANIEL: Kevin Carpenter?

KEVIN: From history class.

DANIEL: European history, or . . . ?

KEVIN: Exactly, European history class. I saw you across the bar just now and said to myself, "Well, if it isn't little Daniel Delmonico from high school in a gay bar. I haven't seen him in years. I know what! I'm gonna go over and mess with his head."

DANIEL: And so you did.

KEVIN: Boy, did I.

DANIEL: Right . . . So. Kevin . . .

KEVIN: So Daniel—sew buttons! Hey, hope I didn't freak your shit too severely or anything.

DANIEL: No, that's . . . Wow, you know . . . I've gotta be honest here. I don't remember you at all.

KEVIN: You don't?

DANIEL: I'm sorry.

KEVIN: No, that's cool. It's not like we were ever friends or anything.

DANIEL: We weren't.

KEVIN: Not at all.

DANIEL: Were we . . . acquaintances even?

KEVIN: Not that I recall.

DANIEL: Well, it was a full class.

KEVIN: And an *enormous* school.

DANIEL: (*not sure about this*) Right . . . But . . . it's good to finally meet you now. After all these years.

KEVIN: (*as they shake*) After all these years.

DANIEL: (*little smile*) You know, this is actually very cool because . . . the whole time I was in high school, I was fully convinced I was the only gay person there.

KEVIN: You may well have been. I'm straight.

DANIEL: Sorry?

KEVIN: Hundred percent hetero.

DANIEL: But this is a gay bar. . . .

KEVIN: I know that.

DANIEL: So . . . what are you doing here?

KEVIN: I don't know, I just wanted a beer. I was walking down the street, wanting a beer, and I saw this place—and hey, I enjoy an old *Golden Girls* episode as much as the next guy.

DANIEL: Okay . . .

KEVIN: Problemo?

DANIEL: No.

KEVIN: Gay people are A–OK by Kevin Carpenter.

DANIEL: Uh-huh . . .

KEVIN: (*low*) Don't worry, I won't tell the old gang your little secret.

DANIEL: What secret?

KEVIN: That I saw you here.

DANIEL: Actually, that's not a *secret* really . . . and . . . what old gang?

KEVIN: Your pals from high school. Daniel's old buds.

DANIEL: But I didn't . . . back then, I didn't have that many close . . . (*suspicious*) Exactly who was in my old gang?

KEVIN: You know.

DANIEL: Remind me.

KEVIN: (*reaching*) Like . . . Mary . . . Bill . . .

DANIEL: I didn't know anyone by those names, Kevin. And our high school was hardly "enormous." And come to think of it, I didn't *take* European history; I took American history, so I'm pretty sure you've got / the wrong guy.

KEVIN: (*cracking up*) GOTCHA! Two for two for the Kevinator! I totally had you going there, didn't I?

DANIEL: (*getting angry*) You did.

KEVIN: All the way.

DANIEL: So you didn't go to my high school. . . .

KEVIN: Negatory. I've never even seen you before tonight. But you were buying it, the whole thing, I could tell. Right up to the Bill and Mary part.

DANIEL: Look! *Kevin!* Why don't you just leave me alone, okay? I said I didn't want to talk to anyone, and I don't know why you're doing this to me. So just . . . let's just say . . . good night.

KEVIN: Hey, I hear ya. Nighty night. (*They both stare forward for a moment.*)

DANIEL: (*still out, low*) How did you know my name?

KEVIN: (*Giggles.*) I knew you were gonna say that. I almost said it along with you, swear to God.

DANIEL: HOW THE HELL DID YOU KNOW MY NAME?!

KEVIN: (*getting angry himself*) Whoa . . . easy there, Paco. *Someone*

left his ATM card at the cash machine next door. With his
name imprinted on it. I called out to you on the street, but
you didn't hear me. *That's* why I followed you in here. I didn't
want a beer. I couldn't give a flying flapjack about *The
Golden Girls.* (*Handing him back his ATM card.*) I was being
Kevin Good Guy. Got it?

DANIEL: Well . . . that was very nice of you.

KEVIN: You bet it was.

DANIEL: (*Hates to say this.*) Thank you . . .

KEVIN: (*still testy*) Damn right about that. (*Then, suddenly bright.*)
Say, lemme buy you a beer!

DANIEL: No, Kevin, please . . .

KEVIN: Come on.

DANIEL: I just want to finish this one and go home.

KEVIN: Oh, come on!

DANIEL: Besides, I mean, if anyone should be buying drinks /
here it's . . . I guess, me.

KEVIN: What're you drinking? Beck's?

DANIEL: I . . . okay . . . fine, yes, sure.

KEVIN: I'll bet you always drink Beck's. I bet you've been drinking Beck's for years.

DANIEL: That's . . . I have.

KEVIN: Well, prepare to break new ground, my friend, because
tonight you are drinking a Bacardi Breezer.

DANIEL: Actually, I'd really prefer a Beck's.

KEVIN: Voilà, Bacardi Breezer it is! (*He pulls bottled Bacardi Breezer
from the inside pocket of the jacket he's wearing, twists off the top,
and hands it to* DANIEL.)

DANIEL: Okay, you . . . so you always bring your own . . . ?

KEVIN: (*insulted*) Jeez, ixnay on the udgment-jay.

DANIEL: What . . . udgment-jay?

KEVIN: I'll have you know I bought this legit from the bartender before I walked over here. (*Significantly.*) I knew.

DANIEL: You knew what?

KEVIN: That I could convince you to drink it. I walked in here just as you were buying your beer at the bar. And I watched as you took the change from the bartender and filed it away methodically in your wallet, making sure all the bills faced in the same direction, in order of descending denomination, and I said to myself, "That guy—Daniel Delmonico from the ATM machine—is knee-deep in some major shit and really needs my help."

DANIEL: I don't always do that / with my money.

KEVIN: Then I looked at you, actually studied you for the first time, and thought, "Not only has he got his pocket change under *way too much* control, he also looks like the kind of guy who only drinks Beck's. Every single time he goes out. He's in a rut, and I'm gonna do my part to pull him out of it. I'm gonna make him switch drinks, if only for a Breezer. It's a baby step, but there you go." So I bought that rum concoction *knowing* I could convince you to drink it.

DANIEL: (*a little wounded*) I'm not in a rut.

KEVIN: Sure you are.

DANIEL: Wait, you know nothing about me. . . .

KEVIN: Please, you're here every Thursday!

DANIEL: (*suspicious*) How do you know that?

KEVIN: (*fast*) Ummmm—I'll bet. I'll bet is all I meant. You just seem like that kind of guy. If it's Thursday night, it's Daniel at this bar. Am I right, or am I retarded?

DANIEL: (*hesitant*) You're right. . . .

KEVIN: And why is that, Daniel? Is your life so empty that you feel you have to cling to these meaningless little rituals?

DANIEL: What? No . . . *No!* It's . . . (*embarrassed to admit this*) *Golden Girls* night here on Thursdays.

KEVIN: Uh-huh. And if you don't mind my asking, what did you have for lunch today?

DANIEL: Sorry?

KEVIN: Lunch, Thursday. What'd you nosh on?

DANIEL: Turkey on wheat toast . . .

KEVIN: And yesterday?

DANIEL: Same thing.

KEVIN: I'm gonna go out on a limb here. I'm gonna extrapolate. It's turkey on wheat toast *every* day, isn't it? Isn't it? It is. It's turkey, isn't it? Isn't it? You've been deeply committed to turkey on wheat toast for about a year now, I'm guessing.

DANIEL: It's . . . a couple of years. Ever since I found out how fattening tuna salad was . . . and this means nothing!

KEVIN: Oh, it means plenty, Daniel. It speaks volumes about you. On the subway platform each morning, where you do stand? Anywhere? Or always in the same exact spot because you know where the train doors will open?

DANIEL: *Look,* just because you bought me a drink doesn't entitle you to grill me like this!

KEVIN: Grill? Who's grilling? Am I holding a cattle prod? Am I anywhere near your nipples? I'm merely observing. And asking. Observing and asking, that's all I'm doing.

DANIEL: Well, I'm leaving. . . .

KEVIN: And what's with this *type* thing? What's that about?

DANIEL: (*Stops at this.*) What . . . type thing?

KEVIN: Apparently, I'm not your type. Or so you said.

DANIEL: You're NOT GAY!

KEVIN: That's not the point. What *is* your type?

DANIEL: I'm not gonna tell you that.

KEVIN: Why not?

DANIEL: Because it's none of your business!

KEVIN: I bet I can guess it.

DANIEL: No, you can't.

KEVIN: Latin guys.

DANIEL: (*startled*) Why would you guess that?

KEVIN: It's Latin guys, isn't it? Isn't it? Isn't it? I'll bet it is. It's Latin guys. Isn't it? Isn't it?

DANIEL: YES! I'M INTO LATIN GUYS! SO WHAT?!

KEVIN: So what? So what? I'll tell you so what, Daniel Delmonico from the ATM machine. So what is you're losing out on a world of possibilities and, and *experiences* that have nothing whatsoever to do with Beck's beer, or turkey on wheat, or Bea Arthur and Betty White and Rue McClanahan. And Estelle Getty.

DANIEL: Really . . .

KEVIN: I don't mean to crawl up on a soapbox here, or into your shrink's chair, but I feel it's my duty as a disinterested third party who just did a good deed on your behalf—so maybe his two cents are worth a dime—to say that you are severely limiting yourself in many aspects of your personal life.

DANIEL: (*bemused*) Oh, am I?

KEVIN: Very much so. In my opinion.

DANIEL: Well, in my own defense, I'd like to point out that I happen to like my life exactly as I've made it. I like knowing what
I'm getting.

KEVIN: But how boring is that?

DANIEL: It's comforting.

KEVIN: (*very loud, in his face*) HAAA!

DANIEL: (*over, screaming in reaction*) HAAAAAAHHHHHH!!!
What the fuck was that?!

KEVIN: *That* was probably the last thing you thought I was gonna
say.

DANIEL: Excuse me . . . ?

KEVIN: After you said, "It's comforting." Of all the responses you
thought that might elicit, I'm betting "HAAA!" didn't even
make the short list.

DANIEL: You're right there. . . .

KEVIN: See! You expect the expected! Loosen up, Dan.

DANIEL: It's *Daniel,* Kev.

KEVIN: Right, fine. *Daniel.* Let's take what happened with us
here tonight—and let's forget about my wife, Viveca, for the
moment. And our daughter, Amber, and Helaine, our little
finch bird. Let's talk theoretically.

DANIEL: Theoretically . . .

KEVIN: A guy walks up to you in a bar. Me. Now you know nothing about this person standing next to you. This stranger could
hold the possibility of, I don't know, a one-night stand that
registers on the Richter scale. Or a one-night stand that's truly

pathetic, but that blossoms into a deep friendship involving marathon phone calls and hilarious e-mails—AND I'M NOT TALKING ABOUT FORWARDED JOKES! Or. OR! This stranger could be the man you were supposed to spend the rest of your life with. The man you've been waiting to meet ever since you had a crush on your fifth-grade math teacher.

DANIEL: I didn't realize I was gay until high school.

KEVIN: Yeah, but think back, I'm guessing there were crushes.

DANIEL: (*considers*) There were misplaced . . . crushlets.

KEVIN: Uh-huh, and so this stranger turns to you. Me, I do that. And I say, "Hey," and you say, "Hey," but that's where it *stops* in your mind because my name probably isn't Hernando.

DANIEL: Kevin . . .

KEVIN: That's no way to wander through the world, my friend. With blinders on. Choices made. Low-fat meals preselected months before the flight. I used to be just like you! Set in my ways at an early age, knowing exactly what my life would hold. And look at me now. I'm in a gay bar on a Thursday night, and I can tell you this—when I woke up this morning, I never imagined for a second I'd end up here.

DANIEL: That's . . . I'm sure that's true.

KEVIN: But . . . (*Glances at his watch.*) Sheesh, I've gotta get going. It's Amber's birthday today. She turned four. She's gonna get her first Barbie in about half an hour.

DANIEL: Wow, really . . . tell her happy birthday for me.

KEVIN: Will do. Hey, you have a good night, Daniel Delmonico. It was cool sharing a drink with you.

DANIEL: Yeah . . . Yeah, it was.

(KEVIN *starts to go, then stops.*)

KEVIN: May I ask you just one more little question?

DANIEL: Sure.

KEVIN: It's an ego thing.

DANIEL: Fine.

KEVIN: And again, we're in theory land, it's just . . . well, now that we've talked, now that you know me a little . . . would you give a card-carrying Caucasian guy like me a chance? (*Then.*) You would, wouldn't you? Wouldn't you? You would. Wouldn't you? Wouldn't you? Wouldn't you? Wouldn't you?

DANIEL: (*laughing, frustrated*) CHRIST, YOU DRIVE ME TOTALLY INSANE!!

KEVIN: See, now, I think that's a very healthy start.

DANIEL: I don't know. . . . I guess you are sort of charming. In a totally psychotic kind of way. Sure, what the hell.

(*Little beat.*)

KEVIN: AND SCORE THREE FOR THE KEVINATOR!!!

DANIEL: No way . . . no fucking way . . .

KEVIN: WHOOSH! KEVIN DOESN'T CHOKE ON THE BIG ONE!!

DANIEL: Hold on, so you're actually . . . ?

KEVIN: Yep, full-on gay. Completely queer. A great big bucket o' nell.

DANIEL: I don't believe this. . . .

KEVIN: I knew you were coming around! I could tell!

DANIEL: Get away from me, okay? Leave me alone forever, starting right now.

KEVIN: What are you talking about? We have a date to go on, cowboy.

DANIEL: Are you insane? No! No, we do NOT!

KEVIN: After *all that WORK?!* Do you have any idea how DIFFI-CULT that was, thinking on my feet like that? I totally forgot little Amber's name there for a full thirty seconds.

DANIEL: There is no way in hell I am *ever* going on a date with you, Kevin . . . if that is your real name.

KEVIN: It's actually Hernando, which is pretty ironic. (*Off* DANIEL's *look.*) THAT WAS A JOKE!!

DANIEL: See, that's why I won't go out with you. *That* is my point exactly. Aside from the fact that you're a complete freak—and that's high on the list of reasons why I won't go out with you—there's also this little problem of me having no idea who you really are! Or what you might pull!

KEVIN: Oh, come on . . .

DANIEL: Come on what? We could get to some restaurant, and you'd tell me that you're really a woman. Or that you're Vietnamese. Or that you're a VIETNAMESE WOMAN! Or, or I'd get you home, and then you'd try to rob me, and this whole thing would turn out to be some extended con!

KEVIN: It's not a con.

DANIEL: You *conned* me into saying I'd go out with you!

KEVIN: I did not.

DANIEL: You did! You lied to me repeatedly!

KEVIN: I didn't lie—fine, you want to know who I am?

(DANIEL *rolls his eyes.*)

KEVIN: I'm a guy who's been coming to this bar on Thursdays for months, who noticed you weeks ago and thought you were certifiably cute, only you've never even seen me. You looked right through me. And fine, maybe I'm nothing special. I know that. But I've seen you making *gay eyes* at Latin men who are far, far less nothing special than I am. And that pissed me off, frankly. So when you left your card at the

ATM machine, it seemed like I was being given this chance. And . . . I just wanted you to *see* me for a few minutes. For one conversation.

DANIEL: AND YOU COULDN'T JUST SAY, "HI, I FOUND YOUR ATM CARD?!"

KEVIN: Sure, but how unoriginal would that have been? And I didn't lie to you, for the record. I *surprised* you. I kept you guessing. And for a while there, near the end, you were pretty intrigued by me, I could tell. You were dancing right alongside me. And I still happen to think you're certifiably cute.

DANIEL: Just . . . stop making all this shit up, okay?

KEVIN: I won't make up any more shit. I promise.

DANIEL: And never make me drink a Bacardi Breezer in public again.

KEVIN: I won't.

DANIEL: Beyond that, I just . . . I don't even know what I'm supposed to say to you.

KEVIN: How about we just . . . let's just . . . (*Turns to him, anew.*) Hey.

DANIEL: (*after a pause*) Hey.

(*The lights fade on them.*)

DEER PLAY

Mary Louise Wilson

Deer Play was first performed at Actors & Writers in Olivebridge, New York, on October 2, 1999, with the playwright directing the following cast:

MADGE	Nicole Quinn
MABLE	Sarah Chodoff
LOCAL MAN	Joe White
DEER	David Smilow

ACT ONE

(*Two actresses meet in Joe Allen's Restaurant.*)

MABLE: Madge! Darling!

MADGE: Mable! Darling!

MABLE: It's been ages!

MADGE: Ages!

MABLE: You. Look. Fabulous.

MADGE: What is that you're wearing? I love it.

MABLE: (*alarmed shout*) You cut your hair!

MADGE: Don't look at my nails!

MABLE: What are you doing now? Are you in anything?

MADGE: In the country, Darling! Up in my little cottage.

MABLE: I will never forget you in "Put Down That Hammer." I
  can't believe that was three years ago.

MADGE: I adore it up there, surrounded by nature—

MABLE: —You were Brrrillliant in that.

MADGE: You can't imagine how glorious it is—the air! The trees!
  Deer grazing in the meadow!

MABLE: Are you up for anything now?

MADGE: I've taken up gardening, Darling! Oh yes, I'm a huge gardener.

MABLE: Were you seen for that new play "Closet"?

MADGE: I'm seeing about being seen. . . .

MABLE: You should be seen. You're perfect for the mother.

MADGE: I've just become so terribly taken *up* with gardening. I'm devoting all my time to it.

MABLE: I had three callbacks. My agent said they loved me but they went in another direction.

MADGE: I'm so preoccupied with tilth and aerating and mulch and bone meal. . . .

MABLE: Oh! I saw "Spatula" last night. Brrrillliant. Absolutely Brrrillliant.

MADGE: You know what the single most important element in gardening is?

MABLE: You should have played the mother. You would have been Brrrillliant.

MADGE: Soil. Rich, friable soil.

MABLE: I can't believe you weren't submitted for that.

MADGE: That, and a really deep hole.

MABLE: Are you listening to me?

MADGE: (*She comes unstoppered.*) Of course I am, Sweetie! I'm just so *involved*—I've turned my whole property into a perennial bed, you know.

MABLE: Really.

MADGE: Yes! I'm creating my own little Sissinghurst, a deliciously disordered jumble of flowering and foliage plantings, punctuated by topiary. I'm going to send climbers up the trees and twine clematis around the phone wires.

MABLE: You don't say.

MADGE: Pots and pots and pots of annuals and herbs everywhere and giant urns dripping nasturtiums and tons and tons of roses! My floribundas are in bud, my rugosas are about to explode, my Frau Dagmar Hartopp is a repeat bloomer, you know.

MABLE: No.

MADGE: Yes! She's doing fabulously this year. I discovered that she likes a bit of whole wheat flour sprinkled around her ankles. You know, my absolute favorite rose was always the Sparrieshoop but now I have to say it's the Schneezwerg.

MABLE: Schwooznerz . . .

MADGE: Schneezwerg. It has beautiful hips. I've planted *Alchemilla mollis* everywhere, and eupatorium and *Campanula persicifolia,* the white variety of course, and geranium "Johnson's Blue" and *Phlox paniculata,* two kinds, Eva Cullum and Dodo Hanbury Forbes. Phlox must never get its feet wet! On the other hand, *Alcea rosea* detests rich soil. What *Alcea rosea* loves is a *wall.* I've been worrying all week about my *Hydrangea anomala petiolaris.* It's got something. I'm going to erect a sweet little potting shed among the lilies—(*During the last two sentences,* MABLE's *eyes close and her head slowly lowers into her salad.*) Mable? You're in the radicchio.

(*End Act One.*)

ACT TWO

(MADGE *and* MABLE *arrive in the country.*)

MADGE: Here we are!

MABLE: We're here?

MADGE: This is it.

MABLE: Darling! It's beyond cute.

MADGE: Come on, get out of the car, come, come, come, come, I want to show you the garden.

MABLE: (MABLE *points.*) *That* is your cottage?

MADGE: That is my cottage.

MABLE: Too adorable. The little *windows*!

MADGE: Come on, leave your bags—

MABLE: I'll just drop them inside—

MADGE: No.

MABLE: I'll just use the ladies—

MADGE: NO! First, my gardenzia— The lilies were just on the verge of bloom when I left last weekend. . . . See, over here I've filled the entire area with Eupitor—wait. Wait a minute. Wait a little minute. What's missing here? My LILIES! My lilies are gone! They can't be. They were just here. Where'd they go? OhmyGodmyGodmyGod my lilies! My beautiful lilies!

MABLE: What are all these stalks here?

MADGE: (*grief-stricken*) And my MALVA! What in hell happened to my malva? And my verbascum! And my (*huge gasp*) my CONEFLOWERS! They're all deCAPitated! (*Moaning.*) My Astrantia "Margery Fish," my filipendula, my *Coreopsis verticillata*! my *Platycodon grandiflora*! Nibbled, nibbled, every goddamn one of them!

MABLE: Looks like a truck drove through here.

MADGE: (*Agamemnon is dead.*) Oh horror, horror! Oh, oh, oh the pity of it! My eupatorium! My thalictrum! My *Alchemilla mollis*! And look! My digitalis, my lysimachia, my darling dianthus, my Cimici—Cimifi—Cis—my Snakeroot—I can't, I can't—

MABLE: What do you say we go inside and have us some gin?

MADGE: And my ROHOHOHSES! Oh no no no no no, not my darling roses! No, no, no, no . . . not my little ones . . .

MABLE: Don't go there, Madge. . . .

MADGE: My Constance Spry, my Blanc de Double de Coubert, my *Moyessii*!—eaten, eaten, thorns and all . . . Oh my precious darlings, who did this horrible thing to you? Who? Who? Oh woe, oh woe-is-me . . .

MABLE: Madge? Madge, come back. I'd like to wash up.

MADGE: (*mumbling, stumbling off*) Blow winds, crack your cheeks. . . .

(*End Act Two.*)

ACT THREE

(MADGE *and* LOCAL MAN *stand in the garden.*)

LOCAL MAN: Okay, lady, whaddaya want me to do?

MADGE: Look at this! Look at this, this *devastation*.

LOCAL MAN: Ho! Looks like the deer done had a four-course meal.

MADGE: DEER did this?

LOCAL MAN: Well it weren't your Aunt Mary. . . .

MADGE: But I feed them! I put hay out in the field for them!

LOCAL MAN: Lady, if you got a plate of oatmeal in front of you and you look across the way and see a T-bone steak sitting there—

MADGE: Well, I want you to fix it so they can't have my T-bone. My flowers.

LOCAL MAN: Lady. You can't do nuttin' about deer.

MADGE: There must be a repellent of some sort!

LOCAL MAN: Oh yeah, but after a while the deer don't care, it don't make no difference—

MADGE: I want you to put up a fence. A ten-foot fence.

LOCAL MAN: (*chuckling*) Lady, deer can jump a twelve-foot fence. From a sitting position. Deer can squoze theyselves underneath. Deer can flatten theyselves and slide through itty-bitty cracks one inch wide. Deer can shinny up fifty-foot flagpoles—

MADGE: All right allright allRIGHT!

LOCAL MAN: The only answer for deer is L-E-A-D. BOOM! L-E-A-D.

(*End Act Three.*)

ACT FOUR

(MADGE's *house*)

(MABLE's *voice is heard behind* MADGE's *stockade fence.*)

MABLE: Who-hoo! Madge? Madge? It's me. Mable. May I come in?

MADGE: (*low monotone*) Suit yourself.

MABLE: The gate is locked.

MADGE: Oh—wait—

MABLE: Was that river there before?

MADGE: It's a moat.

MABLE: I was antiquing in the area so I thought I'd stop by on my way back to the city.

MADGE: Yuh.

MABLE: Where in the world have you been all these months? You disappeared! What have you been up to?

MADGE: Oh—gardening . . .

MABLE: You know I got a leading role on "All the Worlds of Our Days"?

MADGE: I *say* "gardening," more like "The Terminator"—

MABLE: I play a murderess who's having an affair with the presiding judge.

MADGE: The enemy is out there and the enemy is Bambi.

MABLE: The judge turns out to be a lesbian—

MADGE: I lugged bags and bags of hair clippings up from Elizabeth Arden's and threw them all over the roses—I think some of Diane Sawyer's hair was in there—

MABLE: Then she catches me in bed with my attorney—

MADGE: That worked for about two weeks, until they grew to like hairs in their food. . . . Then I tried rotten eggs . . . yellow slime all over the daylilies . . . that kept 'em away for a day or two. . . . Then I hung bars of Irish Spring soap from everything . . . the stench was so bad it kept *me* away. . . .

MABLE: The attorney leaves me for his former wife's stepdaughter—

MADGE: I tried sprays and pellets and goo and mothballs and mesh and cages and—

MABLE: Unbeknownst to me, I marry my father—

MADGE: First they ate the tulips, then the daylilies—just gobbled them up—

MABLE: He finds out, he poisons me, I die horribly—

MADGE: Gobblegobblegobble—

MABLE: And I come back as my twin sister.

MADGE: *Then* the phlox *and* the hollyhock *and* the daisies *and* the campanula, *then* the *roses,* then the *deer*-resistant plants, then the *Christmas* trees—

MABLE: I didn't know they ate Christmas trees—

MADGE: I was pretty proud of my garden. . . . I labored long hours there—

MABLE: We all wanted to *see* your garden—

MADGE: Digging planting watering ferting pinching pruning weeding deadheading—

MABLE: Well, it's late, I better be going—

MADGE: Mulching root-pruning spraying separating propagating—

MABLE: It's a long drive back—

MADGE: Their number is legion, you know—last night there were forty of them standing on my front lawn. Forty! I counted.

MABLE: You really ought to get out more.

MADGE: Every morning there they are staring at me through the kitchen window. Just standing there, staring. And chewing.

MABLE: Go shopping! Join a gym!

MADGE: Two of them were spotted in Home Depot last week. In Lawn Furniture.

MABLE: Are you seeing anyone these days?

MADGE: Who the hell is there to see?

MABLE: There must be *some*body—

MADGE: Oh Mable, the last time I uncrossed my legs bats flew out!

MABLE: Madge, dear—

MADGE: DON'T CALL ME THAT!

MABLE: Sorry, sorry.

MADGE: Excuse me a minute.

MABLE: Where are you going? (MADGE *goes over to her dahlia bed, pulls her pants down, and squats.*) Madge! What are you doing???

MADGE: What does it look like? I'm protecting what's left of my dahlias.

MABLE: What if someone saw you!

MADGE: I have to drink gallons of water every day.

MABLE: Get up. Pull your pants up!

MADGE: I only do this when I run out of coyote urine.

(*End Act Four.*)

ACT FIVE

(MADGE's *house. At night.*)

(MADGE *sits in her nightie on her porch steps in the moonlight watching several deer devouring her garden.*)

MADGE: Look at them. . . . Mangy beasts . . . chewing away. . . . (*Calls to them.*) Enjoy your meal, boys! . . . Dig in. . . . When you've polished off my Lab-Lab vine, why don't you give my nice *Helianthus angustifolius* a taste? Got to get your greens! Look at them looking at me. I could be yodeling, dancing the fandango, they couldn't care less. Either they're extremely nearsighted or they're brain-dead. (*Yelling a little.*) You stupid stupid animals! You've ruined my dream! You've destroyed everything I loved! . . . (*Sees a large male deer standing apart from the others.*) Look at this one, staring at me. What are you staring at, you big idiot?

DEER: You.

MADGE: What?

DEER: I'm staring at you.

MADGE: You're *talking*?

DEER: Your smell is strange. Provoking.

MADGE: Don't come any nearer!

DEER: You two-legs fascinate me.

MADGE: Aren't you afraid of me?

DEER: Are you afraid of me?

MADGE: Well, you are quite—*large* up close. . . .

DEER: I am a very big buckeroo.

MADGE: God! Your *BREATH*!

DEER: Your daylilies are the yummiest I ever tasted. What do you put in them?

MADGE: Say, I've always wanted to ask, what is all that snorting you boys do?

DEER: Feel my antlers.

MADGE: No. I hate you! Go away!

DEER: But, we're in the middle of dinner here.

MADGE: Yeah! Right! What's the special tonight? The Ranunculus Ragout? The Daisy Melange?

DEER: You know, when I see you in your garden down on all fours pawing at the dirt, I get ideas.

MADGE: Beat it.

DEER: Go on, feel my antlers.

MADGE: Oh all right, but then you really must go. (*She puts her hand on his antlers.*) They're quite amazing. Very—horny. (*Shocked, embarrassed giggle.*) Your antlers are. Hornlike. Excellent equipment. (*More embarrassed giggles.*) Oh dear.

DEER: You called?

MADGE: Cut it out.

DEER: Stroke my flank?

MADGE: No. Hey! Don't put your muzzle there.

DEER: Come into the woods with me.

MADGE: Don't be absurd. You're a *deer.*

DEER: Lie with me.

MADGE: No! I can't. It would never work out.

DEER: Come on.

MADGE: Oh God, your *eye*lashes! Don't look at me like that.

DEER: Come on.

MADGE: Your smell! I loooowuu*uuuuuve* it! (*The word "loathe" surrendering into the word "love."*)

(*As they walk off into the woods.*)

DEER: You're so dainty and hairless.

MADGE: I didn't shave my legs. . . .

DEER: I know where there's a secluded flower bed. . . .

(*Music swells.*)

EL DEPRESSO ESPRESSO

Laura Shaine Cunningham

El Depresso Espresso premiered June 2001, as part of Evening "A" of The Hospital Plays at the HB Playwrights Foundation in New York City. The play was directed by Guy Boyd; the set design was by Michael Schweikardt; the lighting design was by John Lasiter; the costume design was by Mary Margaret O'Neill; the sound design was by Jon Kadela; the production stage manager was David Apichell. The cast was as follows:

MO	Patrick Darragh
LIV	Elizabeth Bunch
DR. YOSHIMURA	Toshiro Yamamoto
DR. OBOLENSKI	Christine Farrell

CHARACTERS

MO: A man, youngish, very depressed (should be able to do Irish inflection, slight).

LIV: A woman, youngish, very depressed (should be able to do Jewish inflection, slight).

DR. YOSHIMURA: Handsome Japanese doctor.

DR. OBOLENSKI: Beautiful Russian doctor.

PROPS: Draped coffee cart, Starbucks containers.

MUSIC: Cajun, zydeco cassettes.

(The depression clinic of a well-known New York City hospital. Midnight. A drizzly, dreary spring night. Outside, police and ambulance sirens shrill the call of the city-wild. The sterile room has a sign: "YOSHIMURA-Obolenski Depression Clinic." There are a row of plain chairs, a movable screen, and a draped medical cart. As the lights come up, we see MO, *a depressed young man, slumped in his chair, a crumpled cigarette pack in his hand. His head is low, his hands drag toward the floor. He occasionally fondles himself. He is in a deep melancholia.* LIV, *a young woman, also depressed, enters, in a tentative, diffident manner, backs out, reenters, finally addresses* MO. *She holds a newspaper advertisement, crumpled in her hand, and also a pack of cigarettes.)*

LIV: Is . . . is this . . . the right place? (MO *doesn't respond.*) Is . . . Is this the YOSHIMURA-Obolenski Depression Clinic? I saw the ad. (*She reads crumpled newspaper.*) "Have your eating and sleeping habits changed? Have you gained or lost weight? Do you start to cry for no reason?" (*She sniffles.*) "If you have answered 'yes' to any of the above questions, you may be eligible for a new and innovative treatment program that begins tonight, at midnight at the YOSHIMURA-Obolenski Depression Clinic. You will be paid for your participation." So . . . is this it? (MO *doesn't respond.*) Why did I get out of bed? I should just go home. . . . Now, I'll have to wait hours for the Second Avenue bus. They say it comes every twenty-two minutes after midnight, but they are lying. Oh, the hell with it, I'll take the subway. Oh why don't I just throw myself onto the tracks? And now the fare has gone up. A twenty-dollar fare card and it's all a waste. My fare cards are expired anyway . . . trips I never took. (*She sniffles.*)

MO: (*without lifting his head*) Can't you read? There's a sign.

LIV: (*reading the sign*) Oh, well, now I feel stupid.

(*She sits down, slumps beside* MO. *He reacts, ever so slightly inching away.*)

MO: Do you mind?

LIV: What?

MO: I don't like people . . . touching me. It gives me the heebie jeebies.

(*She inches away.*)

LIV: I'm sorry. I'm sorry. Yeah, yeah, I'm so sorry, sorry I'm alive.

MO: Yeah.

LIV: So where's the doctors? The ad says "Anti-Depression Team." Innovative New Three-Pronged Treatment for Depression.

MO: How would I know.

(*At that moment, we hear clicketty clack of brisk steps and white lab-coated doctors* YOSHIMURA *and* OBOLENSKI *enter.* DR. YOSHIMURA *is a handsome man and* DR. OBOLENSKI *is a stunning woman.*)

DR. YOSHIMURA: Hi! We're so glad . . . you've . . .

DR. OBOLENSKI: Chosen to attend our clinic . . .

MO: I said "I'd *see*."

LIV: You don't have to pay me to participate. You know, maybe this is a mistake. I don't like the lighting . . . too bright. I don't like the color scheme either. Or the feel of the chairs. Or this . . . other . . . individual. (*She indicates* MO.) . . . I think I'll wait for the bus after all. . . .

DR. YOSHIMURA: (*whisper to* DR. OBOLENSKI) Correct his thinking. . . . I'll deal with her. . . .

(Each doctor flanks a patient, consolingly. Dialogue may overlap.)

DR. YOSHIMURA: (*to* LIV) So tell me . . . (*He looks at a card.*) Liv. Have you experienced changes in your sleeping pattern?

LIV: Yes. I used to sleep eighteen hours a day, now it's twenty-three. I'm wearing my nightgown under this raincoat.

DR. OBOLENSKI: (*to* MO) Mo, may I call you that?

MO: I don't care what you call me.

DR. OBOLENSKI: I love the name "Mo" . . . Short for Morton? Or Mohammed?

MO: I dunno. My parents abandoned me after a few years of abuse. They just used to say, I don't want you no *mo.* The name stuck.

DR. OBOLENSKI: So, Mo, change in weight . . . up or down?

MO: I feel a disgusting subcutaneous layer of fat and gristle all over my body, double-roll folds over my belly when I sit on the toilet which is almost all the time. The single thing that comforts me is smoking . . . and they won't let me light up in here. . . .

DR. YOSHIMURA: (*to* LIV) And have you noticed a change in your appetite?

LIV: Yes, it's worse. I want to eat things that are bad for me. Mostly donut holes, and ranchero spicy chips—I know people say I'm thin, even skinny, but when I look in the mirror I see a fat, humongous blob. . . . I wish I could smoke.

DR. OBOLENSKI: (*to* MO) How many times a day do you masturbate?

MO: Why do you want to know?

DR. OBOLENSKI: It's an indicator.

MO: There are intervals when I don't. Isn't that what everyone does when they are left alone for a few minutes in a room? C'mon, don't make it like it's me. Huh?

DR. OBOLENSKI: Of course, everyone does. But frequency . . . can . . . indicate anxiety. So how many times, Mo . . . ? Trust me, whatever you say, I've heard it before, everything has happened to someone, somewhere, *maybe even to me* . . . So? How many times a day?

(DR. YOSHIMURA *pays attention to her, also, attracted.*)

MO: I don't count after thirteen.

DR. OBOLENSKI: Do you live alone?

MO: What do you think?

DR. YOSHIMURA: (*to* LIV) Do you hear voices?

LIV: I don't like to say.

DR. YOSHIMURA: What do they tell you? What do they tell you to do, Liv?

LIV: I don't know. Jump, sort of. Out a window. On a track. It doesn't matter. I won't do it. I have no follow-through.

DR. YOSHIMURA: Do you think you are ready to feel better, Liv? The fact that you came here, on your own, says everything Liv. . . . That is more than half the battle.

DR. OBOLENSKI: Do you feel ready to feel better, Mo?

(*He doesn't respond. He puts unlit cigarette in his mouth.*)

DR. OBOLENSKI: No smoking, Mo.

MO: It's not lit. I only suck the filter.

DR. OBOLENSKI: You arrived early, Mo. . . . That's a sign of optimism. . . .

MO: No, it's not—I had nowhere to go.

DR. OBOLENSKI: I think it is a cry for help.

MO: No it's not.

(*The doctors confer.*)

DR. YOSHIMURA: Listen, this is a good test of the treatment. I would describe both of them as acutely depressed, wouldn't you?

DR. OBOLENSKI: I have seen only a little bit more depressed, back in Sitka, Siberia, where I trained.

DR. YOSHIMURA: You trained in Sitka? I always wanted to go there. Okay. The three-pronged treatment.

MO: Don't give me no placebo. I want the real drugs.

LIV: Right. No placebo, for me, either. I don't want to be in a control group.

DR. OBOLENSKI: Fine! This is good! The two of you! Look at you! Insisting on treatment!

MO, LIV: What is it?

DR. YOSHIMURA: It is the three-pronged approach. We fight depression from without, within, and below. We use drugs, behavior modification, and talk therapy in combination. . . .

DR. OBOLENSKI: First, we explain: Depression in a social context. That it is global, normal. Every culture has a version of depression. I come from Russia where pessimism is accepted as a philosophy. Our great writers teach us that life is hopeless, love doomed, and we cannot trust even ourselves. . . . We betray our innermost consciences, and commit horrendous crimes for which we are eventually punished. We live lives of dread that are fulfilled in agony! (*She sounds chipper.*) So that's normal for us!

DR. YOSHIMURA: And in my country of origin, Japan, a history of oppression and depersonalization has legitimized our rigidity and compulsive conformity. (*He smiles brightly.*) We recognize suicide as a logical solution to our problems: It does solve them! And it is honorable! . . . We have lost touch with the old ways that once sustained us. We are even losing our ethnic physical characteristics as modern Japanese people grow taller and we notice that even our subway cars seem too small for us. . . . We resent living in tiny rooms, on tiny futons. We are not so tiny anymore. Yet, this also makes us disoriented, as we know our respected ancestors would not approve when we drink instant tea.

MO, LIV: What does this have to do with us?

DR. YOSHIMURA: What is your ethnic background?

MO: I think Irish.

DR. OBOLENSKI: Irish. Oh, well, that has its own bleakness, the life of diminished expectations and even those are not met, as the culture conditions individuals to deny themselves pleasure at every slight opportunity. Joy is often confused with sin. There is a morbid preoccupation with the dead. The only satisfaction is in the grim realization that your suffering on this earth will be finite although you may burn in eternity for whatever moment of happiness you mistakenly knew. . . . (*She smiles brightly.*) Right? And alcoholism is a socially accepted way to deal with this state of mind, so you most likely have substance abuse problems on top of your innate cultural and personal despair. . . . Hair of the dog that bit ya—an 'tis a very black dog, indeed!

DR. YOSHIMURA: (*to* DR. OBOLENSKI) That was wonderful. . . . (*to* LIV) And you, your ethnic background and predisposition toward a cultural form of despair?

LIV: Jewish!

DR. YOSHIMURA: "Oy Gevalt!" You see I have studied intensely in Brooklyn and the Bronx to understand the psychology of imagined disaster, constant anxiety, compounded by hysteria and a cultural tendency toward overeating and gasid indigestion as a self-remedy—"in the kishkas!" for your unrealistically high goals for yourself that predestine you to feeling like a failure. . . .

LIV: I didn't think the goals were unrealistic—my parents are both Ph.D.s in physics, and have been happily married and faithful to one another for forty-four years! It's *me*! Give me something!

MO: Yeah, just give me the drugs, too.

DR. YOSHIMURA: (*to* DR. OBOLENSKI) What do you think . . . correct the parental imaging?

DR. OBOLENSKI: (*to* YOSHIMURA) It's worth a try.

(YOSHIMURA *grabs* LIV, OBOLENSKI *grabs* MO.)

DR. OBOLENSKI: (*to* MO) I am your Mama. I give you my breast. Ooh . . . ouchinka, touchinka! Mammala Mammala . . . Kuchy Koo . . .

(*She makes kissy noises,* DR. YOSHIMURA *notices.*)

DR. YOSHIMURA: (*to* LIV, *but also saying this to* DR. OBOLENSKI) How's my little doll? How is Daddy's best girl! I squeeze your cheeks! (*He makes kissy noises too. The patients,* MO *and* LIV, *do not respond.*)

DR. YOSHIMURA: (*to* DR. OBOLENSKI) Patients unresponsive, Dr. Obolenski, want to try the much-needed Significant Other?

DR. OBOLENSKI: It is sometimes effective with those who do not have a Significant Other. . . . (*She looks for his wedding band.*)

DR. YOSHIMURA, DR. OBOLENSKI: (*to their patients*) I love you! I find you attractive!

(MO, LIV, *do not respond.*)

YOSHIMURA, OBOLENSKI: Okay, prong three: Chemical . . . Where's the cart? (*They push the draped cart toward the patients.*)

LIV: Give me something so I can dream, or just go under . . . I want something sensual . . . escapist . . . but nothing that will make me so lethargic I gain weight.

DR. YOSHIMURA: All right, we researched the world over, for a culture that was not depressive, and we fixed on the Cajun, Creoles from New Orleans. They had mood swings but, by and large a cross-section of Cajun people showed them to be very upbeat—singing . . . making love, paddling boats in the bayou, hunting for crawfish and serving them etouffee. . . . Dancing whenever they get the chance. . . . We studied their lifestyle and discovered they drank a particular kind of coffee. . . .

(DR. OBOLENSKI *whips the drape off the cart, and we see a large coffee dispenser, with tall cups, à la Starbucks, large, larger, and humongous.*)

DR. OBOLENSKI: So what will it be? A Grande Latte? Or a Vente Latte? A cappuccino or Frappuccino?

MO: Hey, what is this? Another Starbucks?

DR. OBOLENSKI: You are only partly correct. Starbucks has financed our trial study. We wondered what would happen, if the euphoric effect of lattes and cappuccinos were combined with some basic serotonin uptake drugs such as those usually employed in Zoloft and Prozac? Cappuccino with a dusting of Zoloft and a dash of cinnamon? They come in Large, Larger, and Humongous. We can give you a cup of coffee as big as you are, in a cup with a drawstring waist and you can dance with it, if you feel good enough!

(*Strains of Cajun music, zydeco play. The stunned* MO *and* LIV *sip from giant cups.*)

DR. YOSHIMURA: Go ahead, dance . . . Fay-do-doh? (*He smiles, dances a bit, energetically stamps his feet.*)

MO, LIV: I don't feel like it—I don't want you near me.

DR. OBOLENSKI: (*to* MO) Dance with me. I will squeeze the pain from your body. . . . Hold me tight!

LIV: Sex is no solution. I am always sadder after . . .

DR. YOSHIMURA: This is not sexual, this compassion hug, to press the pain from you as you drink this exceptional coffee. Please try . . .

(*She hesitates, then sips. He presses her to him.*)

DR. OBOLENSKI: Mo, come here . . . this isn't sexual either. . . . I just want to press my pelvic bones against yours . . . We can grind out the agony, Mo. While you have a Grande Latte or an Espresso Depresso.

(DR. OBOLENSKI *moves into a passionate dance hold with* MO, *rubbing her cheek against his.* LIV *starts to move a bit, in place, to music.* DR. YOSHIMURA *swings* LIV *toward* MO, *who is being squeezed by* DR. OBOLENSKI.)

DR. OBOLENSKI: (*husky whisper to* MO) Let go, Mo, let go of the pain. Oh, I feel it. I feel it entering my body . . . (*She twitches.*)

(MO *swigs another espresso, begins to dance by himself. The two doctors gently guide the couple to one another. The patients,* MO *and* LIV, *still stand, listless, oblivious to the softly playing Louisiana Cajun upbeat sound.* DR. YOSHIMURA *sighs, puts his arm around* DR. OBOLENSKI.)

DR. YOSHIMURA: How do you feel, Sasha? A bit burned out?

DR. OBOLENSKI: Oh, yes, I absorbed so much pain. . . . my head and breast are throbbing . . . Oh, Tim, I feel I'm failing them . . . that it is all hopeless . . . that nothing can remedy despair. . . .

DR. YOSHIMURA: I love you like a mother, a sister, a friend, a comrade, a fellow scientist and a sex goddess. . . . So what do you say? Sweetheart?

DR. OBOLENSKI: (*suspicious*) Did you take something?

DR. YOSHIMURA: (*proffering tiny cup to* DR. OBOLENSKI) Medical sample . . . (*sensual whisper*)

(MO, LIV, *begin to dance a bit in place. The music rises.*)

DR. YOSHIMURA, DR. OBOLENSKI: (*Sing Cajun lyric*)

(*The two doctors sip from one cup, then swirl into the dance. Lights out on the foursome, dancing in manic joy, kissing, embracing, swigging coffee, and fay-do-dohing, zydeco music blares. Blackout.*)

EL SANTO AMERICANO

Edward Bok Lee

El Santo Americano was commissioned by the Guthrie Theater (Joe Dowling, Artistic Director). The play premiered at the Guthrie Theater Lab in an evening of short works titled 7/11 in Minneapolis, Minnesota, in July 2001. It was directed by Doug Mercer; the costume design was by Jeannie Galioto; the lighting design was by Paul J. Hackenmueller; the sound design was by Michael F. Bogden; the production stage manager was Julie L. Odegard; the assistant stage manager was Sarah Mitchell; the dramaturg was Michael Bigelow Dixon. The cast was as follows:

CLAY   Kelly Conway
EVALANA   Breean Julian

CHARACTERS

CLAY: A man.
EVALANA: His wife.

TIME: Present.

PLACE: The desert at night.

CLAY: (*driving at night, 80 mph*) that's because in Mexico it's normal to wear a mask. almost everybody does. silk and satin
and form-fitting lycra. it makes the whole body more aero-
dynamic. you oughta see them flying around, doing triple
flips in mid-air. they got these long flowing capes like colorful wings sprouting from their shoulders. they don't talk
much, though. not the great ones. the silence is mysterious.
it adds a kind of weight to them when they climb into the
ring. get a guy with that much gold and glitter on him here
and you know he'd have to talk shit. in Mexico they just
wrestle. the masks come from thousands and thousands of
years ago. fiestas. ancient rituals. slip one over your head and
you could become a tiger or donkey, a bat or giant lizard. a
corn spirit dancing under the clouds for rain. those were
your gods if you lived back then. you'll like it there in Mexico. don't you think you'll like it there? Jesse?

(EVALANA, *brooding, eventually looks in the backseat then faces front again.*)

CLAY: he asleep back there?
      a growing boy needs his sleep.
      yes he does.
      you hungry?

EVALANA: don't talk to me.

CLAY: hard to fall asleep on an empty stomach.

EVALANA: i can't sleep.

CLAY: you ain't tried to.

EVALANA: i told you.
>i have to go to the bathroom.

CLAY: if i stop, you'll try to run again.

EVALANA: where the hell am i gonna run in the middle of the
>desert at night?
>into a goddamn cactus!?

(*She checks her outburst, then looks in the backseat again, perhaps adjusting their son's blanket, then faces front. They drive on for a time.*)

CLAY: (*looking in rearview mirror*) hey there Jesse.
>you have a nice nap?
>we'll be there come morning, so you just sit back.
>how you like that comic book I got you?
>Jesse?
>what's the matter, boy? you not feeling well?
>Jesse?

EVALANA: sometimes he sleeps with his eyes open.

CLAY: like you.

EVALANA: i do not sleep with my eyes open.

CLAY: how do you know?

EVALANA: i know.

CLAY: how?

EVALANA: cause someone would have said something.
>including you.

CLAY: people do all kinds of things they're not aware of.
>my daddy used to wander through the house all night,
buck naked, up and down the stairs. opening and closing
windows.
>carrying only his briefcase chock full of all the vending
machine products he sold.
>combs. candy. chicken bouillon.

my momma warned if we woke him up he'd have a heart
attack.

so we just let him sleepwalk.

he didn't know.

EVALANA: maybe somebody should have told him.

CLAY: he didn't want to know.

(*They drive on.*)

EVALANA: you talk in your sleep.

you snore.

you drool.

and you fart. all night.

(*They drive on awhile.*)

CLAY: i love you, Ev.

EVALANA: jesus, Clay. listen to yourself.

your whole life you been faking it.

fake husband. fake father.

fake man.

that's what they ought to call you:

Fake Man.

(CLAY *drives on for a little while longer through the night, then pulls the
car to a stop on the side of the road and gets out. He walks a good ways
away from the car, holding a flashlight in one hand and a gun in the
other—not aimed at her, but clearly present, under the starlight.* EVALANA
hesitates, then gets out, the flashlight's beam now on her.)

CLAY: (*Directs flashlight beam to place in the brush.*) there's a bush
over there.

(EVALANA, *hesitant at first, then grabs her purse and crosses past* CLAY.)

EVALANA: (*off*) i won't run!

i promise!

(CLAY *thinks, then lowers flashlight beam and switches it off. Dim moonlight. Sounds of desert at night.*)

CLAY: you should have seen me last week, Ev!

Darton, he cut me a break! he didn't have to, but he did cause i been loyal to him all these years! you remember when we used to work at the turkey plant together!

the smell on my hands when i'd come home and try to kiss you . . .

the match was against the eleventh ranked contender! brand new guy, from Montreal! Kid Canuck they call him! long blonde hair, tan, all bulked up in white trunks with a red maple leaf you know where! some rich producer's nephew or something! he was scheduled to wrestle the Sheik in the opening match, but the old guy had a hernia while they was warming up, so Darton, he give me a break and put me on the bill against Kid Canuck at the last minute!

we didn't have time to choreograph much action! i think he was kind of nervous! two minutes in he starts grabbing my hair! hard! for real! trying to get the audience more into it! he wasn't telegraphing his head butts neither! soon enough my nose was a cherry caught under a dumptruck!

the blood all over sure got the crowd into it boy! up till then they was pretty quiet, waiting for the main headliners to come out!

raking my eyes, slapping my face. i told him to ease up, it don't work like that here, but he wasn't listening. dancing around. cursing at me in French. winding his right arm up, then smacking me hard with the left until both my ears are firebells going off.

now I can take just about anything. you know me. i've been pile-drived, figure-foured, and suplexed into losses by the best of them. but on this particular night, something happened. and one pop I took in the mouth shot my adrenaline way up, my blood running all over hell now like carbolic acid, and him twisting my arm for real, not giving a flying fuck about my bad elbow, my bad back, or my five-year-old son, who don't even like to watch wrestling no more cause he's ashamed, cause his friends call his daddy a loser, and he don't know what to say or believe in, and the next thing i knew i had that pretty boy son of a bitch Kid Canuck down hard on the mat in a scorpion leg-lock!!

they had to haul him off on a stretcher!

i was a little dazed yet, and the crowd, they didn't know what to think!

then the referee threw my arm up under the hot lights and before i knew it all the noise in the arena was more like cheering! it was a chemical thing! at first some people in the upper bleachers stood up! and then all of them did! everywhere! stomping, and starting to chant my name! and not cause they hated the other guy! they didn't! they was cheering cause i beat the guy fair and square! he gave up out of pain, right there in the middle of the ring! i had him wrenched in that scorpion leg-lock a good two minutes screaming like a baby, like a cut pig, like a man in real pain! and they knew it! you can't fake that! they'd seen so much phoney bullshit through the years, and they could tell this match was different!

and they appreciated that!

they appreciated being shown the truth, just once in their sorry-ass lives!

Darton threw a wet towel at my face in the locker room.

i went out on a limb for you!, he says. six months of planning and promotion! tens of thousands of dollars! T-shirts! coffee mugs! now who the hell's gonna believe Kid Canuck is a contender for the federation championship when he lost his debut match to you!!

i told him i was sorry, and after a while he put his hand on my shoulder. asked me what i'd been thinking there in the ring. tell me the truth, he says. so i can go home and feel at least a little bad about firing your dumb ass.

and i wanted to say that i did it for you.

for my wife, Evalana, who i never gave nothing to believe in.

and i did it for my boy, Jesse. who only ever got to see his daddy get beat time and again. i wanted to tell him i did it cause my wife and child was out there in the audience.

not living in some other town.

i wanted to say you was both out there watching over me. cause where else would you be?

Ev? Evalana! (CLAY *switches on flashlight and directs its beam onto the "bush" in the desert.* EVALANA *has run off. He directs the flashlight all around, searching in vain.*) shit. (CLAY *turns off the flashlight and sits down on a stone. In the moonlight, he pulls out from his pocket a colorful Mexican wrestler's mask, and slips it over his head. He sits there in the darkness alone for a moment. He then, as a little boy might, twirls the gun on his finger, and pretends what it'd be like to shoot himself in the head. He tries it from a couple different angles, in strange fun. Eventually he places the gun in his mouth, holds it there for a second or two with his hand, then lets go. It remains stuck there in his mouth from here on out. Eventually, out of the darkness of the desert,* EVALANA *reappears.*)

EVALANA: once, when i was about Jesse's age, we took a trip to California. Disneyland. we drove all the way cross country in Daddy's Ford Falcon. Ma said it was the honeymoon she never got. a lot of the highway had just been tarred, and you could feel it. i thought we was was gonna sail on forever into the future. it was somewhere in Arizona that Daddy woke us all up so we could see this great big dam at night. we stood there looking down at the bright lights and roaring darkness. Ma moved off to one side and stared down, a thousand feet.

i knew she wanted to jump.

then suddenly, she pointed at something. "look, Ev," she said. "a rainbow!"

Shane and Darlene came running over, climbing up on the guardrail. but they couldn't see nothing. neither could Daddy.

a few hours later, somewhere outside of Flagstaff i told them i saw that rainbow too. it wasn't just Ma who saw it. I saw it too. Shane and Darlene were asleep now. Ma didn't say nothing. we drove on deeper into the night. then Daddy looked at me. i could see his eyes in the rearview mirror. hovering there in the blackness. "there's no such thing as a rainbow at night," he said. "not a real rainbow anyway."

the next day at dusk we camped on high ground. from where i stood looking down, you could see all the layers of sediment carved in the side of the mountains they cleared away for the highways a long time ago. red, black, brown, white, and sometimes almost blue, like a human vein in the side of a mountain, running parallel to the horizon. i stood there a long time, watching all the layers of earthen rainbows darkening all around me. then slowly, i noticed something. in the far distance, a cluster of fallen stars. only, it wasn't a cluster of stars, but a town. far off the highway, down there in the middle of nowhere. you wouldn't even notice it by day. but at night you could see something. twinkling. i imagined i'd been born in that town, and that that was where we was all heading back to. not Disneyland. but that town shining with tiny stars that weren't really stars, surrounded by rainbows that weren't really rainbows. but erosion. as far as the eye could see. for thousands and thousands of years. both real and imaginary. like that town down there in the valley at night. just barely shimmering. like . . . Eden.

(*We hear the sound of their car start and drive off into the night.* CLAY *in mask with gun still in mouth and* EVALANA *slowly turn to watch the vehicle go, converging closer together as they walk and watch.* JESSE *has driven off into the night. Once the sound of the car has faded into the distance,* CLAY *in mask with gun in mouth and* EVALANA *slowly turn to one another. After a moment,* EVALANA *reaches up and removes the gun from* CLAY*'s mouth and slowly points it at him. Fade to black.*)

EMOTIONAL BAGGAGE

Nina Shengold

Emotional Baggage premiered at Actors & Writers, Olivebridge, New York, on October 28, 2000, where it was directed by the author. The cast was as follows:

DICK	David Smilow
PHYLLIS	Sarah Chodoff
LOUISE VUITTON	Tad Ingram
ROLLO	Joe White
AMBER	Shelley Wyant
MILDRED	Carol Morley
OFFSTAGE "CREW" VOICE	Kevin O'Rourke

CHARACTERS

DICK: An irate Samsonite pullman.
PHYLLIS: A panicky carry-on bag.
LOUISE VUITTON: Attaché case, a drag queen wannabe.
ROLLO: A drug smuggler's duffel, beat-up and beatific.
AMBER: Brassy, an over-the-hill overnight bag.
MILDRED: A dignified, threadbare valise from the South.
OFFSTAGE "CREW" VOICE

COSTUME NOTE: All characters should wear normal human clothing, possibly tending toward leathers, tweeds, and other luggage-like fabrics. They might also have airport stickers, tags dangling from glasses frames, ponytail holders, belt loops, etc. Use your discretion.

(*A near-empty baggage claim carousel at Newark Airport, on which a few stray suitcases circle forlornly. [Actors shuffle around the periphery of the stage shoulder to shoulder, as if swept along by a rotating belt.]* PHYLLIS *stands crookedly, leaning on* DICK *as if thrown there.*)

DICK: This sucks.

(*An attaché case—*LOUISE VUITTON*—sidles after them.*)

LOUISE: *Where* can my pickup be??

(PHYLLIS *and* DICK *turn in unison, facing the side wall as the "carousel" circles upstage.* DICK *looks back over his shoulder.*)

DICK: How many times have you been around?

LOUISE: Please. I've stopped counting.

PHYLLIS: I'm dizzy. My straps hurt. I'm going to catch cold!

DICK: Quit whining. (*Shouts into the wings.*) YO, HEY!!! COME AND GET ME, YOU MORON!!!

LOUISE: Shut up or the redcaps'll grab you.

DICK: Let 'em try it. I'll smash their damn toes. Do you know what I *weigh?* I'm a Samsonite hardbody!

LOUISE: How hard?

DICK: I'm gonna flatten you.

(*He makes an impotent lunge, nearly toppling* PHYLLIS.)

PHYLLIS: Please! I've got mal de mer!

(*The carousel shuts off abruptly. They lurch to a sudden stop.*)

LOUISE: Uh-oh.

PHYLLIS: It *stopped!* The belt, the, the thing . . . it's not—

DICK: (*hissed whisper*) Cheese it, the crew. Look inanimate.

(DICK *and* LOUISE *freeze in place.* PHYLLIS *continues to panic for a beat, then freezes suddenly. Long pause, all tense. Then:*)

PHYLLIS: What—

DICK: Sssh!

(*An exaggerated, stentorian "giant" voice booms from the wings.*)

CREW: (*offstage*) LOOKS LIKE WE GOT US A COUPLE OF UNCLAIMED BAGS. LUG 'EM.

(PHYLLIS *and* DICK *are "lifted" in unison [shoulders pulled up toward the ceiling as if picked up by giant hands], followed by* LOUISE, *who slaps her invisible lifter.*)

LOUISE: Hands *off!*

PHYLLIS: Where are they taking us??

DICK: Lockup. The big house.

PHYLLIS: (*eyes wide*) Not—

DICK: Unclaimed baggage.

(*The unseen hands "throw" them down onto a luggage rack.*)

PHYLLIS: Oh God!

LOUISE: My heart.

DICK: Fuckin' screws!!!

PHYLLIS: (*fearfully*) . . . Who are those other bags?

(AMBER *saunters on, followed by* ROLLO *and* MILDRED.)

DICK: Looks like rough trade. Maybe lifers.

AMBER: Hey, big boy, what's in the bulge? Is that a travel umbrella, or are you glad to see me?

DICK: Fuck off, cowhide.

AMBER: (*casing* LOUISE) Hey, handsome. Nice logo.

LOUISE: I'm Louis Vuitton!

AMBER: Christ. They're *all* gay. (*Eyeing* PHYLLIS.) It's a good thing I swing both ways. Kidding.

(*She barks a short, humorless laugh and plunks into a chair with her arm around* PHYLLIS.)

PHYLLIS: OhGodOhGodOhGodOhGOD!!!

ROLLO: (*sitting on* PHYLLIS*'s other side*) Chill, babe. What are you, a carry-on?

PHYLLIS: Yes! I'm a carry-on! I was made to be carried! I *would* have been carried if *she* hadn't bought so much Duty-Free Tia Maria! I was flying First Class!

MILDRED: So was I, my dear. So was I.

(*She sits with a thud.*)

ROLLO: What're you in for?

PHYLLIS: Beg pardon?

ROLLO: Lost tag, missed connection? You holding?

PHYLLIS: I don't . . . I'm . . .

ROLLO: You're just off the plane from Cancun, right? A little ahem talcum powder packed into the toilet kit? A few wonky Vitamin Cs? Sensemilla-stuffed diapers?

PHYLLIS: I flew down for a Realtors' convention!

ROLLO: Did the beagle sniff you? I hate it when they sniff you.

DICK: Leave her alone or I'll pop you one right in the buckle.

ROLLO: Big man. I'm aquiver. First time in the joint? (PHYLLIS
   nods. ROLLO *nods toward the audience.*) We got some hard cases.
   Watch out for that camp trunk. And Rolf there, that ruck-
   sack, he'd eat you for breakfast. Most of the rest? Just a bun-
   cha lost luggage.

PHYLLIS: So what happens now?

ROLLO: Happens?? In *this* place?

AMBER: We wait. For our legs.

LOUISE: For our pickup.

MILDRED: A gentleman caller to claim us.

ROLLO: Godot. Lefty. Guffman.

PHYLLIS: How long?

ROLLO: Some cases make bail the first night. Some do the whole
   stretch. Thirty days.

PHYLLIS: But . . . I'm carrying beach things rolled in a mesh bag!
   Her tankini's still damp! I could *mildew*!

ROLLO: So what? Little mildew won't kill you.

PHYLLIS: I'm *lined*!

AMBER: I was lined once. Won't last.

PHYLLIS: I have sand in my twill! (*Breaking down in tears.*) This is
   not what I thought it would be like at *all*. You know, when
   you're still in the warehouse, you dream about having somebody to carry you? *Well.* First, she removed all my tags. And it
   says. Right there in capitals: "Do not remove under penalty
   of *law*."

ROLLO: Oh, you poor baby. You're fresh from the store?

PHYLLIS: From a catalog! I was just *ordered*!

AMBER: Fuck me. She's a virgin.

ROLLO: Lay off. Your first trip on a plane? (PHYLLIS *nods*.) And that bitch—if you'll pardon my German—she *lost* you?? (*She nods again*.) That makes me so mad I could split a seam. Hell needs a separate ring for that kinda behavior. We're gonna take care of you, kiddo.

DICK: I *bet* you'll take care of her.

ROLLO: Stow it, you steroid-pumped piece a' petroleum. Can't you see the kid's scared?

PHYLLIS: The luggage compartment was bad enough!

MILDRED: Steerage! I was *flung* cheek by jowl with an R.E.I. backpack. The smell of that bedroll. I thought I'd expire, I most certainly did.

ROLLO: I was next to a *dog*. (*Murmurs all around. This is* bad.) Uh huh, yeah. Flew up from Miami alongside a doped-up Jack Russell. But not too sedated to squirt me.

AMBER: I hate that.

ROLLO: Hey. Piss is piss. Not the end of the planet, you get me?

PHYLLIS: What are you . . . in for?

ROLLO: My asshole missed his plane. Checks me in at the counter, right, goes to the men's room to snort a few lines, meets some dude hawking Ecstasy, next thing you know he's in Boca Raton and yours truly is doing the carousel cha-cha in Newark. Again. I wish he would just fuckin' lose me.

PHYLLIS: You don't really mean that.

ROLLO: Oh no? I came close a few times. Hotel lobby in Bangkok. My asshole puts me down and goes out for a smoke. I was sure I'd be lifted, you know, do a stint on the black market? Wrong. No one looked at me twice. Nother time he was running some kilos offshore a' Key West. I was praying he'd stuff me with cash, hand me over to someone with class. I could've been a container. Instead of a bum, which is what I am.

PHYLLIS: I think you're kind of cute.

ROLLO: Don't melt my heart with that garbage. I'm nobody's treasure chest.

LOUISE: You can say that again.

ROLLO: What's your monogram, kid?

PHYLLIS: P.M.S.

ROLLO: Aw. That's so sweet. My name's Rollo.

LOUISE: I may vomit.

ROLLO: What is your *problem,* Miss Thing? Is your toilet kit leaking?

LOUISE: I am perfectly packed.

ROLLO: Oh yeah? What's that you got rolled in that towel?

LOUISE: That's *personal*!

AMBER: What've you got, x-ray eyes?

ROLLO: You been through as many detectors as I have, you've got x-ray everything.

DICK: This guy's full of shit. He's a con man!

ROLLO: Whatever you need to believe. Though if *I* had those magazines sewn in my lining . . .

DICK: How did you know that??

ROLLO: We ain't so opaque as we think, my man. Not if you know how to look.

DICK: It's a trick!

ROLLO: Hey, I've *done* tricks. False bottoms, lead x-ray blocks. Not any more. I got nothin' to hide. What you see is what is. I've had some hard knocks, done the merchant marine, rode the rails outta Marrakech next to a fuckin' *goat*. Top of the bus,

Guatemala. I ain't sayin' I ain't got some miles on me. But I'm ready to kick all that shit, settle down, have a coupla fanny packs with the right girl. End of the day, it's who you got loving you.

MILDRED: Even love doesn't last. I married a satchel, raised three matching garment bags. Where are they now? Do they call? Do they write?

AMBER: I used to hang out with a weekender bag, name of Morty. The zipper on him. I get goosebumps remembering.

DICK: Dumped you, huh?

AMBER: He would've gone to the ends of the earth for me! He was the genuine article. Leather. Top-grain. They don't make 'em like that anymore.

MILDRED: They're all microfiber. Synthetic.

ROLLO: Uh-oh. Here comes.

ROLLO AND MILDRED: Back in *my* day—

MILDRED: We were valises back then. We were carried by uniformed porters. Cunard Lines. The steamer trunks! *Bandboxes!* Linings of satin and peau de soie. Solid brass fittings.

DICK: Yeah, right. And your ancestors rode on the *Mayflower.*

MILDRED: As a matter of fact, they were portmanteaux. My great-great grandfather is still on display at Mount Vernon.

DICK: Well la di dah.

MILDRED: Thug!

DICK: Dust collector. White elephant!

ROLLO: (*Pulls* DICK *aside, confidential.*) Go easy on her. She's on day twenty-nine of a thirty-day stretch. And the old bag don't know about this, but her legs had a cardiac thirty-five thou in the air over Greenland. He ain't coming back.

PHYLLIS: What . . . what'll happen to her?

ROLLO: The daughter-in-law picks her up, checks her insides for valuables, doesn't find nothing, she sends Portmanteau down the Red Mile.

PHYLLIS: (*in horror*) The Salvation Army??

ROLLO: She got Clearance Sale written all over her tweed.

PHYLLIS: (*rising panic*) I want to get out of here! Somebody CLAIM me!!!

ROLLO: Hey, hey, hey. Kid, that ain't you. You're just outta the warehouse, ya dig? You got miles of blue sky up ahead.

CREW: (*offstage*) CAN I HELP YOU?

LOUISE: (*Tenses, alert with anticipation.*) Hssst! Freeze! It's a pickup!

CREW: (*offstage*) COULD I SEE YOUR CLAIM CHECK?

(*The suitcases sit forward, waiting expectantly.* PHYLLIS *closes her eyes tightly, crossing her fingers.*)

PHYLLIS: Me. Me.

CREW: (*offstage*) YUP. IT'S RIGHT OVER THERE.

(*Loud sound of footsteps. The suitcases hold their breath, hopeful. Suddenly* DICK *is "pulled up" by the shoulder.*)

DICK: Me??

PHYLLIS: (*eyes open*) *Him???*

DICK: (*yelling into the wing*) IT'S ABOUT GODDAMN TIME! WHERE THE FUCK HAVE YOU *BEEN??*

(*He is "carried" off, stiff-shouldered. The others sit stunned.*)

MILDRED: (*quietly heartbroken*) Mercy. My land.

PHYLLIS: *He* got picked up?? Out of all of us? *Him??*

ROLLO: (*Shrugs, mournful.*) As flies to wanton boys are we to the gods. They use us for their sportsacks.

MILDRED: Isn't that . . . ?

ROLLO: Shakespeare. My asshole, he used to shack up with an actress he met down in Isla Mujeres. I carried her scripts.

AMBER: I hate theatre.

PHYLLIS: (*voice starting to tremble*) I'll never get home now.

AMBER: Quit snivelling. We're all on the shelf.

LOUISE: Speak for yourself, Miss Thing. *I* don't intend to remain in this venue.

ROLLO: Drop the attitude, will you? You're luggage.

LOUISE: I'm Louis Vuitton! I'm a French attaché!

ROLLO: You're *Louise* Vuitton, from Paris, Queens. Anybody can see that you fell off a truck.

LOUISE: (*bristling*) I'm hand-tooled!

ROLLO: Is *that* what they call it in Hong Kong? You're Naugahyde, buddy. A knockoff. A fake.

(LOUISE *draws herself up with great, wounded dignity.*)

LOUISE: . . . Well, a girl can dream, can't she?

ROLLO: (*softening*) Sure she can. Plump up your pillow and dream of the Louvre. (*Sotto voce.*) Shit. Me and my big . . . Gets me into more trouble.

PHYLLIS: What do you mean?

ROLLO: I see dead baggage. The future, the past. I can't help it. I always have. Thing is, most people, they don't wanna know.

PHYLLIS: Can you see *my* future?

ROLLO: You're best off not knowing. We're all flying blind. But you know what? We land. Somehow or else—call it kismet or roll of the fuckin' dice—all of us land on the right piece of road.

PHYLLIS: So my Realtor is gonna come back for me, right? I'll be found?

ROLLO: (*Hesitates, doesn't like lying.*) . . . Sure, kid. Of course you will. Here, put your strap on my shoulder.

PHYLLIS: Thanks, Rollo.

(*She settles her head on his shoulder, then puts her thumb in her mouth.* ROLLO *strokes her hair softly.*)

ROLLO: You're gonna get home, kiddo. All us lost chickens. One way or another, we're all goin' home.

(PHYLLIS *sucks her thumb.* ROLLO *stares straight ahead.*)

FAITH

Eric Lane

Faith was first performed by Orange Thoughts Productions in New York City, in April 2003. The author directed the following cast:

MICHAEL   James Georgiades
FATHER   Joel Rooks

CHARACTERS

MICHAEL: Twenties to thirties, average looking.
FATHER: A priest in his forties to sixties.

SETTING: A confessional.

(*A confessional, simply represented by two chairs.* FATHER, *a priest in his forties to sixties, listens to* MICHAEL's *confession.* MICHAEL *is in his twenties to thirties. Average looking.*)

MICHAEL: . . . Bless me father for I have sinned.

FATHER: How long has it been since your last confession?

MICHAEL: Many years.

FATHER: Tell me your sins, my child.

MICHAEL: I have killed someone.

(*A pause.*)

FATHER: Go on.

MICHAEL: Over and over. In my mind. Killed them for what they have done. And I'm scared.

FATHER: Scared of what?

MICHAEL: What will happen.

FATHER: What will happen?

MICHAEL: When it's no longer in my mind but me, actually— not thinking but when it's time—Trying to believe, to find a reason not to—But less and less and wondering—

FATHER: Wondering what?

MICHAEL: Why?

FATHER: Wondering why what?

MICHAEL: How someone could have done this—could have taken so much, when I trusted, believed—Why did I believe—?

FATHER: You were right to have faith.

MICHAEL: Not then. Not in him. He stole from me. Took things—

FATHER: Things.

MICHAEL: Not things. But important—Irreplaceable. Not things.

FATHER: Something closer to you.

MICHAEL: My youth.
       My joy.
       My innocence.
       He took my innocence.

FATHER: He hurt you.

MICHAEL: My soul. He took my soul.

FATHER: No one can take your soul. Only the Lord has that divine power.

MICHAEL: Took it. Pretending he knew things. Secrets. I didn't know.

FATHER: Your soul is still yours. No one can—

MICHAEL: Took it. When it wasn't his to take. To hold. Close. Me not knowing, thinking I should believe. That this is faith. That this is what God wants from me.

FATHER: You must forget.

MICHAEL: How can I forget?

FATHER: You must forgive.

MICHAEL: Forgive?

FATHER: You must.

MICHAEL: No. No forgiveness. Not for this. Not him.

FATHER: The Lord forgives our sins.

MICHAEL: I'm not the Lord.

FATHER: Washes them away.

MICHAEL: Too easy.

FATHER: Offers salvation.

MICHAEL: Only words.

FATHER: And hope.

MICHAEL: No meaning.

FATHER: To those who pray.

MICHAEL: I'm out of prayers.

FATHER: Prayers are answered.

MICHAEL: I can't.

FATHER: Redemption.

MICHAEL: No.

FATHER: Salvation.

MICHAEL: Can't.

FATHER: Hope.

MICHAEL: None.

FATHER: Faith.

MICHAEL: Gone.

FATHER: Joy.

MICHAEL: I can't.

FATHER: Love.

MICHAEL: I can't forgive you. (*A beat.*)
I can't forgive you.

FATHER: Tell me your name.

MICHAEL: You don't get to ask. You don't get to do anything. *You* listen. And *you* pray. For what you've done to me.

FATHER: Who—

MICHAEL: Shut up. (*A beat.*)
You don't even know who I am. Were there so many? You fucking asshole. How many Hail Marys is it going to take to wipe away your sins? Now it's your turn. I want to hear it. Or I tell. Everyone. (*Silence.*)
Now.

FATHER: What, my son—?

MICHAEL: I am not your son. I never was *your* son. I want to hear your confession.

FATHER: I can't.

MICHAEL: Trust me.

FATHER: Only him.

MICHAEL: Where's your faith?

FATHER: My faith is in Jesus.

MICHAEL: Don't even try it.

FATHER: In the Lord Jesus Christ.

MICHAEL: Jesus Christ—

FATHER: In his divine mercy.

MICHAEL: Shut the fuck up.

FATHER: I ask for his forgiveness.

MICHAEL: What about mine?

FATHER: Forgive me if I have sinned.

MICHAEL: "If." What kinda bullshit is that?

FATHER: If I have not seen—

MICHAEL: Fuck you.

FATHER: Not followed—

MICHAEL: How could I have followed?

FATHER: For what I am about—

MICHAEL: What are you about?

FATHER: To do.

MICHAEL: I was five years old. Do you remember? I was five years old.

(*A moment.*)

(*Blackout.*)

FIGHT DREAMS

Alison Weiss

Fight Dreams was presented in workshop at the Ensemble Studio Theatre's Intern Fest (India Cooper, Lab Director) in New York City, in June 2001. It was directed by Moira Squier. The cast was as follows:

BRADLEY	Mark Frankos
DINAH	Gwendolyn Wilson
DR. WERMAN	Michelle O'Connor
JULIO	Christos Klapsis
PHARMACIST	Laura Maxwell

Fight Dreams premiered as part of *Five by Five and One by Ives* (Sara Sessions and Alison Weiss, coproducers) at the HERE Arts Center in New York City, in December 2002. It was directed by Richard Harden. The cast was as follows:

BRADLEY	Roger Del Pozo
DINAH	Alison Weiss
DR. WERMAN	Sara Sessions
JULIO	Christos Klapsis

CHARACTERS

BRADLEY: Twenties to thirties, sensitive, devoted, and whiny.
DINAH: Twenties to thirties, neurotic and pushed to her limit.
DR. WERMAN: Thirties to fifties, intellectual, caring, and businesslike.
PHARMACIST: Any age, lazy and jaded.*
CUSTOMERS: Nonspeaking, all types, annoyed by a long wait in line at the pharmacy.*
JULIO: Twenties to thirties, handsome, powerful, and fantastical.

*CASTING NOTE: In one production of this play, the need for a pharmacist and extras in the drugstore scene was avoided by having Dinah and Bradley pantomime the exchange downstage.

(BRADLEY *and* DINAH *are in bed together, snuggling and kissing.*)

BRADLEY: God, I love you so much. I can't imagine life without you, Dinah.

DINAH: I love *you,* Bradley.

BRADLEY: Do you really love me?

DINAH: I do! (*They kiss.*) Mmmm.

BRADLEY: Pookie? Is something bothering you?

DINAH: (*Kisses him.*) What do you mean?

BRADLEY: You can't hide from me, love. You know how in synch we are . . . Look, just . . . tell me what's making my angel sad, and we'll work on it. We'll work on us.

DINAH: (*totally fed up all of a sudden*) I can't do this anymore.

BRADLEY: Oh come on now! You are the most precious, exquisite—

DINAH: I can't go on like this.

BRADLEY: Like what?

DINAH: IMAGINING YOU!

BRADLEY: *What?!*

DINAH: Ugh, this is pathetic. I can't even fantasize anymore! This is supposed to be my healthy fantasy life, and it's come to this!

BRADLEY: You're thinking too much again, honey.

DINAH: You don't fucking *exist,* Bradley. Hate to be overanalytical here, but it's one hell of a stumbling block in this relationship.

BRADLEY: I don't understand this. Everything was perfect a moment ago. I'm your *fantasy,* for chrissakes. I was doing all the right things. . . .

DINAH: Of *course* you were doing the right things, Bradley. I'm the one thinking them up!

BRADLEY: We were spooning . . .

DINAH: I was curled up on my side, alone. Look, there wouldn't even be enough room for you in this bed!

BRADLEY: Sure there is!

DINAH: Well, maybe if I move the *Times* (*Begins shuffling papers, books, and teddy bears around the bed.*) Oh what the hell am I doing?! I'm a mess! (*Tosses papers, cries.*)

BRADLEY: Maybe you're bored. Are you bored with me?

DINAH: I—I don't know. Maybe I just wish you could do things on your own. Like . . . I always wanted a man with a pulse. And maybe a working set of anatomical features strong enough to sustain human life.

BRADLEY: Good lord, do you even *hear* how demanding you are right now? Will you please just get out of your head, Dinah? I'm here for you!

DINAH: It's just not the same.

BRADLEY: Is it something I said?

DINAH: No, honey—you don't say anything. I haven't created myself.

BRADLEY: Well to be honest, Dinah, it's starting to feel like . . . sometimes you deliberately have me say the wrong thing. Just to liven things up. Creating controversy, is that it?

DINAH: Oh God.

BRADLEY: You know, I'm supposed to be your fantasy here. And you're making me the Bad Guy! How you think that makes me *feel*?

DINAH: I think you might be right. I've got to tell Dr. Werman about this.

BRADLEY: Dinah, no! You can*not* tell Dr. Werman about our problems.

DINAH: (*putting on shoes and preparing herself to leave*) Bradley, I cannot go on battling with you over your existence or lack of existence every time I try to enjoy myself in bed!

BRADLEY: (*panicking*) You know what those doctors do to us, don't you? They kill us. Kill us! Maybe with hours of therapy. Maybe with a pill. (*Mimicking doctors.*) Bradley's not healthy. Bradley's not "Real."

DINAH: (*putting a raincoat over her nightgown*) Dr. Werman is a brilliant woman.

BRADLEY: (*still mimicking*) Bradley doesn't actually "Exist."

DINAH: (*picking up purse, heading out*) Do you hear yourself? Do you hear what that does to me?

BRADLEY: Fine, go! Go to her plush little Upper West Side home office! Stare down into the repeating patterns of her Persian carpet as you rattle off the list of *my* inadequacies! (*Beat.*) Dinah, is this really what you want? She'll take out her pen and her pad. You'll go to the drugstore. The pharmacist will sneer at me. Oh, yes. Pharmacists can see us.

DINAH: Good-bye, Bradley. I wish it didn't have to be this way.

(*She crosses the stage to the office of* DR. WERMAN. DR. WERMAN *enters with her pen and pad and sits down across from* DINAH.)

DR. WERMAN: So . . . you're telling me . . . you fantasize dysfunctional relationships.

(BRADLEY *crosses from bed to* DR. WERMAN'*s office; he sits beside* DINAH.)

BRADLEY: Honey, we're not dysfunctional! We've got a great situation here.

DINAH: Will you shut up! I never asked you to come.

BRADLEY: (*to* DR. WERMAN) This is exactly—see this?! See this sort of behavior?!

DR. WERMAN: (*She doesn't see* BRADLEY.) Dinah? Need a moment to think?

BRADLEY: Dinah please. We can fix this! Don't let her kill me off. Is it the sex? Is that it? If it's the sex, I can improve!

DINAH: (*to* BRADLEY) Oh, of course the sex is fine, Bradley. Which one of us do you think actually *handles* the sex?

DR. WERMAN: Dinah, how are your sexual fantasies? I mean, have those taken a backseat to these—these "fight dreams," we'll call them?

DINAH: (*to* DR. WERMAN) Doctor, I—um—I think I handle that area pretty well. (*To* BRADLEY.) Myself.

BRADLEY: OH! So I get none of the credit, then, is that how it works? Dinah, I am sorry but this is ludicrous. I AM YOUR FANTASY! Where would this alleged sex life of yours be without *ME?!*

DINAH: (*to* DR. WERMAN) But sometimes, Doctor, our most intimate moments—

DR. WERMAN: "Our" most intimate moments?

DINAH: Well, *my* most intimate moments, you know . . .

DR. WERMAN: Yes. I know.

BRADLEY: Oh, this is just rich. Hello! In bed Thursday morning? *My* creative work. Oh, and what about the futon after *Days of Our Lives?* You're telling me I had *nothing* to do with that concept?

DINAH: (*to* DR. WERMAN) Sometimes, Doctor . . . those intimate moments are interrupted by a profound anger inside me that none of it is real, so why bother! Why bother imagining someone else so incredible it can only be a letdown to continue my own existence?

BRADLEY: Thanks for the gratitude.

DINAH: How is that useful in my life? What do I need this for?

DR. WERMAN: Dinah, in fact, a healthy fantasy life can be paramount to one's happiness.

BRADLEY: Yes!

DR. WERMAN: We've discussed this.

BRADLEY: You hear that?

DR. WERMAN: However, if you feel these depressing intrusions of conflict into your otherwise healthy sexual dream life are inhibiting your ability to function—

DINAH: Yes, Doctor. They are.

BRADLEY: How can you be so cold?

DR. WERMAN: Okey dokey. (BRADLEY *begins to tremble as* DR. WERMAN *jots down a prescription.*) I'm going to write you a little three-month supply here. . . . (*Tears sheet off the pad and holds up the prescription.*) This has been shown to help many of my patients gain some extra . . . focus. Still the same old you, just a lot more . . . composed. (*Hands* DINAH *the piece of paper.*)

BRADLEY: (*trembling*) No warmth. No breath . . .

DINAH: (*She takes the prescription.*) Give me strength, doctor!

DR. WERMAN: Now, now. Same time next week.

(*They shake hands,* DR. WERMAN *exits. Lights fade on* DR. WERMAN'*s office.* DINAH, *with* BRADLEY *following, approaches a counter center stage where a* PHARMACIST *appears, chewing gum and chatting on the phone.* DINAH *hands the* PHARMACIST *the prescription, then gets in line and waits. About five annoyed customers are ahead of her, impatient.* PHARMACIST *helps them with superhuman slowness and "attitude" during the following exchange.*)

BRADLEY: Dinah. You don't fool me. You chose Duane Reade on purpose. Look at this line! They'll take hours! You have time to change your mind!

DINAH: I just want to get you out of my head.

BRADLEY: Dinah, honey! Think . . . about us . . . about your feelings . . . about ME. Pookie? This is you . . . and ME.

DINAH: There is no US, there is no YOU, there is no Pookie!

BRADLEY: (*pointing at the* PHARMACIST, *who sneers at him as the guy being helped looks around, wondering what the hell is going on*) She sees me! She sees me, she fucking sees me! Dinah, I need you to work with me here, baby.

DINAH: YOU ARE GOING TO DIE TODAY, BRADLEY! DIE! DIE! DIE!!

(*All turn and look at* DINAH. *After a beat, the* PHARMACIST *knowingly saunters over to* DINAH *with her bag of medicine, takes* DINAH's *money, and gestures for her to leave at once. The other customers, indignant that she's cut the line, ad lib complaints. Blackout on that portion of the stage as they exit.*)

(DINAH *crosses hurriedly back to her bed. She tears open the drugstore bag, opens the bottle, and pops the pill.* BRADLEY *sits with his head in his hands on the edge of the bed.*)

(*Enter* JULIO. *Enough said. After a brief and futile attempt at a stare down,* BRADLEY *exits, defeated.*)

JULIO: Dinah?

DINAH: My God! Who are you?

JULIO: (*removing shades*) Dinah, the name is Julio. And I'll be your socially acceptable, conventionally healthy, and refreshingly masculine fantasy for the duration of your pharmaceutical experience.

DINAH: (*Looks at the pill bottle in awe.*) Sweet nectar!

JULIO: Shhhh. From now on, there won't be any talking.

(*Blackout.*)

THE FIND

Susan Sandler

The Find premiered in New York City on June 5, 2002, at the HB Playwrights Foundation as part of the Theatre's Sixth Annual Short Play Series. Amy Saltz directed the following cast:

PERRY	Bernie Passeltiner
AGNES	Victoria Boothby

(*A man,* PERRY, [*late sixties to early seventies*] *wielding a well-worn metal detector moves down the beach, monitoring the piercing beeps on his earphones. He wears a foreign legion khaki hat and carries a backpack with a small folding shovel attached. His pants are rolled up to his knees.*)

(*A woman,* AGNES, [*late sixties to early seventies*] *sits in a lounge chair, wearing a careful linen beach dress. She is patrician, bronze, and has about her the look of a summer spent in luxury at the beach.*)

(*The man moves the metal detector in careful circles around her. The clunky machinery buzzes loudly.*)

AGNES: Disgusting. (*When she speaks we hear her crisply—British, upper-class, and brittle, thoroughly repulsed by the spectacle.*) *I thought this was a private beach.* (*He keeps buzzing.*) Won't you take your—equipment somewhere else? You're disturbing me. (*He doesn't hear her.*) Dear God, do you mind?! (*He keeps buzzing. She gets up, jabs him on the shoulder, her pointed finger a dagger. Shouting in his face.*) Won't you take this disgusting thing somewhere else. There's six bloody miles of beach here, do you have to do this directly in my line of vision? This is, after all, a private beach.

(*He gestures to his headset. Turns down the volume, slips off the headset.*)

PERRY: What's that?

AGNES: (*at normal volume, crisply*) This is a private beach. Won't you please take your . . . equipment somewhere else.

PERRY: Oh, no, no—No private beaches here. All the beaches belong to all the people. That's how we do things in this country.

AGNES: I am a houseguest of Martin and Regina Duncan. These are the Duncan steps, this is the Duncan boat and I am quite certain that this then is the Duncan beach.

(*She points to the sign on the steps that lead up the cliff to the imposing house.*)

PERRY: First ten feet. After that, it's public property. My property, everybody's property—maybe not yours— You a U.S. citizen?

AGNES: No.

PERRY: Didn't think so.

AGNES: You're just doing this to irritate me. You've got a whole stretch of unmined beach and you're insisting on doing this section, one agonizing inch at a time. Why, may I ask, have you picked this bit of sand?

PERRY: Instinct. You get a feeling in the gut. Like everything else. You know what you know. And I feel like something real good is here.

AGNES: Oh? And what does your . . . gut tell you it might be?

PERRY: Could be gold jewelry, precious stones. A find.

AGNES: Ridiculous. People don't toss their jewelry around in the sand.

PERRY: You'd be surprised. All kinds of things happen. People are careless with their treasures at the beach. They're here under this sky, breathing this air, the sun makes them feel, I don't know, like they could live forever and things don't matter so much. Things are just things—they get lost, they slip away, and it doesn't matter so much.

AGNES: What nonsense. Please, couldn't you just move along. I'm appealing to your better character. I've had a very difficult morning and I would adore the chance to just be alone and have some quiet time. You do understand.

PERRY: They at it again, are they?

AGNES: I beg your pardon?

PERRY: The Duncans. They at each other's throat again?

AGNES: I don't know whatever you mean.

PERRY: I seen 'em down here last month, she coulda sliced him down the middle like a big old bass, that's how steamy she was . . . she's a killer, eh?

AGNES: I don't approve of public disagreements.

PERRY: Well, whether you approve or not, them two's been having it up and down the beach all summer. I'm surprised they're not divorced already.

AGNES: (*It slips out.*) They will be. Very soon.

PERRY: See?

AGNES: My God, how frightful, I shouldn't be gossiping with you.

PERRY: Why not?

AGNES: I don't even know you.

PERRY: (*extending his hand, warmly*) Perry. Perry Geddis.

AGNES: (*bristling, not taking his hand*) Mr. Geddis, I am not in the habit of gossiping about my host and hostess. It's vulgar, it's rude and I am thoroughly ashamed of myself. Good day.

(*She moves off toward the steps leading up the cliff to the house.*)

PERRY: Wait, wait—don't let me chase you off. I can imagine how rough it must be for you up there. Please. I'll move along. (*She hesitates.*) I mean to say, I'm sorry I disturbed you. Please Miz—? (*She turns.*)

AGNES: Agnes Barton-Caufield.

PERRY: You related to Michael Caufield in Chattam? No, no of course not.—How could you be—I mean, well—We used to fish together—Good man, Caufield. Good friend. He came all the way to the island to see me after Madeline died. Tried to get me out on his boat. Good man.

AGNES: Yes, well—

PERRY: Please, take your seat, enjoy the sunset. (*She moves slowly back and sits.*) So where are you from?

AGNES: My family home is Shropshire, but I'm—I'm visiting friends here in the States.

PERRY: You mean the Duncans.

AGNES: The Duncans and—and others.

PERRY: Oh, I see. You're making the rounds.

AGNES: I hadn't thought about it in those terms—but yes, I suppose one might say I was "making the rounds."

PERRY: We get a lot of that here. You got a home on this island, you got friends all over. Suddenly they're your best friends. Can't wait to see you, spend quality time—that means at least a week—enough to justify their airfare. Well, me and Maddie finally put a stop to it, whole summer there she was cooking, cleaning, changing sheets, like she was running a B&B and where were those dear friends in the middle of winter, I want to know. Yup, we put a stop to it. Even family can be freeloaders—Oh, sorry, I didn't mean to—I mean, I'm sure your—your situation is—. Well, I don't think the Duncans worry much about their houseguests, huh? They got a whole separate house for you, probably got your own separate maid. All you have to do is show up at dinner.

AGNES: Making the rounds, as you say, is a bit more complicated than it sounds. One does not just show up and act cheerful, one must play by one's hosts' rules, however ridiculous, however humiliating. One must learn to speak carefully with the staff, not too familiar, not too removed, a tone that says, please may I have some little comfort, without presuming to be in fact the lady of the house, one must understand that there is an art to being a good guest. And by that I mean, not just a good guest who doesn't ruffle feathers, or require too much attention, but a guest who gets invited BACK, that's the whole of it, you see, one wants to establish the pattern, the expectation—Oh, it's July, this must be Agnes. Can't wait to see dear, jolly Agnes. She listens to all our woes, laughs at our tired jokes, our excruciatingly boring family stories that God knows she's heard a thousand times, and will no doubt hear many more times—and while she certainly can carry off a bit of the old glamour and does have a whiff of royalty— her mother was Lady Frampton, her sister married a duke— she is a rather poor relation and we do get to feel sorry for dear Agnes—sorry and a little superior to the poor soul, and yes, we also get the added satisfaction, of feeling better about ourselves for having given the poor dear a bit of a break from the nasty summer heat of what is rumored to be her painfully modest London flat, barely a maid's room, that no one has ever seen, nor will they ever see.

(*Silence.*)

PERRY: Where do you go from here?

AGNES: Newport. The Gambols—then back to the Vineyard and then up to this utterly beautiful private island off the coast of Maine, and while I do detest these people, they have the most wonderful chef and a very sweet little guest cottage— it's a good distance from the main house. There is absolutely nothing to do there and the house has no library to speak of, and all they do is fish and drink and play cards, but I do have a good deal of time to myself.

PERRY: Well, I suppose that's something. (*Pause.*) There's always a price, eh?

AGNES: Always.

PERRY: Well, I'll be seeing you, Agnes. Enjoy the sunset.

AGNES: Thank you, Mr. Geddis.—Perry.

(*He smiles, puts his headset on, and starts down the beach, buzzing in a careful grid.* AGNES *picks up her book, starts to read, puts it down, and stares out at the horizon.* PERRY *turns, starts back.*)

PERRY: Wouldn't you just like to give her a feel?

(*He takes the headset off, extends it to her.*)

AGNES: I think not.

PERRY: Oh, come on, give her a try. When was the last time you had a chance to be a certified treasure hunter?

AGNES: I'm rather pleased to say—never.

PERRY: No one's looking. You know you want to— (*He moves closer.*) Just give her a little feel. Give her a little listen. (*He takes off the headset.*) It's not just the treasures you know, it's the stories that taste so good. After I get a good find, I like to think up the stories myself—sometimes it's like these two young lovers have this argument, and she's so hurt she wants to hurt him back. So she throws the ring, the thing that tied them together, right into the ocean and it's swallowed up. It's gone—then later, maybe years later, the shoreline reshapes itself, ocean piles the sand high here—destroys the dunes there, and that ring suddenly lands ten inches down, directly below your feet.

(*He slips the headset around her neck—holds the detector out for her to take.*)

AGNES: It's—it's awfully sweet of you. But I don't see myself engaged in this occupation. It's simply not what I do. Ever. (*She starts to hand the headset back—then suddenly hears—*) What's that sound?

PERRY: That's her heart beating. Hmm, she's purring. She's ready
  for something big.

AGNES: Oh?

(*He slips the headset on, smiles blissfully.*)

PERRY: Oh, yeah. Something big. Very near.

AGNES: Well, let me hear.

(*She takes the headset, puts it on.*)

AGNES: Oh, yes—I certainly hear that—oh—it's very interesting,
  isn't it. It gets louder over here, doesn't it. Uh huh. Yes. Just
  over here and then—

(*She moves the wand over the sand cautiously, carefully, scanning the
beach square foot by square foot with the look of a pro.* PERRY *smiles,
watching her.*)

PERRY: My Madeline, she never went hunting with me, but when
  I'm home with the prize, she's all for it. She'd have the table
  cleared off, "Watcha got today, honey?"

(AGNES *takes her headset off, suddenly aware that he's talking, not hearing.*)

AGNES: What are you saying there?

PERRY: I said, we'll have another hour of good light after the
  sunset.

AGNES: Just an hour, that's all?

PERRY: Yup, looks like.

(*She puts the headset back on.* AGNES *is fiercely into the search now,
moving across the sand in careful circles. She turns to* PERRY, *her eyes
blazing, the headset still in place, she can hear only the* Tick-Tick, *we
hear it faintly now, too.*)

PERRY: (*to himself, as she moves the wand*) —Oh, it's big time. The
  first find, you're hooked, Agnes. You're hooked.

AGNES: *(excitedly, not hearing him)* Well, come along then.

(AGNES circles the beach. We hear the ticking with her now as it draws her closer and closer to the target.)

(PERRY watches her, beaming as the ticking grows louder and louder and louder. . . . Blackout.)

THE GRAND DESIGN

Susan Miller

The Grand Design was done as a reading at New York's Town Hall on September 11, 2002, for Brave New World, a benefit commemorating 9/11. Starring Marsha Mason and Scott Cohen, directed by Cynthia Croot.

CHARACTERS

JOSH: Mid/late thirties. Smart. Underlying (and not so underlying) angst. Governed by his questions—the joy and difficulty of what he searches for and what he finds—and an abiding sense of humor.

FRANCES: Josh's mother. Late fifties/early sixties. Whatever her son has—trace it back! She is also, like him, in the process of discovery.

Their rhythms are bantering, intimate, passionate.

TWO–THREE PEOPLE: Any gender. Diverse. They sit somewhere on the periphery of the stage almost as if watching the action until they become part of it.

TIME: The present.

PRODUCTION NOTE: There are three slides shown at the beginning of the play and one slide near the end. The illustrations from which to make the slides appear at the end of the script.

With a minor adjustment of words in the opening, the play can be done *without* the use of slides.

(*Lights up.* JOSH *leans against a desk. He is charismatic and relishes talking about what he knows and what he struggles to know. A slide goes up, depicting what he's about to tell us.*)

JOSH: The first page of the Dutil-Dumas message, sent from a transmitter in the Ukraine. To signal other civilizations. The message was encoded using a system called Lincos that starts with simple mathematical ideas and builds to complex information about who we are.

(*Beat.*)

In case there's anyone out there.

(*Another slide.*)

April 5, 1973. *Pioneer 11* is launched into deep space, carrying a message in the form of a six-by-nine inch gold plaque showing human figures, Earth's location in the universe, and a diagram of the hydrogen atom.

(*Beat.*)

In that same year, on the day before *Pioneer 11* makes its voyage, the ribbon is cut on the tallest building in the world. One hundred ten stories high on sixteen acres in lower Manhattan. "A living representation," according to the architect, "of man's belief in the cooperation of men . . . and through this cooperation his ability to find greatness."

(*Another slide.*)

November 16th, 1974. The Arecibo Observatory in Puerto Rico sent this message toward a cluster of stars 25,000 light-years away. A string of 1,679 bits, or ones and zeros, it can be assembled into a pictogram showing the figure of a man, a telescope, the numbers, DNA, and the solar system.

(End slides.)

1977. My personal favorite: gold plated L.P.s—remember phonograph records—in aluminum cases launched on board *Voyager I* and *II*. With, of course, instructions on how to play the records.

(He breaks into a dance to a lush arrangement of Sinatra. After a few bars, the music stops.)

Items missing from *Voyager*, Dutil-Dumas, Arecibo, and all previous messages that have traveled through space and time: The sign over Auschwitz. ARBEIT MACHT FREI. Work makes one free. A slave ship carrying the first of fifty million people Africa will lose to slavery or death en route. The hole in our ozone layer. A small woman refusing to sit at the back of the bus. Yen. Francs. Dollars. Money.

(A blank slide goes up.)

(His struggle.)

2003. What? What's the message this time?

(A woman, his mother, speaks to the audience from another part of the stage.)

FRANCES: My son is kind of a poet scientist. He has a grant to come up with a message to alien civilizations. To let them know who we are. The human race. He's hit a wall. And I've left town. On foot.

JOSH: My mother is walking. She is walking with no clear purpose all across the United States. It's her response to the situation. To turning a certain age. To my breakup. It's her memorial to the nature of our times.

(Beat.)

She calls me from the road.

FRANCES: (*a succession of calls*) I'm on the Eleanor Roosevelt Trail. I'm standing outside a church on top of a hill in Ohio where the underground railroad connected.

I don't know where I am. But, I see cows.

I'm covering ground. I'm walking past the things I know.

(Beat.)

I met this person who picks the places to stop. To stop along the way. You know when you get directions—on your computer. What's that called—map something? Well, they actually send people out to find interesting things to do along the routes. I just never thought of that. There are all kinds of jobs I never thought about.

JOSH: Look, I'm sorry. I'm sorry things didn't work out and I didn't give you grandchildren and—

FRANCES: (*to audience*) He thinks I'm out here because he failed in his marriage. I'm out here because I failed. To know what to do next. I was sad. And I started walking. I was walking in circles all around the house. Finally, I just took it outside. I'm not the only one out here. There are mothers walking all over the place.

(Beat.)

I'm worried he won't find love.

(The phone rings in his house. Although they begin talking to each other, as if on the phone, this is dropped shortly and they just address each other directly.)

FRANCES: Hi, Sweetie!

JOSH: Mom? Where are you?

FRANCES: If I wanted to be located, I would stay home.

JOSH: Are you just walking aimlessly or do you have some kind of plan?

FRANCES: I do have a plan. To walk aimlessly. All right, the story so far. I just had the most delicious, sinful piece of pie. They use shortening and whole eggs. I don't care. Because while I eat my pie or have my coffee, I'm not drowning in the facts.

(Beat.)

How are you coming with your memo to alien civilizations?

JOSH: See, when you say it like that—

FRANCES: Like what?

JOSH: Like how you said it.

FRANCES: Like how I said memo or how's it coming?

JOSH: Anyhow, it's more like an equation. You know? Which lays out the thing to be discovered or proven. It's not necessarily what we are—it's what we could be.

FRANCES: That's lovely.

JOSH: For a lie, you mean.

FRANCES: Well, maybe it's a lie we need.

JOSH: I do, I guess. I need it.

(Beat.)

See, the big discoveries—gravity, particle theory, chaos, DNA—they place us. They put us in the physical world. But they're just descriptions. Of our physical properties. Our propensities. What we're capable of—what's possible, what we've already accomplished, I mean how do you—first I thought, well, fucking, of course. Sexual congress. For them to see how we do it and how much we like to do it. But, fucking causes so much confusion and anxiety. And what if they interpret two figures expressing their ardor as some kind of cruel rite? And the truth is, fucking doesn't last, anyhow. And then what about madness, disorders of the mind, bodies that aren't whole?

(Beat.)

I should just tell them to be human is to impose yourself on the world. This is how I see it, so this is how it is.

FRANCES: (*A beat.*) Or—you could take this grant money and give it away to actual people. So they could eat, go to school, and maybe collectively expand and redefine the concept of what it is to be human.

JOSH: Okay, sister, listen, didn't I give up my beautiful SUV when you were on your moral imperative not to drive big gas-guzzling automobiles thus entrenching us in a relationship with oil-producing nations and consequently undermining what we tout to be our own unique position of being free in the world?

FRANCES: I was quoting. I didn't come up with that myself, which is disturbing, but I don't always see how things fit, and I'm always completely thrown to learn there's this relationship between a simple thing like buying a car or a carton of milk and the decline of civilization.

JOSH: Well, just put your two cents in about this, would you. And help me out here. Is it sentimental to think there is anything we have in common with everyone else on earth?

FRANCES: I don't know. I mean, what everyone wants to know is, who am I going to be. And then who am I going to be with who'll make it not so terrible to *be* me. And if you have children, who are they going to be and who are they going to be with and how do I keep them safe.

(Beat.)

You know, maybe the story of one person is all they need to know about us.

JOSH: Where the hell are you?

FRANCES: In my tent.

JOSH: You are not in any kind of a tent.

FRANCES: In my tent outside of my room at the motel. You don't think I'd really pee in the open, do you? You should go outside. It is an alarmingly beautiful night.

JOSH: I can't.

FRANCES: Did you open my letter yet?

JOSH: (*avoiding*) I just haven't had a chance—

FRANCES: I know you're carrying it around in your pocket and it's getting smushed and I need you to read it.

JOSH: I know you want me to read it, Frances. So it must be important. And that, of course, brings up my morbid fear of important letters.

FRANCES: Josh.

JOSH: And I don't really have the time right now.

FRANCES: (*retreating*) Okay.

JOSH: I'm in over my head with this thing.

FRANCES: Look, if they have a sense of humor, they'll see the irony. Or they'll receive it like the French do when you try to speak in their language.

(*A beat.*)

Tell me—show me what you've got so far.

JOSH: (*a moment*) All right. But, just—you know, I'm still working on it.

(*After a moment, as a kind of living slide show, an actor steps forward from another part of the stage and stands with arms outstretched.*)

That we're—incomplete. That we long for. That we miss our chances. And we're born to repeat: If only. If only!

(*A second actor comes forward to join the first. They join hands.*)

FRANCES: (*acknowledging what she sees*) How it is to hold someone else's life in your own.

(*Beat.*)

Can you add a dog? I think we need them, somehow.

(*One of the actors holds the other in his arms, as if that person were wounded or ailing, in need.*)

JOSH: That we're moved. That we can meet another person's sorrow or subjugation with an answering cry and a wish to make it better. Not because we're thinking, "That could be me" but because that is me.

(*Beat.*)

You know, if you put a group of six-month-old babies in a room and one starts to cry, pretty soon they all start crying. They can't differentiate. They are all one living, breathing, wailing, sobbing, suffering being.

(*Another actor comes forward and joins them. They stand still, as their faces show different reactions to something we don't see.*)

The chemistry of the brain changes with certain events. Once you witness an atrocity—or hear a cruel remark. When you cause the disappointment in someone's eyes. Or see an act of courage. There's a shift. Now your brain's accommodating this new information. You're still pulled to the earth by gravity. And your blood type is still O positive. But what happens to other people is placing itself in your cells. It resides in you now. And you're not the same. It changes you forever.

(*The actors move to the rear of the stage, where they sit.*)

FRANCES: Come outside. Be with me, tonight.

(*After a moment, he walks "outside." They both stand under a starry sky.* JOSH *looks up toward the heavens, addressing the unknown civilizations.*)

JOSH: Okay, I have some questions for *you*. Do you have pets? Do you marry? Is there gender? Does it matter to you if another of your species, group, tribe, community, has different markings? Do you have prisons? Are you kind? Do you sleep? Do you have mothers?

FRANCES: (*Joins in speaking out to the universe.*) This is who we are! Hurtling through time, tumbling, stretching, moving through time to what we're meant to be—this is us, becoming!

(*Beat*—*to* JOSH.)

Please open the envelope.

JOSH: (*a moment*) Fine. (*He retrieves the letter from his pocket and opens it.*) I see something that looks like a house. And little stick figures in crayon.

FRANCES: The other side.

(*He turns it over and starts to read out loud.*)

JOSH: The last will and testament of—(*as he realizes what it is*) my one and only mother! Jesus. I don't want to see this. I don't want to think about it.

FRANCES: Well, you have to.

JOSH: Why?

FRANCES: You're my executor, beneficiary, and medical proxy. And when you have children—

JOSH: Would you please—with the children.

FRANCES: It could happen.

JOSH: Are you all right? Should I be worried? I'm worried.

FRANCES: I'm fine. It's just something a person has to do. I'm all right.

(*A beat. As* JOSH *looks over the will. And turns it over.*)

JOSH: So, what's this drawing?

FRANCES: Something you did as a child. You drew a house. Next to other houses. Because you said our house needs those other houses. So you drew a house. With people inside. Small people. And big people to take care of them, to give them an example, to accompany them on their way.

(*Beat.*)

What makes us human is other humans.

(*A moment.*)

JOSH: (*to audience*) After my mother dies, some years from now, and I've married my first wife all over again. And a simple child's drawing has gone into space—I tell my daughter the story of one person. Walking. Looking at things. Listening to other people's stories. Wanting to know.

(*He turns back to her. They are on their phones again.*)

FRANCES: I love you, Josh. I love you so much.

(*The slide of* JOSH's *childhood drawing goes up.*)

OTHER ACTORS: (*Each speaks a line in turn.*) In Wonder. In Awe. In Loss. In Gratitude. In Sympathy. In Release. In Pain. In Honor of. In Memory. In Celebration. In Mourning. In Difficulty. In our Stumble and Fall. In each Attempt. In Remission. In Rapture. In the Beginning. In the End. In IT.

JOSH: (*beat*) I love you, too, Mom.

(*The light narrows to frame the drawing. Until, lights fade.*)

Slide 1
DUTIL-DUMAS

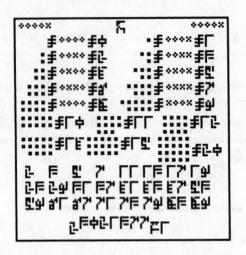

Slide 2
PIONEER 10 and 11

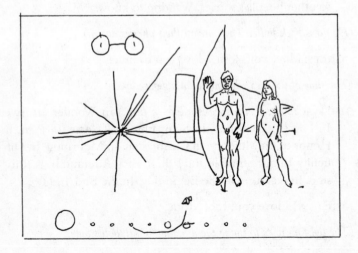

Slide 3
ARECIBO

Slide 4
CHILD'S DRAWING

KITTY THE WAITRESS

Christopher Durang

Kitty the Waitress was first presented in an evening called *Nine Lives* at the Juilliard School, Drama Division, in New York City, on February 21 and 22, 1997. The evening was a series of nine plays, all about the lives of a cat. The other eight plays were by Hilary Bell, Ron Fitzgerald, Daniel Goldfarb, Jessica Goldberg, Bob Kerr, David Lindsay-Abaire, Marsha Norman, and Alexandra Tolk. The evening was directed by Elizabeth Gottlieb; the program coordinator was Richard Feldman; and production stage manager was Scott Rollison. The cast for *Kitty the Waitress* was:

HOSTESS	Claire Lautier
MR. O'BRIEN	Peter Jacobson
KITTY	Greg McFadden*
WAITER	Erin Gann
VERONIQUE	Pamela Nyberg
VETERINARIAN	Dave Case

*NOTE: The part of Kitty is meant to be played by a woman. For the purpose of the *Nine Lives* evening, we chose to have the cat in each play played by the same actor, necessitating having a male actor play the waitress in my play and a fading female cat star in Bob Kerr's play. The other seven plays all had a male cat in them. Greg McFadden did a terrific job as the waitress in my play; but especially if you present the play on its own, I prefer that Kitty be played by a woman.

CHARACTERS

HOSTESS: Gracious and French.
MR. O'BRIEN: American.
KITTY: The waitress, seductive and French.
WAITER
VERONIQUE: Another waitress.
VETERINARIAN

(*Scene: A restaurant on a tropical island. An American man,* MR. O'BRIEN, *enters. He is in his early thirties to early forties. He is greeted by a friendly, effusive French woman, who is the* HOSTESS *and owner of the restaurant. She has a French accent.*)

HOSTESS: Oh, Monsieur Au Briand, comment ça va?

O'BRIEN: Fine, merci.

HOSTESS: Did you 'ave a lovely day at the beach?

O'BRIEN: Yeah, yeah. My ex-wife won total custody of our kid today. I get to see him for two hours when he turns twelve, and then again when he's sixteen.

HOSTESS: Oh, Monsieur, quelle dommage. Well, forget your troubles here on our beautiful island, and we at this restaurant will do all we can to soothe you.

O'BRIEN: Thank you. I'm feeling kind of gloomy.

HOSTESS: Oh, Monsieur. We lighten your troubles for you. Forget your wife, forget your child. You are in tropical paradise.

O'BRIEN: Yes, thank you. I am in paradise, right.

HOSTESS: Your usual table, Monsieur?

O'BRIEN: Yeah, I mean, oui.

HOSTESS: Oui, Monsieur. (*Guides him to his table; motions for him to sit:*) S'il vous plaît. (O'BRIEN *sits.*) Veronique will be your waitress tonight, Monsieur. Bon appétit.

O'BRIEN: Thank you. (*The* HOSTESS *goes away. After a moment,* KITTY *enters. She is very seductive, seductively dressed. She walks over to* O'BRIEN's *table, and then stands in front of him. Whenever she stands, she has a pronounced curve to her posture; she pushes her lower body forward. It seems seductive, but also a little weird. It should seem odd and explicit, but not like a contortion; her stance should be comfortable for her. It's just her pelvis pushes forward.* KITTY *is extremely flirtatious in her manner as well, in a very generalized way. She speaks in a French accent.*)

KITTY: Bonjour, Monsieur. My name is Kitty, I will be waitress ce soir.

O'BRIEN: I thought my waitress's name was Veronique.

KITTY: No, Monsieur. My name is Kitty. Je m'appelle Kitty, le chat d'amour.

O'BRIEN: Well, okay. Hiya, Kitty.

KITTY: Bonjour, Monsieur. (*She moves her lower body around in a circle, seductively.*) Would you like something to drink, Monsieur?

O'BRIEN: (*responding to her flirtatiousness*) A bottle of water. A bottle of wine. A hunk of cheese. Et vous, Mademoiselle.

KITTY: (*Laughs seductively.*) Et moi? Oh, no, Monsieur. Non, non, non. Kitty is not on ze menu.

O'BRIEN: Well, why are you standing that way then? Pull your private parts in. (KITTY *stands straight for a moment, pulling in her lower body so that her pelvis does not thrust forward. However, this posture is difficult for her. The "pelvis out" one is the one that feels natural to her. However, for now, she does her best to stand straight.*)

KITTY: Would you like to 'ear the specials, Monsieur?

O'BRIEN: Okay. Shoot.

KITTY: Tonight we 'ave filet of red snapper avec un sauce of artichokes et sardine. We 'ave Mahi Mahi avec un sauce de Mieu Mieu, in honor of ze French actress Mieu Mieu. The fish is flown in by aeroplane from ze island of Maui.

O'BRIEN: Mahi Mahi from Maui avec Mieu Mieu sauce.

KITTY: Oui, Monsieur. (*Unable to stand straight anymore, she reverts to her old posture, and lets her lower body thrust out again with relief; she explains seductively:*) I 'ave ze bad posture, Monsieur.

O'BRIEN: No, it's charming in its way. It's just I haven't had a woman in over a year. And your posture upsets me.

KITTY: (*flirting*) I do not know what you mean, Monsieur. (*Back to the specials.*) We 'ave mussels meunière, we 'ave salade du Crab, we 'ave tuna grille avec Gerard Depardieu sauce; et finalement, we 'ave le specialité de la maison, le filet du soleil avec roast mouse et parakeet gratinée. Meow, meow, c'est une grande delicacée. (*Shakes her lower body at him in ecstasy.*)

O'BRIEN: Kitty, please. I told you, I haven't had a woman in a year.

KITTY: Oui? Quelle dommage, Monsieur. Et what would you like from ze menu zis evening?

O'BRIEN: Well, the specials sound interesting, especially that Maui Maui fish served with Muck Muck sauce. But what I would like is a good old American hamburger, cooked rare, with French fries and cole slaw. I hope you don't think badly of me by my order.

KITTY: Pas de tout, Monsieur. Kitty does not judge. Kitty loves all choices, she sees no difference between any of zem. But let me tell ze kitchen of your wishes. (*Screams out, a bit vulgar.*) Hey, Mario! Gimme a Number 42, with grease and slaw, bloody! (*Back to* O'BRIEN; *flirtatious and French again.*) Anything else, Monsieur, you wish from Kitty? (*She waves her lower body at him again.*)

O'BRIEN: Not right now. Thank you very much.

KITTY: Oui, Monsieur. (KITTY *walks away seductively, exits. A young* WAITER, *cute, comes on, holding a basket of bread. He comes over to* O'BRIEN *and, like* KITTY, *sticks out his lower body and waves it at him.*)

WAITER: (*waving his lower body seductively; French accent*) Would you like a basket of bread, Monsieur?

O'BRIEN: What?

WAITER: Basket, Monsieur? (*Waves his lower body with energy.*)

O'BRIEN: No, go away. I'm not interested. (WAITER *puts bread on table, walks away, annoyed or disappointed in the response; exits. To himself.*) What island am I on exactly, I wonder? (KITTY *appears right, across the stage from* O'BRIEN. *She holds a bottle of wine and a glass.*)

KITTY: I am bringing you ze wine, Monsieur. (KITTY *raises the bottle and the glass into the air. The* WAITER *comes back, next to* KITTY, *and begins to play the bongo drums.* KITTY *begins to dance toward* O'BRIEN *with the wine, but with very slow, samba-like movements, always leading with her lower body. It is a seductive, strange dance she is doing. Her dance does take her toward the table, but it will take a very, very long time for her to actually get to* O'BRIEN *if she keeps going at this slow, seductive, rhythmic speed.* KITTY *smiles delightedly while she does this dance, and keeps moving her hips and that pelvic area of hers.*)

O'BRIEN: (*Stares for quite a while; eventually becomes impatient.*) Faster, faster! I haven't got all day. (*The bongo rhythm goes much faster, and* KITTY *speeds up her dance movements and gets to his table much faster. The dance, sped up this way, looks much less sexy and much more peculiar, silly, an odd and unnecessary way to cross a room.* KITTY *arrives at the table. The* WAITER *finishes the bongos with a definitive thump, and exits.*)

KITTY: Sometimes it takes a very long time to get across ze room.

O'BRIEN: Ah yes. Does it? (KITTY *puts the wine glass on the table, and holds up the wine bottle.*)

KITTY: Your wine, Monsieur. (KITTY *tries to pour the wine into the glass. However, the bottle is corked and nothing comes out of the bottle.*) It ees not coming out, Monsieur.

O'BRIEN: Well, do you have a corkscrew?

KITTY: (*blushingly flirtatious*) Oh, Monsieur . . . a cork . . . screw??? Oh, Monsieur, you make Kitty blush avec your obscenities. (*Laughing like a schoolchild.*) Screw, screw? Oh, my, I am beside myself!

O'BRIEN: (*sort of annoyed*) Do you have a corkscrew to open the wine?

KITTY: (*Thinks; not flirtatious.*) No, I don't.

O'BRIEN: Well, take it away then.

KITTY: (*Calls offstage for* WAITER.) Gaston! (*The* WAITER *comes back and plays bongos again, so that* KITTY *can dance off with the wine. She dances away quickly this time. She and the* WAITER *exit right. Another waitress,* VERONIQUE, *enters from left. She goes up to* O'BRIEN's *table.*)

VERONIQUE: (*Speaks with an over-the-top Cockney accent.*) 'Allo there, guv-nor! I'm your waitress, Veronique. 'Ow would you like a nice plate of beef and Yorkshire pudding, eh, ducks? Or a lovely cheese and tomahto sandwhich. Or a lovely shepherd's pie?

O'BRIEN: I'm sorry, your name is Veronique?

VERONIQUE: That's me name. I live in a flat with me mom, underneath the loo at Victoria Station. I come 'ere in the tube, and in the mornings I eat digestive biscuits.

O'BRIEN: I see. Kitty was waiting on me before.

VERONIQUE: We don't 'ave no Kitty 'ere, sir.

O'BRIEN: But she was just here. She did a dance to the bongo drums.

VERONIQUE: Bongo drums. Blimey, sir . . . your imagination is runnin' away with you.

O'BRIEN: She was just here. She walks funny.

VERONIQUE: Uh huh. Whatever you say, guv.

O'BRIEN: Never mind. Do you have a corkscrew?

VERONIQUE: What for?

O'BRIEN: For a bottle of wine. Oh that's right, she took the wine away.

VERONIQUE: We don't serve wine 'ere, sir. 'ow about a lovely lager, or a bit o' ale, or a nice cup a' tea served with a delicious bit of digestive biscuit.

O'BRIEN: Never mind. I'll wait for Kitty.

VERONIQUE: You'll wait a long time then, guv'nor. (*Exits left.*)

O'BRIEN: (*wanting* KITTY; *calling toward right, where she had exited*) Oh, waitress! Oh, waitress! (VERONIQUE *comes back on.*)

VERONIQUE: Yes?

O'BRIEN: No, I wanted Kitty.

VERONIQUE: (*threatening a punishment*) Do you want me to bring you your check?

O'BRIEN: Well, I haven't even eaten yet.

VERONIQUE: Then don't go on about Kitty please. Now you eat your bread and water, and if you're well be'aved, maybe Matron will reinstate your privileges.

O'BRIEN: What? Matron? Privileges? Am I in a play by Pirandello?

VERONIQUE: I'm sure I don't know, sir. (*Exits.*)

O'BRIEN: (*calling, a bit softer*) Kitty. Oh, Kitty. (VERONIQUE *is back in, in a flash.*)

VERONIQUE: What did you say?

O'BRIEN: Nothing. I said absolutely nothing.

VERONIQUE: All right, then. (*Exits.*)

o'brien: (*Waits a few seconds; then calls plaintively.*) Kitty . . . oh, Kitty. . . . Here, Kitty, here, Kitty . . . I miss you. Oh, Kitty . . . (veronique *comes back on, leading in the* hostess *and pointing to* o'brien, *indicating there is some issue.* veronique *exits.*)

hostess: Monsieur Au Briand, my apologies. Veronique has told me that the kitty was bothering you. I am so sorry.

o'brien: What? No, no one was bothering me.

hostess: I 'ave taken care that the kitty will bother you no more. We 'ave called up ze veterinarian, and 'e will put kitty to sleep momentarily.

o'brien: Put her to sleep? I don't know what you mean.

hostess: Please, do not feel bad. Many other guests have objected to the cat before . . . she rubs against the legs, they are allergic, she makes them sneeze. She makes the bus boys play the bongos. She has been warned; it is only right she be put to death.

o'brien: Good God, where is the vet? I must stop this.

hostess: But your dinner, Monsieur . . .

o'brien: I don't want her death on my conscience. My ex-wife can't be right about me. I don't destroy all women I meet, do I?

hostess: I am sure I don't know, Monsieur.

o'brien: The address of the veterinarian . . . quickly, quickly!

hostess: Soixante-cinq, rue du chat du mort.

o'brien: Oh, God. (o'brien *runs off. Lights change, and we are in another part of the stage. The* veterinarian, *in a white coat, is standing over* kitty, *who is in a fur coat* [maybe] *and lying on a cot. The* veterinarian *has just finished giving* kitty *a shot from a hypodermic.*)

veterinarian: Bonne nuit, Kitty.

o'brien: Wait, wait . . . don't give her a shot. She was my waitress. I loved her.

VETERINARIAN: Too late. Ze kitty kat is on her way. Au revoir, kitty kat. (*Exits.* O'BRIEN *kneels by* KITTY's *side.*)

O'BRIEN: Kitty, Kitty, I'm here, don't die.

KITTY: Good-bye, Monsieur. You did not love Kitty, and so the doctor, he give me a shot. It ees time to leave. I 'ave danced enough.

O'BRIEN: Oh, Kitty, no. I realize now. You're my reason for living.

KITTY: Oh, Monsieur, do not try to cheer up a dying kitty. I am past it. I 'ave 'ad a full life. I 'ave lapped ze milk. I 'ave arched ze back. I 'ave eaten ze mouse, I 'ave chased ze parakeet. It ees time for Kitty to move on.

O'BRIEN: No, I have nothing.

KITTY: We 'ave Paris, Monsieur.

O'BRIEN: We do? I don't remember anything about Paris.

KITTY: Well, zen we 'ave nothing, Monsieur. Oh, the sodium pentathal is working. Au revoir, au revoir, I am leaving . . . life number . . . five, it is ending. Oh God, four more to go. So many disappointments, so many ze twists and ze turns. How difficile is la vie du chat. Oh . . . oh . . . c'est finie. (KITTY *dies.* O'BRIEN *moans in sorrow and bows his head. The* VETERINARIAN *comes in and gives* O'BRIEN *a hypodermic shot of something.* O'BRIEN *cries out in pain and looks surprised.*)

O'BRIEN: Ow! What are you doing?

VETERINARIAN: I am sorry, Monsieur. My mind, it wandered. I did not mean to give you a shot. But it is too late. Good-bye. (O'BRIEN *looks shocked, then falls over dead.* VETERINARIAN *shrugs, what can you do? Lights out. End.*)

LEFT TO RIGHT

Steven Dietz

Left to Right was commissioned and premiered by the Guthrie Theater in Minneapolis, Minnesota (Joe Dowling, Artistic Director) and was presented in An Evening of Short Plays, July 2002. It was directed by Melissa Kievman; dramaturgy was by Edith-Nicole Lenz; the costume design was by Sarah Mitchell; the lighting design was by Paul J. Hackenmueller; the sound design was by Michael F. Bogden; the production stage manager was Joelle Oetting. The cast was as follows:

ANGIE	Bridie Harrington
DEE	James Eixler
RON	Adam Richman
SCOTT	Rashaad Ernesto Green

CHARACTERS

ANGIE
DEE: Angie's friend.
SCOTT: Dee's husband.
RON: Scott's friend.

SETTING: A long table. Four chairs behind it. All facing the audience.

(*Seated at the table, from left to right:* ANGIE, DEE, RON, SCOTT. *There is only one thing on the table: a cup of coffee, which is directly in front of* ANGIE. *The rest of the table is bare. After a moment,* ANGIE *takes a sip of the coffee. She turns to* DEE.)

ANGIE: That's good coffee.

DEE: Shade grown.

ANGIE: Really?

DEE: The beans.

ANGIE: Right.

DEE: Kept in the dark.

ANGIE: What do you know.

DEE: Another cup?

ANGIE: I'm sleeping with your husband.

DEE: Are you?

ANGIE: Mm-hmm.

DEE: I see.

(*Silence.*)

ANGIE: I feel awful.

DEE: I know.

ANGIE: Really, Dee, I just—

DEE: I know.

ANGIE: No, please, let me explain—

DEE: I mean: I know. I've *known*. I've known this, Angie. I have *been knowing this.*

(*Silence.*)

ANGIE: Did he *tell you*?!

DEE: What do you think?

ANGIE: So, how on earth did you—(*Stops.*) We're friends, Dee.

DEE: Yes, we are.

ANGIE: I can't believe you'd do this to me.

DEE: Excuse me?

ANGIE: I can't believe you'd keep this from me. That you *knew.* That you have *been knowing this.* And you don't say a word. You just let me go on about my—

DEE: You can't believe that.

ANGIE: I trusted you, Dee. I thought we were friends.

(*They are looking at one another. After a moment . . .* DEE *turns immediately to* RON.)

DEE: She didn't know I knew.

RON: So: boom?

DEE: What?

RON: So, just—boom—you told her.

DEE: Yes.

RON: Wow.

DEE: Boom. (*Silence.*) Could *you*?

RON: Hmm?

DEE: Tell Scott. Could you tell Scott about us?

RON: He's my *best friend*.

DEE: And he's my *husband*.

RON: Exactly.

DEE: So? (*Leans in.*) Could you?

(*Silence.*)

RON: We go on a trip. Every year Scott and I go on what we call The Trip.

DEE: Yes, I know.

RON: And this is the thing you *don't* know: whatever happens on The Trip—whoever we meet, whatever we do—any, you know, *commandments* that get a little bent or broken—all of it stays on The Trip. We leave it right there—and we come home *clean*. (*Pause.*) You keep your friend's secret and you keep your friend. It's as simple as that.

SCOTT: I'm thinking Tahoe. (RON *turns immediately to* SCOTT.) Tahoe or Miami Beach. What are you thinking?

RON: For The Trip.

SCOTT: Yes, for The Trip.

RON: I haven't thought about The Trip.

SCOTT: And don't say Prague.

RON: I won't—

SCOTT: Every year: "Prague."

RON: I said I won't—

SCOTT: Like we're gonna—what?—like we're gonna have FUN in Prague?! I mean, c'mon. We don't make The Trip to LEARN SOMETHING, Ron. I think you know that. We don't make the trip to COME HOME BETTER PEOPLE. We make the trip—

RON: Yeah.

SCOTT: I mean, even the years when NOTHING HAPPENS on The Trip—still—the reason we make The Trip—

RON: I *know.*

SCOTT: I know you know.

RON: Okay.

SCOTT: So, I'm thinking Tahoe.

RON: Or Miami Beach.

SCOTT: Now you're talkin'.

RON: How's Angie? (SCOTT *stares at him.*) Does your wife know? (SCOTT *stares at him.*) About Angie. Does she know about Angie?

SCOTT: How do you know about Angie?

RON: You told me.

SCOTT: I did no such thing.

RON: There's this girl named Angie—you said. You don't know her—you said. Friend of Dee's. And we've been sort of, you know . . . *seeing* each other.

SCOTT: Jesus, Ronnie—

RON: Those were your words. (*Silence.*) Does she know?

SCOTT: Is that a threat?

RON: No, it's—

SCOTT: Like you'll—what—like you'll TELL HER?!

RON: Hey, I didn't—

SCOTT: My wife who you do not even *know*—not *really*—never made the effort—not really—all these years, Ronnie— Christmas, New Year's, birthdays by the lake—all these years and *you never made the effort to know her*—

RON: Hey—

SCOTT: People like you—my wife is *wasted* on people like you.

RON: HEY—

SCOTT: Your loss, pal. Dee is a remarkable woman.

RON: I know that.

SCOTT: Bullshit.

RON: I KNOW THAT.

SCOTT: THE HELL YOU DO.

RON: I HAVE MADE AN EFFORT!

(*Silence.*)

SCOTT: Meaning what?

(*A bell rings—or a whistle blows—and they ALL stand and rearrange themselves at the table, sitting in a new order. Left to right:* RON, DEE, SCOTT, ANGIE. *Beat. Then:* RON *immediately turns to* DEE.)

RON: Haven't I made an effort?

DEE: More than you should have. More than both of us should have.

RON: (*troubled*) Why would he say that?!

DEE: How should I know? He's *your* friend.

RON: He's *your* husband. (*Beat.*) It just—I mean, you have no idea—it just *eats at me*.

(*Silence.*)

DEE: You want me to *ask him*?

RON: (*quickly, eager*) Could you?

DEE: You've got to be kidding.

RON: Dee—

DEE: You're taking me to *bed* three days a week, but you want me to ask my husband why you never tried to be my *friend*?!

SCOTT: How should I know? (DEE *turns immediately to* SCOTT.) How should I know? That's just Ron. Lives in a box. Doesn't reach out. It's his loss.

DEE: Do you? (*Beat.*) Do you reach out?

SCOTT: Say again.

DEE: To *my* friends. Do you . . . *reach* a little? A little more than I know. A little more than you should?

ANGIE: What did you say?

(SCOTT *turns immediately to* ANGIE)

SCOTT: The phone rang. Saved my ass.

ANGIE: Who was it?

SCOTT: What does it matter?

ANGIE: It matters.

SCOTT: How does it matter?

ANGIE: It might matter. It just might matter.

SCOTT: I don't care who it was—it rang—saved my ass—Dee changed the subject.

ANGIE: Just like that?

SCOTT: What are you—

ANGIE: Just: BOOM—NEW SUBJECT.

SCOTT: YES.

ANGIE: And you don't think it *matters*—you think it could have been just ANYONE on the phone.

SCOTT: It wasn't just ANYONE. It was NO ONE. There was NO ONE on the phone. I answered. THEY HUNG UP.

ANGIE: *Now.*

SCOTT: What?!

ANGIE: Now, you *get it.*

(*Bell or whistle, as before, and they ALL rearrange themselves again: Left to right: DEE, SCOTT, RON, ANGIE.*)

DEE: That was a week ago.

SCOTT: Yes.

DEE: You expect me to remember a phone call from a week ago?

SCOTT: Was it Ron?

DEE: What? (*Silence.*) Why would it be Ron?

(SCOTT *turns immediately to* RON.)

SCOTT: Was it you?

RON: Why would it be me? (*Silence.*) If I called your house, why would I hang up?

(*Eye to eye.*)

SCOTT: That's what I'm asking. (*Silence.*) Do you know why we go on The Trip, Ronnie?

RON: What kind of ques—

SCOTT: You think we go on the trip to *fuck around*—is that it?

RON: I'm not gonna talk about this. You're not—

SCOTT: (*overlapping*) We go on The Trip—*we go on The Trip to stay friends.* The day we stop going on The Trip—the day we stop knowing something about the other that we're not supposed to know—well, that day, Ronnie, that day we are *done*.

RON: Whatever you say.

SCOTT: *Did you call my house?*

(*Silence.*)

RON: (*simply*) Hey, I met Angie. (*Beat.*) She's nice.

ANGIE: What can it hurt?

(RON *turns immediately to* ANGIE.)

RON: Right.

ANGIE: A little get-together. Casual. Just the four of us. Sounds great.

RON: Good.

(*A beat. A shared smile.*)

ANGIE: You got my number from Dee, didn't you? (*Beat.*) Well. I'm glad. Dee talks about you all the time. Says you're the one friend of her husband's who really *makes an effort*.

RON: Scott.

ANGIE: Hmm?

RON: I got your number from Scott.

(*Silence. She stares at him.*)

ANGIE: (*to* RON) Would you pass my coffee? (RON *looks at* DEE. DEE *lifts the coffee. It is handed to* SCOTT, *then to* RON, *then to* ANGIE.) Thanks. (*She does not drink the coffee. She merely looks down into the cup.*)

RON: What does it matter?

ANGIE: Hmm?

RON: Who I got your number from. It doesn't matter.

ANGIE: (*simply*) It might. It might matter. (*She takes a sip of her coffee.*) Just the four of us.

RON: Right.

ANGIE: Casual. (*Beat.*) When?

RON: Next week. When Scott's back from his trip. (*Off her look.*) Tahoe. (*Beat.*) Business, I think.

(*Silence.* ANGIE *smiles.*)

ANGIE: Dee told me all about those trips.

(ANGIE *takes a long sip of her coffee.*)

RON: (*quietly*) Really.

ANGIE: (*re: the coffee*) And this. Dee told me all about this. Said you're the one who turned her on to it.

RON: What are you talking ab—

ANGIE: Shade grown. (*Beat.*) Kept in the dark.

(*End of play.*)

THE LEVEE

Taylor Mac Bowyer

The New York premiere of *The Levee* was presented by Vital Theatre Company (Stephen Sunderlin, Artistic Director. Sharon Fallon, Managing Director). Marc Parees directed the following cast:

KEITH   Al Hasnas
PAIGE   Denis Joughin Casey

(*Two o'clock in the morning. August in the central valley of California. Lights up on a small kitchen.* KEITH, *late thirties/early forties, is fixing the sink. He wears boxer shorts and a dirty T-shirt. There's the sound of a car driving up.* KEITH *stops his work, not bothering to get up from under the sink.* PAIGE, *late thirties, comes in. She is still in her polyester-blend work dress, nylons, and sensible high-heel shoes from her day job. She carries a purse and is drunk. She stumbles into the kitchen and sees* KEITH.)

PAIGE: Jesus Christ. (*Louder than she needs to be.*) Hello there.

KEITH: Shhhhh.

PAIGE: Someone sleeping?

KEITH: I was getting worried.

PAIGE: Were you?

KEITH: Couldn't sleep.

PAIGE: And so you thought you'd fix the sink?

KEITH: Needed fixing.

PAIGE: So accomplished you are.

KEITH: You've been drinking.

PAIGE: Am I not allowed?

KEITH: Just different.

PAIGE: You shouldn't have waited up.

KEITH: Wasn't sure where you wanted me.

PAIGE: To sleep?

KEITH: Didn't want to assume. Did you drive home like that?

PAIGE: I skipped. Thank you for being here. Vows and all. You could be so many other places. Should I be handing you something? Isn't that what bystanders are supposed to do? Hand the dirty handymen something?

KEITH: I got it.

PAIGE: Come out come out wherever you are.

KEITH: Maybe you should sit down.

PAIGE: You're concerned. (PAIGE *attempts to sit but falls on the kitchen floor.*) No laughing. I love this floor. So cold. Like silk pillows. Went to the baby doctor today.

KEITH: You didn't tell me. . . .

PAIGE: Hopes.

KEITH: So.

PAIGE: It took.

KEITH: And you thought you'd go get sloshed to celebrate?

PAIGE: Of course the problem isn't the conception.

KEITH: Still.

PAIGE: Still.

(KEITH *puts his hand on* PAIGE's *belly.*)

KEITH: Can you feel it?

PAIGE: Like it's swimming around? No. Feels like the absence of something larger. You notice, my body's so used to being pregnant I don't even have morning sickness anymore?

KEITH: Might not happen again.

PAIGE: My miscarriages.

KEITH: It might work yeah?

PAIGE: A woman at work quit her CPA job, declared bankruptcy and is now working at Dairy Queen. I thought that was something only men did. Aren't women supposed to just be happy to *have* the high-paid office job—midlife crisis to hell. We're developing a whole new area of land. Farmers be damned. Building more track housing. Here's to another inception. (*Seeing his arm for the first time, which has a brand-new tattoo on it.*) What the fuck did you do?

KEITH: Took you a while.

PAIGE: No. You don't get to destroy . . . how could you?

KEITH: My body.

PAIGE: No. Not your body. My body. ALL MINE.

(PAIGE *tears her nylons off in an attempt to cause some bodily harm without actually hurting herself. She cries.*)

KEITH: Shhhhhh.

PAIGE: Don't do that. I'm fine. Things are lovely for me. The doctors bet on a girl. I don't know about that. What would I do with a girl?

KEITH: We.

PAIGE: Let's just take it one second at a time. No celebration. Not yet. Fix the sink. I'll be wanting to throw up in it later.

KEITH: You okay?

PAIGE: You can sleep on the couch. Or come to bed. Whatever you'd like. I'd like to give up, you know. Get a dog. I do it by rote now. Don't even know if I want it anymore. At one point I wanted it more than anything. More than you. Remember? Baby ultimatums.

KEITH: I'm older.

PAIGE: Now it's all turned around—

KEITH: I can handle—

PAIGE: Now you want it more than—you don't even look at me—just my midriff.

KEITH: That's not true.

PAIGE: What goes around . . . please let it work Keith. Please let it work. Please please please. Whatever you'd like. I won't wait up.

KEITH: Shhhhhh. You stink like booze.

PAIGE: Not sexy?

KEITH: Not right now.

PAIGE: I have a mint somewhere.

(*She dumps the contents of her purse on the table, which include, among other things, a pack of cigarettes.*)

KEITH: You're smoking.

PAIGE: No comments.

KEITH: Just thought . . .

PAIGE: Didn't do much good to quit.

KEITH: Just thought.

PAIGE: Woman at work just found out she's pregnant. You can imagine how tippy toe that makes everyone. Parties when I'm out of the room that suddenly hush into sorrowful looks every time I walk in. Should never have told anyone. I can hear her talking on the phone, everyone can hear her talking on the phone, and she's telling her mother, her mother no doubt, that the doctor says the baby should be twenty inches but only eighteen inches if she continues to smoke and she says to her mother, "Two inches, I can sacrifice two inches," they have a good laugh and she hangs up to have a puff. I swear they do it sometimes just to get more breaks.

KEITH: That's not why you do it?

PAIGE: Were you really worried?

KEITH: It's two o'clock in the morning.

PAIGE: Did you call the police?

KEITH: I worried.

PAIGE: File a missing persons report?

KEITH: Didn't know what to do.

PAIGE: So you fixed the sink.

KEITH: Needed fixing.

PAIGE: Daddy hates tattoos. Says they keep you working-class.

KEITH: He's no better off than us.

PAIGE: Still hates them.

KEITH: Tired of not being enough.

PAIGE: Supposed to consult me about stuff like that right?

KEITH: Didn't feel like it.

PAIGE: We stopped being friends huh?

KEITH: Been working two jobs.

PAIGE: And then coming home to fix the sink.

KEITH: Needed . . .

PAIGE: Fixing, I know. No time for me.

KEITH: I was home.

PAIGE: But not me, I was off getting hammered.

KEITH: I should finish up. (PAIGE *sits and cries.* KEITH *sits with her for a while and then gets behind her on the chair and starts making soft motorcycle noises.*) rmmmmmmmmmm. (*Pause.*) rmmmmm-rmmmmmm.

PAIGE: Where are we?

KEITH: The miracle mile.

PAIGE: At sunset.

KEITH: Hot summer night.

PAIGE: Like now.

KEITH: Right.

PAIGE: Passing all the homeless men and abandoned shops.

KEITH: rmmmmmmmmmmmm.

PAIGE: So much wind.

KEITH: Blowing your hair in my face.

PAIGE: In your mouth.

KEITH: Can't see.

PAIGE: So I'm your eyes.

KEITH: Right.

PAIGE: Faster.

KEITH: You got it.

PAIGE: Faster than the eyes can focus. Everything zooming by.

KEITH: rmmmmmrmmmmm.

PAIGE: So beautiful. You feel that baby girl—all them lights just stretching on out as you pass 'em.

KEITH: Think she can see 'em?

PAIGE: Where to now?

KEITH: The levee.

PAIGE: Up on top.

KEITH: Even faster.

PAIGE: Dodging all them bugs.

KEITH: That's why you're in front.

PAIGE: So chivalrous. Come and get me buggies. NOTHING CAN TOUCH ME NOW.

KEITH: You'll wake the neighbors.

PAIGE: Fuck 'em. Where'd my soundtrack go?

KEITH: Sorry. (KEITH *continues to make motorcycle noise.*)

PAIGE: Gravel looks like the sea when it goes by fast. You can just dip right in if you want. Tumble and discombobulate into little stones.

KEITH: Hold on tight.

PAIGE: No rules. Not today. (PAIGE *stands up on the chair.*)

KEITH: What are you doing?

PAIGE: Acrobatic art.

KEITH: You should get down.

PAIGE: The Hippodrome Stand.

KEITH: Baby won't be too happy if I let you break your neck.

PAIGE: You'd never let me.

KEITH: Can't see with your ass in the way.

PAIGE: Thought you liked my ass.

KEITH: You're gonna bust it wobbling like that.

PAIGE: Besides I'm your eyes right?

KEITH: Can't be doing that kind of stuff.

PAIGE: You concentrate on driving.

KEITH: Just get down.

PAIGE: Sourpuss. (KEITH *picks her up off the chair like a newlywed.*) HA.

KEITH: Ha yourself.

PAIGE: Such a man.

KEITH: Playing the concerned father. (*He sets her down on the table.*)

PAIGE: So good you are. When can we do it for real?

KEITH: Once I get my bike.

PAIGE: How much longer?

KEITH: Once you have the kid, once we figure out the money situation.

PAIGE: Will there be a horn?

KEITH: Always is.

PAIGE: A horn to say good-bye with. And for the fun of making noise and for the fun of just pressing.

KEITH: If you want.

PAIGE: I want to move. I don't want her growing up here. There's nothing here, only leftover dust that doesn't know where to go. Used to grow stuff. Used to have a purpose but doesn't anymore. I don't want that for her. Can we do that?

KEITH: We can decide when she comes.

PAIGE: Cause she might not? I miss making love to you just cause. Will you come to bed tonight? Will you clean me up and put me to bed. I must look pretty awful huh? Have I failed too much to know what to do with me?

KEITH: We're gonna have a baby.

PAIGE: And then everything will be okay?

KEITH: And she'll have ten fingers and ten toes and tons of hair.

PAIGE: Cause all the babies on your side of the family have tons of hair, when they're babies.

KEITH: Right. Paige?

(PAIGE *puts her hand up her dress and pulls it out—there is blood.*)

PAIGE: Spotting.

KEITH: Let's get you to the hospital.

PAIGE: Stupid little girl.

KEITH: Baby.

PAIGE: Stupid little weak little girl.

KEITH: Baby let's go.

PAIGE: Don't want to.

KEITH: I'll call an ambulance.

PAIGE: Don't want it.

KEITH: Might be all fine.

PAIGE: Tired of investing so much.

KEITH: Could just be spotting.

PAIGE: She doesn't want to grow into this. Doesn't want this. Can't force things. Tired of investing. Don't have any more to give. Everything already used up. What if she scraped her knee? I don't have any more to give. Any more caring. I'm tired. Want to let it go.

KEITH: Baby.

PAIGE: Just want to let it go.

KEITH: Please don't.

PAIGE: Can we let it go?

KEITH: Please.

PAIGE: Just let it go.

KEITH: There might still be time.

PAIGE: Stay here.

KEITH: They could help.

PAIGE: Just stay here.

KEITH: Let her die?

PAIGE: Just rest here.

KEITH: Here.

PAIGE: Just here.

KEITH: With you?

PAIGE: Yes.

KEITH: Just here.

PAIGE: Yes.

KEITH: I'm so sorry.

PAIGE: Just here.

KEITH: I love you.

PAIGE: So sorry.

KEITH: Okay.

PAIGE: So so sorry.

KEITH: Okay.

(*Lights out.*)

MARRED BLISS

Mark O'Donnell

Marred Bliss was commissioned and first produced by Actors Theatre of Louisville, Kentucky. It premiered on May 26, 1987. It was directed by Larry Deckel; the set design was by Paul Owen; the lighting design was by Cliff Berek; the costume design was by Kevin McLeod. The cast was as follows:

JANE	Denise Campion
DINK	Nick Phelps
JEERY	David Beach
ALAS	Amanda Rambo

SETTING: The front porch of Jane's family home.

(*At rise:* JANE *arranges roses in a vase.* DINK *sits on the glider, reading the paper or just enjoying the evening. It's a typical midwestern scene.* JANE *is a pretty, prissy, inhibited young woman, wearing starched, modest clothes.* DINK *is a regular lug who's been talked into marriage but is willing to turn himself over to it.*)

JANE: Darkling?

DINK: (*looking up from his paper*) What is it . . . Dulling?

JANE: I thought we'd have ruses for the centerpieces. For us and for all the guest tables. Ruses *are* traditional.

DINK: Ruses it is. (*He returns to his reading.*)

JANE: (*after a restless pause*) Oh honey, just *sink!*

DINK: What do you want me to sink about?

JANE: In less than forty-eight horrors, you and I will be moan and woof! (*Grins.*) Isn't it amassing?

DINK: It *is* amassing. (*Lowers his paper thoughtfully.*) So much has harpooned in just a few thief years!

JANE: It steams like only yesterday that you were the noise next door.

DINK: And you were that feckless-faced cod sitting up in the old ache tree!

JANE: And now we're encaged! I can hardly wait till we're marred!

DINK: Oh, Hiney! (*Makes to enfold her in his arms.*)

JANE: Now, now! I'm sure the tame will pass quickly till our hiney-moon! (*Eases out of his grasp.*) I'll go get you some of that nice saltpeter taffy that Smother brought back from A Frantic City. (JEERY, *a sexy, slouching sailor, appears at one corner of the stage.*)

JEERY: Hello? . . . Any him at home? (*He carries a tiny bouquet.*)

JANE: Oh my gash! It's Jeery, my old toyfriend!

DINK: Jeery! That bump! What's *he* brewing here?

JANE: Oh, Dueling! Try to control your tamper! I'm sure he means no charm! Don't do anything you might regress! (JEERY *approaches.*)

JEERY: Hollow!—Revised to see me?

JANE: Hollow, Jeery.

DINK: Hollow. (*Pause.*)

JEERY: I'm completely beware that I'm out of police here. But— (*Looks to* JANE.)—for old climb's sake—Jane—I brought you this little bunch of foul airs. A token of my excess steam. Lots of lack to you. And much lack to you too, Dink.

JANE: (*unsurely*) Wail . . . (*Decides to accept the flowers.*) Spank you, Jeery.

DINK: Spank you very much.

JEERY: My shaft is at rancor in the harbor, and they gave me whore leave. I heard you were engorged, and I just wanted to slop by and pave my regrets.

JANE: (*uncomfortably*) Well, blank you!

DINK: Blank you very much.

JANE: (*uneasy with this standoff*) I think you two have already messed, haven't you?

JEERY: Oh, we've thrown each other for years!

DINK: We went to the same cruel . . . Till Jeery dripped out to join the Nervy.

JANE: Of course. I remainder all that now! (*She is eager to lessen the awkwardness.*) Um—Do you haunt to sit down?

JEERY: Well, only for a menace. (*He sits with them on the glider.*) I'm hooded over to Pain Street. There's a big trance at the Social Tub. I'll probably go and chick it out. (*Awkward silence as they sit on the crowded glider.*) Wail, wail, wail . . . So when do you two tie the net?

JANE: The day after temerity!

JEERY: That soon?

DINK: (*curtly*) We've been enraged for over a year.

JEERY: Well, concatenations!

DINK: Rank you very much . . . (*Tense pause.*) . . . Jeery, it's getting awfully lout! You don't want to miss the trance! (*From the other entrance comes* ALAS, *a provocatively dressed woman with elaborate hair and a loose manner.*)

ALAS: Hell's own? Hell's own?

JANE: (*aside*) Oh no! Is that who I slink it is? Why won't she let us align? (ALAS *advances.*)

ALAS: Hell's own, every burden! Hell's own, Dink!

DINK: (*uncomfortable but heated*) Hell's own, Alas! . . . Fantasy seething you here!

JANE: (*tartly*) I thought you'd be at the Social Tub trance, Alas. Aren't you on the degradation committee?

ALAS: (*Offers a gift-wrapped bottle.*) I may stoop by there later. I sinfully wanted damn pain for you—I hype you enjoy it.

JANE: (*suspicious*) How sweet of you. (*Takes bottle, puts it aside.*) You know Jeery, don't you, Alas?

ALAS: Yes, we mated years ago. How's the Nervy, Jeery?

JEERY: Great! I was born to be a soiler. (*Another awkward silence as they regard her.*)

DINK: (*to* ALAS) Um—Would you like to hit with us, Alas? Jane, you don't grind if Alas hits with us, do you?

JANE: Well, the glider's getting awfully clouded!

ALAS: (*airily*) I'll just loin against the railing! (*She poses against the pillar seductively.*)

DINK: No, here, have my seed! (*Stands.*)

JANE: Dallying! (*Pulls him back into his seat.*) I think she'd rather remain stunning!

DINK: (*getting agitated*) Jeery, you could awful her *your* seat! Don't they teach you manners in the Harmed Surfaces? (JEERY *bristles.*)

JANE: (*to avoid a scene*) Look, qualm down! Maybe we should admit this is an awkward saturation! I have complete face in you, Dink—But I think it's in power taste for your old street-part to come around so soon before our welding!

ALAS: (*offended*) I can't bereave this! There's no reason to be sub-species, Jane!

JANE: (*affronted*) No?

ALAS: This is a Good Wall visit, that's all! You're just high-stung!

DINK: (*chiming in his objections*) And what about Jeery here! I don't luck having him luring at you!

JEERY: (*contemptuously*) Oh, relapse, Dink! Afraid she'll realize her Must-Ache before the Sorrow-Money? (*To* ALAS.) He's in debt, it's a mortgage of convenience!

JANE: (*frightened by this sudden passion*) Toys, please! Clam your-self! (*Earnestly, to* DINK.) Dink, don't drought yourself this way! Where's the strong, stabled man I'm taking to be altered? You know I lug you, I'll always lug you. (*Puts her arms around him maternally.*) I want ours to be a beautiful cremation-trip. But it has to be based on *truss*. (*Hugs him even more suffocatingly, and not erotically.*) I want to be able to *truss* you.

DINK: (*too independently to suit* JANE) All I did was offer Alas my seed. You act like I rammed off with her!

JANE: (*Feels dressed down before company.*) Well, maybe you'd rather ram off with her! She's been trying to reduce you since she got here!

ALAS: (*angry*) Don't spike like that to me! I bitter go.

JANE: (*her insecurity making her hysterical*) Stew where you are, you're the claws of this! You *slot*!

ALAS: (*sneering at* JANE) —What a little squirrel! I have nothing but potty for you!

(*The women suddenly slap each other; the men must intervene.*)

JEERY: (*restraining* ALAS) The whole tissue is ridiculous! Fighting over a man who's in doubt up to his ears!

DINK: At least I'm not diddled with funeral disease, you bellow-jellied bull-bottomed sin of the beach!

JEERY: You sod-damned cowbird!

(*The men fight; now the women must intervene.*)

ALAS: Boys! Stomp it! Stomp it this minute!

(*There is momentary silence as they all recover from their wounds.*)

JANE: Why are we having such trouble trying to communicate?

DINK: (*taking the lead*) . . . Look. Alas . . . I heave nothing but harpy memories of our time together. I depreciate your good winces, but Jane and I are to be marred, and that's that. (*He looks to* JANE *to match his definitive renunciation.*)

JANE: (*taking* JEERY'*s hand briefly*) And . . . Jeery . . . I leave you very much. You know that. But that's all winter under the fridge. (*Turns to* ALAS.) Alas, I'm sorry I lost my torpor.

ALAS: (*with dignity*) I understand. And I axe-up your apology. Anyway, I'm getting marred myself. To Henry Silverstone.

JANE: (*impressed*) The banker! But he's rather old for you, isn't he?

ALAS: Luckily, he's in very good wealth. (*A car horn honks from off-stage.*) There's my chauffeured limbo now. I'd better get golden. Conglomerations, and gall the best! . . . Goad bye!

DINK: (*feeling bested*) Bile!

JANE: (*feeling outdone*) Bile!

(ALAS *exits.* JEERY *now feels superfluous.*)

JEERY: Her own limbo! . . . Well, I guess I should leave you two lifeboats alone!

JANE: Thanks for the foul airs, Jeery! Enjoy the trance!

JEERY: Maybe I'll meet my future broad!

DINK: (*as if to a buddy*) That's the right platitude!

JEERY: So long! Have a lot of skids!

DINK: Bile!

JANE: Bile! (JEERY *goes.*) He's a good spore, isn't he?

DINK: (*reluctantly*) I gas so.

JANE: (*hugging him consolingly*) But you're the *uphill* of my eye!

DINK: Oh, hiney! (*He holds and tries to kiss her, but she resists him.*) Oh come on! Plead? Pretty plead? (*She relents and gives him a peck, then quickly raises* ALAS'*s gift bottle between them.*)

JANE: Oh look! A vintage battle of damn pain! Let's celibate! (*She pops it open and pours some of it into two empty lemonade glasses on the porch table. She raises her glass.*) I love it when those little troubles get up your nose!—Here, let's test each other! (*They toast.*) To *ice!*

DINK: To *ass!* (*They drink.*)

JANE: Oh, galling! Our life together is going to be *blitz!*

(*Blackout.*)

MEN'S INTUITION

Itamar Moses

Men's Intuition was first presented as part of the 8×10 festival, an evening of short work by NYU and Columbia M.F.A. playwrights, in the PSNBC space at the HERE Center for the Performing Arts, produced by Ethan Youngerman and Winter Miller, on May 10, 2002. Isaac Hurwitz directed the following cast:

WENDELL	Cameron Francis
ERIC	Johnathan F. McClain

CHARACTERS

WENDELL: A male college student, skinny, rumpled clothing.
ERIC: His roommate, hockey jersey, backwards cap.

SETTING: Eric and Wendell's dorm room, on a large college campus.

TIME: Evening.

(*Lights up on a dorm room: two desks, two chairs, two computers, two twin-sized beds, two piles of dirty laundry, two doors, one of which leads to the hallway, and one of which leads to a closet.* ERIC, *nineteen, hockey jersey, backwards cap, is seated at one of the desks, with papers, pens, a calculator, and an open economics textbook in front of him.* WENDELL, *also nineteen, in jeans and a button-down, is pacing.* ERIC's *desk is by the front door.* WENDELL's *desk is by the closet door. A hockey stick leans against the wall by the closet.*)

WENDELL: So? Did you figure it out?

ERIC: No. Dude, you gotta give me a clue. It's, like, impossible.

WENDELL: Just keep in mind that every word counts. It's important to employ exacting attention to detail with respect to the given circumstances.

ERIC: Oh. (*Pause.*) What?

WENDELL: Do you remember what the question was?

ERIC: Oh, um. There's two guards. One always lies, one always tells the truth. And there's, um, two doors. One leads to certain death, and one leads to freedom. And you gotta . . . I have to figure out . . . you can ask only one question, and you have to figure out . . . I don't know.

WENDELL: That's all right, Eric, we can try a different one.

I know it's a little bit difficult to conceive of, after all:

Someone who always lies.

ERIC: Dude, I don't see why I have to do *any* of these. This isn't even what the test is even about.

WENDELL: Hey, *you* asked *me* for help, uh, man, so if you don't really—

ERIC: No, I know, I know, so, like, thanks, or whatever, but could we at least do it faster, though? I gotta get out of here. I'm going out tonight.

WENDELL: A little bit of patience is required for this. Let's do another one.

ERIC: Aww, maaaan . . .

WENDELL: Three lightbulbs are attached to a wall at eye level.

ERIC: Could you just explain to me how it works? Like, what's in the book?

WENDELL: There is an adjacent room containing three switches, each of which operates one of the lightbulbs. Each room is visually inaccessible from the other.

ERIC: Visually what?

WENDELL: Inaccessible. You can't see one from the other.

ERIC: Wendell, I gotta say—

WENDELL: Do you want to pass this test or not? Listen: Eric—

ERIC: Call me E.

WENDELL: I'm not calling you E.

ERIC: Everyone else does.

WENDELL: I'm not starting to call you E just because your god-damn coach—

ERIC: I don't have a lot of time, okay?

WENDELL: Which is why it's important that we hurry up and—

ERIC: Dude! It's an econ midterm! What the fuck do these brain tweezers have to do with economics?

WENDELL: "Teasers."

ERIC: What?

WENDELL: "Brain *teasers.*" And the reason I am doing this, as I
    thought I explained, is that much of the material is intuitive.

ERIC: Oh. (*Pause.*) It's what?

WENDELL: You just, sort of . . . You either get it or you don't,
    Eric. These puzzles will place you in the appropriate state of
    mind to . . . get it.

ERIC: I don't—

WENDELL: Okay, so: There's three lightbulbs attached to a wall at
    eye level.

ERIC: Why are lightbulbs attached to a wall at eye level?

WENDELL: I don't know.

ERIC: Is it, like, a strip club?

WENDELL: No.

ERIC: Cause that'd be sweet. (*He chuckles to himself.*)

WENDELL: It is not a strip club. They're attached to the wall
    because they just *are,* okay? There's an adjacent room with
    three switches. You, uh, you *can't see* the lightbulbs from the
    switch room, okay? Operating the switches however you like,
    and then going to check the status of the bulbs only once,
    how can you determine which switch operates which bulb?

    Got it? Go.

ERIC: Wendell—

WENDELL: Go.

(ERIC *tries to get to work, scribbles some notes, drums his fingers, plays
with his hat, and gives up more or less immediately.* WENDELL *simply
stares at him.*)

    It doesn't look like you're making much progress.

ERIC: Wendell, dude, no, all right? Enough. Just explain to me how economics works. I'm supposed to meet this girl later. Just *explain* it to me.

WENDELL: A girl? Well. That *is* important. I'll do what I can to speed this up. (*He stands, slowly.*) Shall we try just one more?

ERIC: I don't know. (*Standing.*) If this is all you're planning to make me study, I should really just—

WENDELL: You can't *go*. Didn't your coach say, if you don't pass this class, you can't, you won't be allowed to—

ERIC: Yeah, but, this isn't helping. I gotta—

(ERIC *heads for the door.* WENDELL *moves quickly and blocks his path.*)

WENDELL: One more.

ERIC: No.

WENDELL: One more, one more, all right: Here it is. Listen carefully: There's a gun in a desk drawer.

ERIC: Dude—

WENDELL: And you fucked my girlfriend.

(*Pause.*)

ERIC: What? (*Pause.*) Hey. Hey, let's go back to the one with the two guards—

WENDELL: You heard me.

ERIC: What are you talking about?

WENDELL: You know what I'm talking about.

ERIC: Who told you that?

WENDELL: So it happened.

ERIC: Dude, no, I asked who *told* you that. (*Pause.*) She's not your girlfriend.

WENDELL: Oh, is that right? Why don't *you* teach *me* something, what do *you* call a girl that somebody is going out with? What's *your* term for that? Is it, like, "Ho," or something, Eric?

ERIC: Call me E.

WENDELL: No.

ERIC: You went out with her *one time*. You didn't even kiss her.

WENDELL: Just tell me what happened. I want to hear it from you.

ERIC: Dude, no. (*Pause.*) I ran into her at a party.

WENDELL: No. Tell me exactly what happened, Eric.

ERIC: E.

WENDELL: *I'm not fucking calling you E!*

ERIC: Hey, keep it on the ice!

WENDELL: *What!?*

ERIC: Keep it on the ice, dude.

WENDELL: *What ice!?*

ERIC: It means "calm down."

WENDELL: If you want me to calm down, then tell me what happened.

ERIC: We talked at the party. I thought she was cute. She asked me back to her room. That was pretty much that.

WENDELL: *No. No. Tell me everything that happened!*

ERIC: What the fuck is wrong with you? It didn't even *matter*. It was just this *thing*.

WENDELL: What did you *say* to her? What *hand gestures* did you make? What were you *wearing?* When did she laugh, how did you make her laugh? Tell me every word you said, *every single word—*

ERIC: (*overlapping*) *Why?* Why do you want to know all that stuff?

WENDELL: *Because I don't understand!*

> You went to a party? That's your fucking explanation? You probably weren't even planning on it, some *buddy* of yours drags you, "Hey, E, let's go to this party," you so then you, you *run into* this girl. And you talk. And, and, and what happens *then*? What fucking *alchemy* takes place at that point, to turn, to turn *that* into . . . into *this*?

> Can you just *explain* it to me? Because I don't get it.

ERIC: I don't know what to tell you, man. It just happened.

WENDELL: Is she the girl you're meeting later?

ERIC: What? Oh. No. That's a different girl. (*Pause.*) Are you going to get out of my way? Wendell?

WENDELL: No.

ERIC: Dude, don't make me have to, like, move you.

WENDELL: I wouldn't try that if I were you.

ERIC: What are you talking about?

WENDELL: You weren't listening, Eric. To the last puzzle.

ERIC: What, the thing about the drawer? The gun in the—

(*A quick beat. Then,* WENDELL *jerks, as though he's going to run to his desk, but* ERIC *sprints there first and opens the drawer. He laughs, high-pitched, a bit relieved.*)

> You had me goin' there, man. You really had me goin' there. (*He chuckles, tension draining.*) I'm sorry, okay? I really am. I'll make it up to you. I'll take you out, we'll meet some girls. I'll hook you up. Tonight's kind of no good, this is really just a thing for the hockey team, but, seriously, next weekend maybe, okay?

(*As he talks,* ERIC *turns his back on* WENDELL *to open the closet. He takes out his letterman jacket and puts it on.*)

And, you know, thanks for the help with the studying. Even if we didn't get to the actual, you know, econ. Coach'll work somethin' out, I guess.

WENDELL: You didn't pay close enough attention, Eric. You have to listen to every single word.

ERIC: What?

WENDELL: I didn't say the gun was in *my* drawer.

(*Another quick beat, but this time* ERIC *is much too far away.* WENDELL *pulls open* ERIC'*s desk drawer and pulls out a gun. He points it at* ERIC'*s head.*)

ERIC: Dude, what the fuck?

WENDELL: You're not leaving, Eric.

ERIC: That is not real.

WENDELL: Listen to me—

ERIC: That is not real, man. Is that real? That is not real. Is that *loaded*?

WENDELL: Who knows? That wasn't in the given circumstances of the brain teaser. You can only work with what you have. So. What now?

ERIC: Quit fucking around, man. I'm sorry, all right? Just tell me what to do. I'll do anything you say, just tell me what to do.

WENDELL: You were about to leave, Eric, you've obviously got it all figured out. You don't need me to teach you anything. What's the solution? How do you get through the door? Huh? What do you think you can—

(*Suddenly,* ERIC *grabs his hockey stick from where it leans against the wall by the closet. He swings it with incredible precision and knocks the gun from* WENDELL'*s hand. A brief moment of stunned motionless silence from both of them as the new circumstances are absorbed. Then* ERIC *charges, stick held out in front of him body-check style, and slams*

WENDELL *up against the front door. He punches* WENDELL *in the stomach.* WENDELL *drops to the ground, where* ERIC *kicks him several times.*)

(*A silence. Both of them are breathing hard.* WENDELL *curls up into a ball.* ERIC *throws his stick away, and looks around for the gun. He picks it up from the floor where it fell, and hefts it, curiously. He finds a plug in the "cartridge" and pulls it out. Water spills onto the floor.* WENDELL *sees.* ERIC *puts the water gun down.*)

WENDELL: (*weakly, with a rueful chuckle*) Blam. (*Pause.*) Nice slapshot.

ERIC: I'm an All–American wing. (*Pause.*) Wendell. Wendell, I . . . uh . . . You shouldn't have done that, man. You didn't need to, uh . . . to do that.

(ERIC *sits, not sure what to do. A long pause. Breathing. At last . . .*)

Wendell?

WENDELL: Mhm.

ERIC: So . . . uh . . . what's the answer? To the thing with the light-bulbs?

WENDELL: Are you kidding me?

ERIC: No. Tell me. What's the answer? Just explain it to me.

WENDELL: You turn on two of the switches for a few minutes. Then you turn one of them off, and go into the other room. One of the bulbs will be on, easy. But this way you can also figure out which of the other two was on before you came in.

Because you feel it. And it's warm.

(*They stare at each other,* ERIC *down at the floor, and* WENDELL *up from it. Fade to black.*)

THE MOON PLEASE

Diana Son

The Moon Please premiered as part of Brave New World (J. Dakota Powell, Producing Artistic Director) at Town Hall, New York City on September 11, 2002. Christopher Smith directed the following cast:

CIEL   Gloria Reuben
JAY   Frank Wood

CHARACTERS

CIEL: (pronounced "seel") Mid to late thirties.
JAY: Mid to late thirties.

SETTING: A small one-bedroom apartment in New York City. The only physical set piece needed is a door. A few props the actors need to put their hands on: a couple ties, Ciel's bag, a breast pump, Jay's bag.

TIME: The morning, September 11, 2001.

(JAY *walks in as* CIEL *looks through a stack of papers.*)

CIEL: I'm missing a page. I'm—(*Riffles through report.*) The page with the pie chart. It should be right here.

JAY: What color is this tie?

CIEL: I can't go in there without that page. You know how Schaefer is, he's gotta have his visual—god*damn*it, I can't believe this is happening to me today. (*Notices* JAY's *tie.*) Brown. It doesn't go.

JAY: This tie is brown?

CIEL: Yes.

JAY: It's not blue?

CIEL: No. (JAY *stares at the tie, willing it to turn blue.*) Wear your maroon tie . . . the one with the squiggly stripes. (*Riffling again.*) Fuck!

JAY: Just print another copy, honey, it doesn't have to be—

CIEL: I can't print it out. The baby's been sleeping so lightly lately and our shitty little printer makes such a fucking rack—

JAY: She's gotta get used to our noises. Remember what the doctor said? I mean, this is a one-bedroom apartment. We've all gotta share the space.

CIEL: I know that but I just can't deal with her being awake when I leave and I have to leave in . . . (*checks watch*) ten minutes at the latest. Can you wait until Georgia gets here?

JAY: What time is she supposed to come?

CIEL: (*checks watch*) Twenty minutes ago.

JAY: I can't be late to my interview—I mean, they're not gonna hire someone who can't even come to the interview on time. Maybe you should call her.

CIEL: What time's your interview?

JAY: Nine.

CIEL: What about my pie chart?

JAY: Print it at the office.

CIEL: I forgot to pack my pump. (*Heading for the kitchen.*) We're not meeting at the office. We're doing the pitch at a conference room in—

JAY: (*leaving for the bedroom*) You better call Georgia.

(CIEL *returns to the living room and picks up the phone.*)

CIEL: Be quiet when you're in there, please.

(JAY *passes into the bedroom, which is just another part of the stage. We see him gingerly take down a tie and freeze when he hears the baby stir.*)

(*As she dials.*) It's just that it took me forty-five minutes of nursing to get her down. (*Touching them.*) My nipples feel like I've been rubbing them against a cheese gra—(*into phone*) Hey—what are you still doing home? It's 8:20, you said you'd be here twe—(*Silence as* CIEL *listens. At the same time, we see* JAY *peer into the baby's bassinet and watch her breathe—as if it were possible the next breath won't come.*) Georgia . . . It's going to take you half an hour just to get here. I have to be all the way downtown by nine o'—(*She drops the phone [still holding it] and covers her eyes. She puts it to her ear again. Meanwhile,* JAY *can't resist the temptation to touch the baby ever so slightly, to establish a connection without waking her.*) I can't believe you. This is my first day back at work! I have to pitch to the client in front of my boss who *you know* is just looking for the chance to fire my new mother ass. How can you *do* this to me, Georgia? To my *family*?! I'm the only one making any money, what are we gonna do if I get fi—(*Sees* JAY *reenter with the new tie. Doesn't pursue this line of thinking.*) You are totally irresponsible. I can't—no, forget it, I'm so pissed at you, I don't—no, I don't even want you to come. Stay in your fucking bed—(*She slams down the phone.* JAY *waits for her to make the first move.*) She's with some guy she met at a party—they've been fucking all night. . . .

(JAY *does not immediately respond. It's been about five months since he and* CIEL *have had any kind of sex. He can't show it, but it sounds kinda great to him.*)

JAY: Oh.

CIEL: His dick was still inside her until about fifteen minutes ago. I can't believe her.

JAY: I guess that's what we get for not hiring a real babysitter.

CIEL: You don't think it's better for the baby that we have a friend, someone we know and trust, to stay with her? Instead of some stranger—

JAY: A stranger might be here right now. (CIEL *doesn't want to start this now. She heads back to the kitchen to get her pump.*) So, is she coming? Over?

CIEL: No! I don't know.

JAY: Ciel, we're never gonna be able to move out of this one-bedroom apartment unless I get a job and start making some—

CIEL: (*turning around*) I wasn't volunteering you to stay home, Jay.

JAY: . . . *You're* gonna stay home? (*Long silence.*) Fuck it, I'll blow off my interview.

CIEL: That's not what I'm saying, Jay. I know how anxious you are to get back to work.

JAY: I think she's starting to notice me. Lately. You know what I mean? (CIEL *doesn't know the right response*—) For the first couple of months I felt like all she cared about was breast-feeding, breastfeeding, breastfeeding . . . and, like, I was just some *guy* who couldn't get a job and was hanging around being mommy's helper. But lately . . . I can tell that she, like . . . I don't know, maybe knows who I am.

CIEL: Are you saying you want to stay home with her? Be a stay-at-home dad? Because that would be even better than—

JAY: I don't know. It's a big commitment, I gotta . . . it depends what happens at this interview—which I'm lucky to even *have* . . . there're so few computer jobs right now.

(CIEL *heads for the phone.*)

CIEL: I'll call Georgia back. Tell her to haul her ass here in a cab, I'll call Shaefer on his cell phone, tell him I'll be a few minutes late, but that I'll definitely be—

JAY: No, you go. (CIEL *stops dialing.*) It's more important that you be there on time. It's your first day back. If you're late, Shaefer's gonna leap to all kinds of conclusions, about how you're not committed to the job—

(CIEL *stuffs the report in her bag and picks up her keys.*)

CIEL: If I leave now I can print my pie chart at the client's office.

JAY: What floor are they on?

CIEL: The two hundred seventy-fifth, or something like . . . I have it—(*She fishes through her purse for her datebook.*)

JAY: They only go up to one hundred ten.

CIEL: When I was at NYU, they had these old-fashioned elevators in Main building that were operated by this incredibly grumpy—he wasn't even old—man. The elevators could fit like thirty people and you had to shout over everyone's heads

what floor you wanted: seven, please; eleven please; thirteen . . . And somebody would inevitably say "the moon,
please." Typical freshman humor . . . but sweet, really. Whenever I'm in the towers, I think about that. I want to say it.
"The moon, please." (*Finds her datebook.*) Ninety-fifth floor.
I'll call Adler's assistant on my way and tell her I need her to
print something out. (*She slams the datebook shut and kisses* JAY
on the lips.) Thank you, honey. Good luck on your interview. I'll call you after lunch. (*As she opens the door.*) I'll call
Georgia right now!

JAY: (*indicating the baby*) Sssh!

(CIEL *cowers, reprimanded. She waves good-bye and leaves.* JAY *heads for
the phone and dials.* CIEL *walks back in.*)

CIEL: I forgot the pump.

JAY: (*into phone, tentative*) Hi Kathy, this is Jay Coleman, I have a
nine A.M. interview with you and I'm going to be a few
minutes late. Sorry for the inconvenience . . . okay, thank
you. Bye.

(CIEL *returns from the kitchen with the pump on her shoulder. She pats
it and smiles at* JAY *as she passes through. He hangs up the phone. She
waves at* JAY *as she puts her hand on the doorknob.*)

CIEL: (*whispering*) Bye again.

JAY: You look happy.

(CIEL *swings the door open, then turns to look at* JAY. *She closes the
door then walks closer to him.*)

CIEL: What?

JAY: What?

CIEL: (*on edge*) What did you say?

JAY: You look happy. You look psyched to be going to work.

CIEL: What do you mean by that?

JAY: (*shrugs*) . . . What I said.

CIEL: I look happy to be going to work?

JAY: Yeah, you—what's wrong with that?

CIEL: Are you saying you don't think I have conflicted feelings about going back to work?

JAY: No, I . . . *Do you?*

(CIEL *steps closer to prevent her from yelling.*)

CIEL: Jay . . . I think I'm going to kill you. How dare you accuse me of—

JAY: *Accuse*—

CIEL: Our daughter's not even three months old yet! She can't even totally hold her head up. She's still half moosh and I have to leave her for ten hours a day! You think I *want* to go back to work?

JAY: I don't know. I've never heard you say you *didn't* want—

CIEL: How can I . . . You say it as if— . . . You don't have a job, Jay. How can I even fantasize about staying home with her when you're not bringing in any—

JAY: How am I supposed to make any money if I can't even go to a job interview on time. I mean, how long do you think we're gonna all be able to live together in this tiny apartment? We can't afford to move to a two-bedroom on your salary. At least not in the city, which you insist we stay in.

(CIEL *slams down her bag.*)

CIEL: Go to your interview.

JAY: Yeah, right.

CIEL: Go. Fucking go. I'd love to quit my job. I'll call Shaefer right now—tell him to fucking pitch to a client without me.

Without my goddamn pie chart. (JAY *can't tell whether to take her seriously.*) Go to your interview, Jay.

(*After a pause.*)

JAY: All right. (*He slowly gathers his stuff as* CIEL *watches. Maybe looking for a watch that he's already wearing.*) Are you gonna call Georgia—

CIEL: Don't worry about it.

JAY: Because if she can—

CIEL: Maybe I'll call her, maybe I'll stay with the baby myself. Maybe I'll get fired, maybe Shaefer will be completely sympathetic. Who knows?

(JAY *goes to kiss her before he leaves.*)

JAY: I'll see you later.

(CIEL *watches him walk to the door. He opens it—then leaves.* CIEL *exhales. Thinks a beat. Her mind races—what has she gotten herself into? She starts for the phone—then stops. She walks into the bedroom and looks at the baby. She picks her up gingerly, desperately hoping not to wake her—and rests her against her shoulder.* CIEL *turns to the baby and inhales her scent deeply. As if it were an elixir. Then, she sees* JAY *come back into the apartment. She eases the baby off her shoulder and with kabuki-slowness, lowers her back into the bassinet. Makes sure the baby doesn't wake then walks into the living room.*)

CIEL: Jay . . . ?

JAY: I'm sorry, you're right. It was totally insensitive of me to accuse you of not feeling ambivalent about going back to work.

(*Slight pause.*)

CIEL: Okay . . . (?)

JAY: You have worked so hard to get to your position and you deserve to come back with a bang. Show Shaefer and all his misogynistic cronies they can fuck off—yes you're a mother but you're also the most kickass vice president they have. (*Long pause.* CIEL *doesn't move.* JAY *starts to take off his tie and shoes.*) How many ounces of milk do we have in the freezer? I think I saw at least five or six of those bags and those are each eight ounces. That'll get us through the day. How much do you think you'll pump this afternoon?

CIEL: . . . I don't know.

JAY: You'll be able to do it in the bathroom, right? Or your office—that might be better. More private. Do you know where the Bjorn is? It's such a beautiful day, I was thinking of taking the baby out to the park. Maybe even see if she likes the swing—

CIEL: You're forcing me to go to work.

JAY: (*now he's mad*) What!?

CIEL: You're, like, pushing me out the door. And you have the nerve to talk about what a great day you're going to have with the baby while I'm locked in my office with two plastic cones clamped to my breast—hoping I don't leak breast milk all over my—

JAY: Ciel, you should have seen your face *light up* when you were walking out the door knowing you were going to work all day.

CIEL: Jay, just because you're too scared or, or, or . . . laz—

JAY: You're worried that all your new mommy friends are going to think you're a terrible mother just because you like to work, but face it, Ciel, you're a workaholic. You love it.

CIEL: (*rage causing volume*) How dare you fucking tell me I love to work. I *have* to work—

JAY: (*simultaneous*) The status, the power—

CIEL: This is the third job interview you've blown off.

JAY: Even when I had a job you were working all the time. You didn't even want to take the full three months off—!

(*Their voices rise recklessly.*)

CIEL: That was *before* I had the baby—

JAY: Oh, so, what? You've had a personality transplant since you gave birth?

CIEL: You don't think giving birth is a transformative—

JAY: You've been working this whole time from home! You've been preparing this pitch for months!

CIEL: It's my account! I've been kissing this client's ass since the new year!

JAY: (*simultaneous*) You just couldn't stomach the idea of Shaefer giving Grace Chan this account.

CIEL: Grace Chan couldn't deliver this account if it was a pepperoni pizza. *I* did all the leg work, *I* developed the relationships, and I deserve the goddamn commission—

JAY: So, go!

(*After a pause,* CIEL *grabs her bag and hooks it onto her shoulder.*)

CIEL: (*calmly*) I am the youngest person in my position. I am the only woman, the only person of color and I got where I am because my work is excellent. Just . . . let me nail this account and . . . and then we'll—

(*The baby starts to cry.* CIEL *and* JAY *both look at each other. Then, they both start for the room.*)

JAY: I'll get her—

CIEL: No, I'll get her.

(*They stop.*)

JAY: If you pick her up, she's going to freak out when you leave. (*A cell phone rings.*) That's your phone.

CIEL: What time is it?

JAY: 8:35. If you take a cab, you could be there before nine.

(CIEL *looks at* JAY *then continues toward the baby's room. The cell phone continues ringing. She picks up the baby and nestles her into her chest. The baby wails harder. She can feel the tension.*)

CIEL: Okay, it's okay. Sshhhh . . . (*As* CIEL *relaxes, the baby's cries settle into more of a whine.*) Thatta girl. Mama's here. (CIEL *looks up at* JAY, *whose concern for the baby is stronger than any anger he may feel.* CIEL *lowers her bag off her shoulder. She exhales and looks up—there's so much to lose—She rests her head against the baby's and looks at* JAY.) Mama's gonna stay.

MY RED HAND,
MY BLACK HAND

Dael Orlandersmith

My Red Hand, My Black Hand was commissioned by Long Wharf Theatre, New Haven, Connecticut, and given its world premiere presentation there on October 10, 2001.

It was directed by Sarah Peterson; the set design was by Frank Alberino; the costume design was by Stacey Galloway; the production stage manager was Tracey J. Yang. The cast was as follows:

DAUGHTER   Mary Hodges
FATHER   Jack Burning
MOTHER   Sandra Mills Scott

CHARACTERS

DAUGHTER: Indian and black, aged late teens to mid-twenties.
FATHER: Native American, late fifties to mid-sixties.
MOTHER: Black, late fifties to mid-sixties.

NOTE: The reference in the script "boom, boom, boom boom!" should be spoken like the John Lee Hooker song "Boom, Boom!" The other reference, "Gonna shoot it right down," also should be spoken/performed in the spirit of the song. Note that "sport high-heeled shoes" and "sporting high-heeled shoes" are references to Chuck Berry's song "Sweet Little Sixteen." Please note also that the stage is bare. If there is a need for chairs or musical instruments that is fine, but no more than that.

DAUGHTER: My hands / red / black
Dance to Rhythms
Different / Various / similar rhythms

My Red Hand it dances to the
Rhythm of my Father's Blood / His
Blood Beat / His red
Man beat
PURE RED MAN

FATHER: My father / his mother /
Tlingit from Alaska /

DAUGHTER: Died giving birth to him
She died /
But she still whispered to him /
My father / his father

FATHER: Santee Lakota

DAUGHTER: My father half Tlingit
Half Lakota dreamer

FATHER: Transported
Transported
to Boston

DAUGHTER: He / my Father crying for his
Father / Drumming up the
Rhythm of his Father Through

Pent up Angers
Wearing Eagle Feathers

FATHER: Sign of the Eagle

DAUGHTER: Sign of Scorpio—Nov. 4 / His birthday
My Father /

FATHER: Eagle Born

DAUGHTER: Scorpion
beat his
hands to the rhythm of
his Father's Ghost

FATHER: His Father / My Grandfather
Spent
Depleted
American Dreams / Stomped into the
Dirt of the Res /

DAUGHTER: His American
Dream /

FATHER: to pick up
a Guitar
To be a Blues Man
To be a Red Man / Blues Man—

DAUGHTER: My Father's Father / My Grandfather

FATHER: Ghost danced Lakota Style

DAUGHTER: to
his father / my Great Grandfather's rhythm
but he closed his eyes and also
Ghost dances with

FATHER: Robert Johnson /
Mississippi John Hurt
Blind Lemon Jefferson

DAUGHTER: He / my Grandfather couldn't leave it /

FATHER: The Res—

DAUGHTER: They wouldn't let him leave it /
                 The Res /

FATHER: —"you're not True to
                 your own"

DAUGHTER: —they said

FATHER: "you're not proud to
                 be a red man"

DAUGHTER: they said—

FATHER: "If you leave / Don't come
                 back /

DAUGHTER: Don't come back
                 to the Res"—they say

                 He / my Grandfather Looked
                 into my Father's Eagle eyes
                 A Child's eyes / knowing
                 eyes / an old child's eyes /
                 His eyes—my Grandfather's eyes
                 Said

FATHER: "Take the world / make
                 it yours / Rock the world
                 You can Rock

DAUGHTER: Rock

FATHER: Rock

FATHER/
DAUGHTER: Rock the World"

DAUGHTER: My Father Glides Eagle-eyed from the
                 Res and the Tlingit island /

FATHER: Leather-jacketed /Eagle-
               eyed /

DAUGHTER: Blues and Tlingit / Lakota riffs
               dripping from his fingers /

FATHER: Chuck Berry /

DAUGHTER: Tlingit riffs
               dripping from his fingers /
               Leather-jacketed and Guitar ready
               Just like Chuck Berry or

FATHER: Link Wray

DAUGHTER: —Link Wray

FATHER: —a Shawnee
               from North Carolina

DAUGHTER: —A RED / Blues
               Rock 'n' Roll man /

FATHER: —a cool man

DAUGHTER: My Father cool—Just like Link Wray

FATHER: Slick

DAUGHTER: —Just like Link Wray
               Ghost dances Lakota Style / Tlingit Style
               and Rock 'n' Rolled / a Steady
               Rock 'n' Roll bop

               and Somebody on the Res says
               "How could you do that / Leave /
               us / How could you? /
               You're not proud of your own
               kind" / Somebody on the Res says /
               they say "wanna be a white
               boy? / Wait till they call you a FeatherHead" /
               Someone on the Res says

               My Father stares straight ahead

FATHER: Eagle-eyed /

DAUGHTER: proud and
                 Eagle-eyed
                 Outside

FATHER: —Standing Tall

DAUGHTER: Inside—Rumbling
                 The voices of the Res rumbled /
                 inside of him but he continued to
                 dance /

FATHER: Ghost dance /

DAUGHTER: The Res voices Got Louder /
                 He continued to Blues dance /
                 Blues / Red / Blues / John Lee
                 Hooker dance / he had to
                 take the voices and shoot them
                 down / Vodka
                       Tequila
                       Bourbon
                 Hide himself in a woman's
                 Skirt / to kill the voices
                 Vodka
                 Tequila
                 Bourbon
                       Another woman's skirt / gonna shoot
                                           it right
                                           Down!

                 My Black Hand—

                 My Mother's hand / A Black Girl

MOTHER: Girl from Virginia / my mother /
                                           a
                 Sharecropper Black Girl from Virginia /

DAUGHTER: Her mother / my Grandmother
                 Lynched /

MOTHER:	it is Hard Time Virginia /
DAUGHTER:	no Different from Hard Time Mississippi
MOTHER:	"Don't walk anywhere except in Dark Town"
DAUGHTER:	they told my mother
MOTHER:	"Just stay in Dark Town"
DAUGHTER:	—they told my mother
MOTHER:	"Dark Town" was where the Dark people lived
DAUGHTER:	they weren't Black Then They were colored then and where they lived was "Dark Town" My Mother / Sharecropper Black Girl / Big Black Girl Knew about Trees
MOTHER:	Knew about the Bodies that hung from those trees
DAUGHTER:	and the people who wore billowing white sheets My mother's bare feet
MOTHER:	were blistered from Tar and Dirt Roads /
DAUGHTER:	Those feet Shifted themselves
MOTHER:	into high heels /

DAUGHTER: She wanted to Chuck Berry Bop
                         in her high heels /
              She wanted

MOTHER: to "Sport high-heeled shoes"

DAUGHTER: She wanted

MOTHER: her hair slicked back
              pressed and curled /

DAUGHTER: She wanted

MOTHER: to Lip Balm
              her lips—"Ruby" Red Just Like
              The Ray Charles Song /

DAUGHTER: She wanted

MOTHER: to snap her fingers /
              Slick headed and curly sporting
              high-heeled Shoes to the
              rhythm of cities /

DAUGHTER: She wanted to Enter a
              New Rhythm
              Explore

MOTHER: —not just the
              Rhythm of Southern men
              Clinging to Mojo /

MOTHER/
DAUGHTER: She wanted a city

DAUGHTER: She leaves Dark Town
              Slick / curly headed
              high heels and fingers snapping and
              clicking /
              She goes to Boston /
              sporting high-heeled shoes

FATHER/
MOTHER: There are Dances /

DAUGHTER: yes
            There are Dances
            People will always Dance

            My Father sees her /
            He sees her at a dance /
            His Eagle eyes / connect to
            her Brown / Black Girl Eyes

FATHER: Eagle-eyed RED man /

MOTHER: red-lipped high-heeled Black Girl

DAUGHTER: The Hucklebuck Dance
                    meets
            The Ghost Dance

            And the Colored People / Before
            They were Black / The
            Colored people said

MOTHER: —"Whachoo doin'
            with him / Some Red Man /
            What do you want with him /
            Some Red Man / That FeatherHead
            dancer / whachoo doin'
                    with him"

DAUGHTER: And the Skins on the Res
            said

FATHER: —"You didn't get
            an Indian Girl / one of our
            Girls / Got a Dark /
            Darker / NIGGER Girl / not
            a Girl from the Res /
            What are you doing with her /
            Why didn't you Get a Girl
            From the Res! /
            Come back to the Res!" /

DAUGHTER: They—my Father
             my Mother

             They both hear the voices /

FATHER: Voices from the Res /

DAUGHTER: The Tlingit Voice that whispers in his ear

MOTHER: Voices from the Virginia Fields

DAUGHTER: They—both—my Mother and Father
             try to Ghost Dance / Blues Dance
             Drink away the
             Voices

FATHER: —Western / Northern Red voices /

MOTHER: Southern Black voices

DAUGHTER: They dance
             Snap their fingers
             Guitar Lick / try to
             Shoot it on Down

FATHER: Vodka

MOTHER: Tequila

DAUGHTER: Bourbon

             They try to shoot the voices down /

FATHER: Boom

DAUGHTER: Boom

MOTHER: Boom

DAUGHTER: Boom /
                        Shoot them all Down—
             A year later—they marry—
             A year after that

I crash through amniotic Fluid
and blood /

I crash but
silently my mother says

MOTHER: —"She's so quiet" /

DAUGHTER: my Mother says

FATHER: —"Makes no noise"

DAUGHTER: my Father says
I hear his voice but rarely—him / he usually
Speaks through guitar fingers / his fingers speak
on his guitar I see him /
longhaired / this man / red man who just spoke /
my father—this red man
this big red man / beautiful man
I am a part of him
My Father

I hear him

But

I can't speak
But I can hear
I can't explain / I'm a baby
But I feel it
I feel them
Turning on themselves
Turning on each other
not always with words
There's looks

MOTHER: shrugs

FATHER: silence

MOTHER/
FATHER: more silence /

DAUGHTER: I feel it /
              I feel them
              Shooting Themselves
                              Down—

FATHER: Boom

MOTHER: Boom

FATHER: Boom

MOTHER: Boom

DAUGHTER: Later   I'm a child
                       not a baby / a child
              I see it / smell it

FATHER: Vodka

MOTHER: Tequila

DAUGHTER: Bourbon

              I hear it my Mother's
              Black Southern voice slurry / shot-down voice

MOTHER: I love
              him / He's my husband /
                       my man / I'm
              NEVER Gonna Leave / I love him!

DAUGHTER: The Black Southern / voices /the
              voices are now Black from
              the Virginia Fields / The 1960s
              and the voices are now Black
              tell her / my Mother

MOTHER: —"your child
              is a Nigger / FeatherHead / a Nigger Feather-
              Head"—

DAUGHTER: My Mother/ she Vodka

MOTHER: Tequila

DAUGHTER: Bourbon

MOTHER/DAUGHTER: Cries

DAUGHTER: I hear it in my
               Father's voice—more so
               in his fingers / Fingers
               sliding up and down his guitar
               Vodka
               Tequila
               Bourbon crying

FATHER: Lakota / Tlingit guitar / Blues   a shot-down
                                        Red
                                        Blues
                                        Bruised
                                        Man

DAUGHTER: His voice thundered / sometimes
               there was thunder in his voice

FATHER: "She's my wife / I love her /
               Never Gonna give her up /
               I love her!"

DAUGHTER: I grow up—my body
               can make a
               child
               I Do not but I can—make a child

               A child / a life / can come through me
               can come crashing through amniotic
               Fluid and Blood /
               It can come silently
               It can come thunderously

               My Grandfather / Long Dead
               Ghost dances in the hills /

His wife / my Grandmother
calls me—"Dark Girl
          Monkey Girl
          animal / Dark / Monkey
          Girl! / The
elders don't want you /
WE don't want you!" She says /
my Grandmother says
My cousins on my mother's side /
My Black hand side says—

MOTHER: "You're Black / what's this
               Indian / no such thing as
               HALF BLACK!"

DAUGHTER: They / my cousins / my Black hand
               mother side cousins say put
               down my Father's Tlingit walk / Ghost dance /
               put aside sweet guitar licks and
               the Red / Blues of my
               Grandfather / Put aside
               his slick / sleek
               Rock 'n' Roll res / Boston Bop /
               Put it Down /
                    Shoot in on
                         Down

               My Red hand / my Father's
               hand / His mother / my
               Grandmother / cousins
                    Don't call my name
                    I'm the "dark" / Monkey Girl /
               Don't have a name—
               An uncle / he calls my name /
               says my name /
               only him / my Father's Brother /
               my uncle / he says

FATHER: "Drop the
            Black Blood / walk like a
            Skin / Drop the Dark / Darkey
            walk / You're a SKIN"

DAUGHTER: How can I drop the
            walk of Southern Black
            Girls / the walk heated / hip
            walk of Southern high-heeled Black
            Girls

MOTHER: (*repeating*)   You're Black / no such thing as HALF
            BLACK

FATHER: (*repeating*)   Walk like a Skin

DAUGHTER: I answer to the voices
            I answer to the voices in
            Dark Town /
            I answer to the voices in
            Black Town / The Town where
                        Black people live
            I answer to the voices My Grandmother's Tlin-
            git voice
            That whispers in my ear
            I see / dance with my Grandfather /
            We sing a Red man Blues
            I am Tlingit / Lakota and Blues
            I am an electric slider / Tlingit / Lakota Ghost
            Dancer
            I've got Red / Black hands

            I answer to all the voices

            I know that Blind Lemon Jefferson did the
            Ghost dance with Robert Johnson
            and Robert Johnson before
            selling his soul to the
            devil pulled out the

Mojo and gave it to my
Grandfather who kissed it
and passed it on to my Father who
passed it to me—I've got Red / Black hands

Don't tell me not to Ghost
dance on the Res
Call for my ancestors
on the Res /
whisper Tlingit secrets to my Grandmother /
dance / Link Wray style
Down at the Res /
I will rock the Res

I've got

FATHER: Red /

MOTHER: Black

DAUGHTER: hands
Don't anybody expect me to
     Shoot it
     Shoot
     Shoot
     it
     on Down

NIGHT VISITS

Simon Fill

Night Visits was first presented by Actors Theatre of Louisville, Kentucky, in January 2000. It was directed by Sullivan Canaday White; scenic design was by Tom Burch; lighting design was by Andrew Vance; costume design was by Jessica Waters; the dramaturg was Kelly Lea Miller; and the stage manager was Nichole A. Shuman. The cast was as follows:

TOM	Tom Johnson
LIZ	Samantha Desz
EMILY	Rachel Burttram

CHARACTERS

TOM: A second-year resident in medicine, twenty-eight.
LIZ: A nurse, twenty-seven.
EMILY: Gentle, looks about twenty-three.

TIME: The present.

PLACE: An examination room in a hospital.

(*A hospital examination room. White. Patient gowns hang all over. We hear wind outside.* TOM *lies on the examining table, asleep. Twenty-eight. In a doctor's outfit.* LIZ *enters. Twenty-seven. Nurse's uniform. Quiet moment to herself, then notices the gowns and* TOM.)

TOM: (*eyes closed*) I'm not seeing patients anymore, Liz. (*Quickly, lightly, sounding upbeat and energetic.*) It's over. It's over. It's over. It's over. It's over. It's over. It's over. It's over. It's over. It's over. It's over. It's over. It's over. It's over. It's over. Do you have a problem with it being over? You better not. Is it not really over? I don't think so.

LIZ: Tom. One more. That's all.

TOM: Seeing one patient in your thirty-fifth hour of being awake is the equivalent of seeing fifteen hundred in your first.

LIZ: You can't refuse to see patients. You're a resident.

TOM: Shit. (*He gets up.*) You look . . . nice.

LIZ: Got a date.

TOM: Doctor?

LIZ: No.

TOM: Yes. Yes. YES! Good for *you*.

LIZ: You are such a freak. (*Looks out window.*) Windy outside.

TOM: It's a bad night.

LIZ: I know. We all do.

TOM: . . . What? Oh. I'm . . . fine.

LIZ: We all loved Katie, Tom.

TOM: Yeah. Thanks. No, I mean it.

LIZ: She was a great nurse. I wish I'd known her more.

TOM: You're okay, Liz. I hate to admit it. (*He hits her lightly on the arm.*)

LIZ: You are such a freak. (*Beat.*) This patient—Doug gave her a shot of methicillin, he's busy now. Watch her ten minutes, see if she's allergic. She was . . . in a car . . .

TOM: Look. Katie's accident was a year ago.

LIZ: To the day.

TOM: I'm not really doing anything to this patient anyhow.

LIZ: You mean that?

TOM: (*very dramatic*) Have I *ever* lied to you before?

LIZ: Yeah.

TOM: No, 'bout something serious.

LIZ: Yeah.

TOM: You're—you're—you're— (*Jokingly, he grabs a tiny knee hammer.*)

LIZ: You gonna test my reflexes? You are such a . . . !

TOM: What!

LIZ: (*Beat. Softly, with great fondness.*) Little boy. This patient. The accident involved only her. After it, she disappeared. They found her in a church. Sitting on the floor. Surrounded herself with lit wish candles. Hundreds. She'd been there hours. When they asked her why, she said, "I'm cold." (*She gives him a chart. He stares at her.*) Emily. I know, I know. She's odd, this one. Another sweet nobody. Passed a psych consult, but otherwise, she won't talk. Here twenty-one hours. Won't leave 'til she feels she's "okay." She's a little banged up, but fine. She could go now. She won't. Bring her upstairs when you're done. (*Beat. Studies* TOM *with suspicion.*) No.

TOM: I'm good at this. She'll feel better. She'll leave.

LIZ: Won't work. We tried everything. Social services was called. They'll be here soon. (*Looks at robes.*) I wish we had another free room.

TOM: You didn't carry those up from a broken dryer at three in the morning.

LIZ: Dr. Pitnick, that was nice. Someday you'll make a good nurse.

TOM: I'll get her to go.

LIZ: Won't happen. (*Looks him up and down.*) You need a compliment. Badly. (*Beat.*) Serious now. You okay?

TOM: Funny. When Katie died, I prayed every night for a month.

LIZ: What about?

TOM: If I told anyone, Liz, I'd tell you. (*Lightly.*) It was very self-involved. (*Beat.*) I'm fine. Thanks. Have a good date. You're not as cute as you think you are.

LIZ: (*smiles*) I'll send her down. See you tomorrow. (*She exits. Pause. The sound of wind. He looks out the window. He is overcome and starting to break down. A knock. He recovers himself.*)

TOM: (*cheerful*) Dr. Pitnick's house of optimism and laundry! (EMILY *enters. She looks about twenty-three. Gentle. Bruised face and arms.* TOM *grins. A quick patter. His "routine."*) Just kidding. There's no optimism here. Don't mean to be unprofessional. I expect you to stay silent. (*Looks at chart, then her arm, checking where the shot was given.*) Hope that didn't hurt too much. I hate shots. We're gonna get you to feel okay. I usually do this by showing patients how impressive they are in comparison to me. Some patients protest. For good reason. I expect you to stay silent. They call me the funny doctor. (*To self.*) This is like one of my dates in high school. (*Looks at her.*) Did I detect a glint of humanity? (*She smiles a little.*) I bet no one upstairs tried to crack you up. Their mistake. Do you feel sorry for yourself? (*She shakes her head.*) You ought to. You gotta listen to me. But if you talk to me, you get to listen to me less. 'Round here, I'm considered aversion therapy for introverts. (*Whispers.*) Of course, being the funniest doctor 'round here is a weak claim. (*Beat. Back to normal.*) Look. I know what you went through was serious. I know. I do. But sometimes when you think you're alone, when you most think that, you . . . aren't. (*Beat.*) Sorry. I'm expecting a lot here. I mean, it's not like you're God or anything. No offense. (*Silence. He raises his hands in surrender, looks out the window. Pause.*)

EMILY: Why would I be offended you don't think I'm God? That's pretty queer.

TOM: I'm not the one who surrounded myself with wish candles in a church.

EMILY: Does that unnerve you? Dr. Tom?

TOM: (*beat*) How'd you know my name was Tom?

EMILY: (*mock mystical*) Woo woo. (*Beat. She points at his name tag.*)

TOM: Oh. Wow. I need some sleep. Sorry. I shouldn't say that.

EMILY: (*lightly teasing*) C'mon. This is all about you. (*Beat. Sincere.*) You look tired. You okay?

TOM: Great. My patient's asking me if I'm okay. Are you?

EMILY: You want me to leave, don't you?

TOM: I . . . (*Looks at her face and arms. Gentle.*) These bruises'll disappear on their own in a few days. They hurt?

EMILY: No, they feel great. Sorry. Not that bad. Thanks. You're nice.

TOM: I'm only nice when I'm tired.

EMILY: How often you tired?

TOM: Always. You're gonna be fine.

EMILY: I'm not important. What?

TOM: Nothing.

EMILY: What?

TOM: (*warmly ironic*) I *WISH* someone'd said that in your chart! (*She smiles.*)

EMILY: You're weird.

TOM: I know.

EMILY: When the accident happened, I hit a divider, everything stopped. I didn't know where I was. For some reason, I thoughta my dad. He died four years ago. Nothing to do with cars. I . . . loved him. After he was gone, I never felt his loss. I . . . Something happened. (*Pause.*)

TOM: You tell anyone this?

EMILY: Do you count? (*Beat.*) I got out of the car, looked around to make sure no one was hurt. Then I ran. (*Silence.*) You all right?

TOM: Yeah. Sure. I'm gonna get you outta here. In good shape.

EMILY: (*lightly*) I'm a nobody. And I dress poorly.

TOM: What's the one thing you could do to give your life meaning?

EMILY: Accessorize? (*Beat. He smiles. She looks off.*) You can't see wind.

TOM: What?

EMILY: You can't see it, but it's there.

TOM: (*beat*) Is it? When the accident happened, who were you with?

EMILY: That's an odd question.

TOM: Who were you with?

EMILY: Why?

TOM: Answer it!

EMILY: No one! (*Beat.*) I was hurt, and for the first time I felt, *knew*, I'm with no one. My father, he's really . . . gone. . . . (*Pause.*) You understand what I'm saying?

TOM: (*Thinks with care, then nods slowly.*) I'm sorry. (*Beat.*) You okay?

EMILY: (*Upset. Snippy.*) With doctors like you, who needs accidents!

TOM: Sorry.

EMILY: I . . . No, don't feel bad for me. I don't. My father . . . I loved him.

TOM: Did he love you?

EMILY: Yes, but that's not as important.

TOM: You okay?

EMILY: Keep asking that, and you won't be.

TOM: (*softly*) Sorry.

EMILY: Stop apologizing, you didn't kill him. (*Beat.*) When I left the accident, a few blocks away I passed a homeless woman. I asked her for the nearest good church. One that was honest, that wasn't about exclusion. She said nothing. I asked again, and she goes, "Here." (*She points to her heart.*)

TOM: (*softly*) Oh.

EMILY: You enjoy helping this nobody?

TOM: Who? You?

EMILY: You know a lot about this. (*Beat.*) Who was it?

TOM: You're my patient.

EMILY: So? There's doctor-patient privilege. I won't tell anyone.

TOM: I'm trying to make *you* all right.

EMILY: You're almost there. This'll help. Or don't you open up to nobodies?

TOM: Is this a trick?

EMILY: Yes. You got me to like you.

TOM: (*Beat.*) My wife Katherine. She was a nurse here in pediatrics. We grew up together in Brooklyn, but in high school I was too shy to ask her out. We ran into each other when she'd graduated from college, at a reading of James Joyce by an Irish actor. Joyce was her favorite writer. She and I dated. At that point, I was well on my way to becoming the "funny doctor." She was quiet and funnier, in that good way the most serious people are. After two months, I proposed. Now that was funny. She didn't answer. We kept dating. Every day for two months after that I proposed. Silence. I thought, "This woman either likes me or is totally insensate." At the end of that time she gave me a copy of *Finnegans Wake,* her favorite book. At college I'd read it and almost finished. The first page, that is. But I loved her so much I slogged through the book. Boy, did I love her. On page fifty, at the bottom, in pencil, someone'd written something. I looked closely. It said, "Yes. I'll marry you." (*Pause.*) I called her up and told her Joyce had accepted my proposal of marriage. (*Pause.*) She was driving to Riverdale, a favor, to pick up a friend's kid at school. I know she was starting to think about children herself. She said she wanted them to have "my looks and her sense of humor." Another car, an old lady who shouldn't have been driving, who had a history of epilepsy . . . and . . . you know the rest. The other woman lived. (*Beat.*) I asked Katie once why she wrote "yes" to me on page fifty. She said, "I knew you loved me, but I wasn't sure how much." (*Pause.*) Don't look so serious.

EMILY: (*gently*) The line you draw between yourself and other people, it doesn't exist. Not how you think. You know that, you'll let her inside of you, even if she's gone.

TOM: (*softly*) Hey. Thanks.

EMILY: (*with affection*) You gonna believe that? Or are you just another punk doctor? (*Long pause.*)

TOM: Yeah, I do. (*Beat.*) Yeah. (*Beat.*) What do you charge? I don't know if my insurance covers this.

EMILY: This was good.

TOM: I can't treat you for premature nostalgia. It isn't my specialty. You gonna stay or go?

EMILY: Quiet in here.

TOM: (*Light. Gentle.*) That tough being a nobody? (*She smiles.*) Funny. When Katie died, I prayed every night for a month. It was very self-involved.

EMILY: No, it was just about her. You asked that she be okay. You never worried about yourself. That's incredibly rare, even for people who love each other. *And* you're a nonbeliever.

TOM: (*Beat.*) How'd you know that?

EMILY: Who listens to prayers?

TOM: I don't get it.

EMILY: Who listens to prayers?

TOM: Nobody! (*Beat. A slow realization.*) Nobody. You could leave the hospital now.

EMILY: Thanks for the permission. (*She gathers her things.*) Oh, and Tom?

TOM: Yeah?

EMILY: Your insurance doesn't cover it.

(*She leaves. Pause. The sound of wind. He looks out the window. He opens it. When the wind enters the room, the robes fill with air, as if inhabited by ghosts. They sway beautifully. Tableau. Blackout.*)

NINE TEN

Warren Leight

Nine Ten was first produced by Lindsay Bowen, Kevin Chinoy, Tina Fallon, and Kurt Gardner for The 24 Hour Plays as part of a benefit for Working Playground. It was conceived, written, rehearsed, and performed at the Minetta Lane Theater on September 24, 2001. Tom Gilroy directed; set design was by Susan Weinthaler; lighting design was by Andrew Merriweather; and music was provided by Mike Doughty. The cast was as follows:

LESLIE	Mary-Louise Parker
JOHN	Robert Sean Leonard
KEARRIE	Natasha Lyonne
NICK	Andre Royo
LYRIS	Rosie Perez

(*Jury Duty Grand Hall. Morning.*)

(JOHN, *a slightly awkward bond trader, sits on a bench. Very neat, buttoned down. He reads a perfectly folded* Wall Street Journal. LYRIS TOUZET, *a dancer, enters, almost spills her coffee on him.*)

LYRIS: Is this Part B?

JOHN: What?

LYRIS: Part B, or not part B?

JOHN: Ah . . . that is the question.

LYRIS: Are you making fun of me?

JOHN: No no. Um, let me look at your . . . (*She hands him a slip of paper, he reads it.*) Where you are is where you're supposed to be.

(*She sits next to him. He needs a little more personal space than she does.*)

LYRIS: Why do they call us at eight thirty? It's like, nine already, and they haven't said anything.

JOHN: They build in a grace period.

LYRIS: They what?

JOHN: They say eight thirty so that most people get here by nine. And around nine ten they start calling names.

LYRIS: You knew this, and you came at eight-thirty?

JOHN: Eight actually.

LYRIS: Eight A.M.? You must hate your wife.

JOHN: I don't see her much. We both have to be at work at six.

LYRIS: You punch in at six?

JOHN: Well, I don't . . . punch in exactly. But, the desk opens at six so . . .

LYRIS: Your desk opens?

JOHN: Sorry. Trading desk. Bonds. Euros, mostly. From my desk, I'm up so high, on a clear day, you can see Europe.

(*At a bench opposite,* NICK THERON *works the* Times *crossword puzzle as* LESLIE RUDIN *arrives, pissed off and hyper.*)

LESLIE: Part B?

NICK: Must be.

LESLIE: Have they called any—

NICK: Does it look like it? (*She looks to the court officer's desk, downstage left.*) Every once in a while this guy comes out and says we should wait. Which is . . . helpful.

LESLIE: I tried to get out of it on the phone and they said it was my third postponement and I had to come down here in person on the day of and that I wasn't going to get out anyway. And I finally get here—do they just change the names of the subway lines for spite lately?—and there's a line a mile long to get through security and they go through my purse like I'm a serial killer and it turns out if I want to smoke I'm going to have to go down and outside, and then wait on line again for them to check my bag. This just sucks.

NICK: I'm going to tell the judge that I'm a felon. He won't even question it. And he'll tell me felons can't serve. I'll act offended at this. And then he'll just let me go back to my life.

LESLIE: (*impressed*) That's good.

NICK: Racial profiling. A two-way street.

(*Over to* JOHN *and* LYRIS.)

LYRIS: My brother's in the same building. Security guard. You probably don't know him.

(KEARRIE, *a tough businesswoman, enters, rushed.*)

KEARRIE: Part B?

LYRIS AND JOHN: Or not part B?

KEARRIE: It's too early for cute. (*They look at her, she means it.*) Have they started to give out postponements yet?

LYRIS: No one gets a postponement.

KEARRIE: I'm on a flight tomorrow. (*Pulls something out of her bag.*) I've got a ticket.

(JOHN *takes another look at her.*)

JOHN: Kearrie?

KEARRIE: What?

JOHN: It's me, John. . . .

KEARRIE: Right. John. That narrows it down.

JOHN: John McCormack. From Wharton.

(KEARRIE *still doesn't place him.*)

LYRIS: (*to* JOHN) You sure leave an impression.

JOHN: Story of my life. (*To* KEARRIE.) Case study: Euro-economic unity.

KEARRIE: You got an A, I got a B plus. Even though we worked together.

JOHN: (*to* LYRIS) You know about Irish Alzheimer's . . . you forget everything except your grudges.

KEARRIE: You went to Gold and Strauss when we graduated, right?

JOHN: Still there.

KEARRIE: (*grades him a loser*) You're kidding. You are not still at—

JOHN: Just the last ten years. Kearrie this is—

LYRIS: Lyris Touzet. Spiritual dancer. And healer.

JOHN: Lyris this is Kearrie Whitman. We went to Wharton together. Class of 91.

LYRIS: I must have missed you two by like . . . one year.

(LESLIE *and* NICK. *He has no hope of attending to his crossword puzzle.* LESLIE *must talk or die.*)

LESLIE: I'm out in the Hamptons. One week after Labor Day. Paradise found. The assholes are gone. The beaches are empty. The water is warm.

NICK: Sharks are hungry.

LESLIE: No sharks in the Hamptons. Professional courtesy.

NICK: Touché.

LESLIE: I think I'll stay another day. Then I remember . . . fuck me—eight thirty summons. Drive in at midnight. Get stuck in traffic. The L.I.E. has got to be the only road in the world that has traffic jams at two A.M. By the time I get to my garage it's locked for the night. You ever try to find a space on the right side of the street at two A.M.?

(*Back to* JOHN *and* LYRIS *chatting.* KEARRIE *plays with her Palm Pilot.*)

JOHN: It's funny, I always wanted to be a spiritual dancer.

LYRIS: You're making fun of me.

JOHN: I'm not. . . . swear to god. But what is a—

LYRIS: I heal people, through movement. Rhythm. Every person has their own . . . pulse. Below the surface, that—

KEARRIE: Fuck me!

LYRIS: I help them to get in touch with their inner—

KEARRIE: (*Turns to them.*) Fuck me fuck me fuck . . .

JOHN: What's hers?

(KEARRIE *now rants in their direction, about her Palm Pilot.*)

KEARRIE: Money on the table. I've got a watch list. It's programmed
to signal me when there's a discrepancy between euro prices
and ADRs. The spread is sitting there. Sitting there. It's
blinking—buy me. Buy me. I try to buy and my damn signal
fades. What's the point of fucking having a watch list if you
can't follow up on it. This whole building should be wired.
This city is . . . in the stone ages.

LYRIS: (*to* JOHN) Some people are harder cases than others.

(*Over to* NICK *and* LESLIE.)

NICK: My neighborhood, downtown, they're *always* filming.
Some sequel to a sequel to a disaster flick. *Mortal Danger
Times Four.* Whatever. Which means like—

LESLIE: They take every parking place. Big lights up—

NICK: —all night long.

LESLIE: Idiots in walkie-talkies saying don't walk there. On your
own street. Call the cops to complain, they don't care. No
one in this city cares. The film crew can be, like, setting off
concussion bombs, and nobody does anything.

(*Back to* JOHN *and* LYRIS.)

JOHN: (*to* LYRIS) I can't.

LYRIS: Everybody can move. Even you . . . Stand up.

(*He doesn't.*)

LYRIS: (*loud*) STAND UP!

(NICK *and* LESLIE *hear this. Look over to* JOHN *and* LYRIS. JOHN *doesn't want to attract attention, so he stands.* JOHN *and* LYRIS *now overlap with* NICK *and* LESLIE. KEARRIE *is in her own world.*)

LYRIS: (*to* JOHN) Just start to, sway a little . . . from your hips.

LESLIE: (*to* NICK) That is sick the way he's flirting with her.

(JOHN *sits back down.*)

JOHN: I can't.

LYRIS: Yes you can.

NICK: (*to* LESLIE) How do you know it's his fault?

LESLIE: (*to* NICK) It's always the guy's fault. I date cops. Believe me. I know.

JOHN: (*to* LYRIS) I don't like to. Move. I like things as they are. I've had the same job for ten years.

KEARRIE: (*on her cell phone, to her office*) Here? It's a fucking hell-hole. What do you think? Ah-huh. Ah-huh. Ah-huh. Look— keep that on hold.

JOHN: (*to* LYRIS, *oblivious to* KEARRIE) Same office, same view. Married my junior high school sweetheart. We take the same train to work. We have the same lunch. Tuna. On rye. No mayo.

LYRIS: No mayo?

JOHN: It's not so bad, once you get used to it.

KEARRIE: (*into phone*) Yeah as soon as they call roll, I show my plane ticket . . . and I'm out of here.

(*Now, from downstage left, a court officer enters.*)

COURT OFFICER: Hello folks. Welcome to New York County Jury Duty. Before you all come up to me . . .

KEARRIE: Excuse me, I have a flight to—

NICK: I have a record—

COURT OFFICER: (*He drowns her out.*) —with your reasons for why you shouldn't be here, let me tell you: I've heard them all. On the bright side, most of you will get to go back to your life in two or three days.

(LESLIE, NICK, KEARRIE, JOHN, *and* LYRIS *all groan. Two days is eternity.*)

COURT OFFICER: And we are as happy to have you, as you are happy to be here. First things first. Check your summons, and be sure you're in the right place. This is Civil Court. Part B. 60 Centre Street. Today is Monday, September 10th . . . Two thousand and one.

(*Blackout.*)

PLAYWRITING 101: THE ROOFTOP LESSON

Rich Orloff

Playwriting 101: The Rooftop Lesson premiered on September 8, 2000, on an actual rooftop, as part of Ten Stories Up, a festival of short plays produced by Word-of-Mouth (Seth Kramer, Artistic Director). Melanie S. Armer directed (and quite nicely). The cast was as follows:

THE TEACHER	Whitney Porter
THE JUMPER	Taylor Ruckel
THE GOOD SAMARITAN	Todd Wilkerson

Playwriting 101: The Rooftop Lesson was named "Best of the 2002 Delaware Short Play Festival" and was a cowinner of the 2002 CrossCurrents Five and Dime Playwriting Contest.

NOTE: The characters can be of either sex, but the Jumper and Good Samaritan should be of the same sex. References are written as if the characters are male, but that can be changed.

TIME: The present.

PLACE: The rooftop of a large urban building.

(*As the play begins,* THE JUMPER *is on the ledge of the roof and is about to jump.*)

THE JUMPER: I'm going to jump, and nobody can stop me!

(THE GOOD SAMARITAN *enters quickly.*)

THE GOOD SAMARITAN: Don't!!!!!

(THE TEACHER *enters and stands to the side.* THE TEACHER *points a clicker at the others and clicks, freezing the action.*)

THE TEACHER: (*addressing the audience*) A typical dramatic scenario: Two people in conflict—at least one in deep inner conflict—with high stakes, suspense, and affordable cast size. How will this situation play out? That depends, of course, on the level of craft and creativity in that remarkable art form known as playwriting. Let's rewind from the start—(THE TEACHER *clicks, and* THE JUMPER *and* GOOD SAMARITAN *return to their places at the top of the play, quickly reversing their initial movements.*) And see what happens.

(THE TEACHER *clicks again to resume the action.* THE JUMPER *is on the ledge of the roof and is about to jump.*)

THE JUMPER: I'm going to jump, and nobody can stop me!

(THE GOOD SAMARITAN *enters quickly.*)

THE GOOD SAMARITAN: Don't!!!!!

THE JUMPER: Okay.

(THE TEACHER *clicks to freeze the action*.)

THE TEACHER: Not very satisfying, is it? Where's the suspense? Where's the tension? And what audience member will want to pay today's ticket prices for a play whose conflict resolves in forty-five seconds? But most importantly, where can you go from here?

(THE TEACHER *clicks to unfreeze the action*.)

THE GOOD SAMARITAN: Gee, you could've hurt yourself.

THE JUMPER: Gosh, you're right.

THE GOOD SAMARITAN: Want to grab a brew?

THE JUMPER: Sure.

(THE TEACHER *clicks to freeze the action*.)

THE TEACHER: Without intense oppositional desires, more commonly known as "conflict," there is no play. When Nora leaves in *A Doll's House,* nobody wants her husband to reply—(*upbeat*) "Call when you get work!" So let's start this scene over—(THE TEACHER *clicks.* THE JUMPER *and* GOOD SAMARITAN *rewind to their initial places.*) maintaining conflict.

(THE TEACHER *clicks again*.)

THE JUMPER: I'm going to jump, and nobody can stop me!

(THE GOOD SAMARITAN *enters quickly*.)

THE GOOD SAMARITAN: Don't!!!!!

THE JUMPER: Fuck you!

THE GOOD SAMARITAN: (*giving an obscene gesture*) No, you asshole, fuck you!

(THE TEACHER *clicks and freezes the action*.)

THE TEACHER: Let's rise above profanity, shall we? It alienates conservatives and makes liberals think you're second-rate David Mamet. (*Clicks.*) Rewind . . . And again: (*Clicks.*)

THE JUMPER: I'm going to jump, and nobody can stop me!

(THE GOOD SAMARITAN *enters quickly.*)

THE GOOD SAMARITAN: Don't!!!!!

THE JUMPER: Why not?!!!

(THE TEACHER *clicks.*)

THE TEACHER: Oooo, you can just feel the suspense rising now, can't you?

(THE TEACHER *clicks again.*)

THE GOOD SAMARITAN: Because suicide is a sin!

(THE TEACHER *clicks.*)

THE TEACHER: Big deal. Theatre is written by sinners about sinners for sinners. Nobody goes to *Othello* to hear, "Iago, you're so naughty!" Always let the audience form their own judgments. Rewind a bit. (*Clicks.*) Now let's try a different tack. (*Clicks.*)

THE JUMPER: Why not?!

THE GOOD SAMARITAN: Because I love you.

THE JUMPER: I didn't know!

(THE TEACHER *clicks.*)

THE TEACHER: I don't care! Let's see if we can find something less clichéd.

(THE TEACHER *clicks again.*)

THE JUMPER: Why not?!

THE GOOD SAMARITAN: Because if you jump there, you'll land on my little girl's lemonade stand. And my little girl!

(THE JUMPER *looks over the ledge and moves over two feet.*)

THE JUMPER: Is this better?

(THE TEACHER *clicks.*)

THE TEACHER: Now what have we gained? Be wary of minor obstacles. Unless, of course, you need to fill time. Again.

(THE TEACHER *clicks again.*)

THE JUMPER: Why not?!

THE GOOD SAMARITAN: Because life is worth living.

THE JUMPER: Mine isn't!

(THE TEACHER *clicks.*)

THE TEACHER: Excellent. We don't just have a plot anymore, we have a theme. Theme, the difference between entertainment and art. No theme, add a car chase and sell it to the movies. But with theme, you have the potential to create something meaningful, something memorable, something college students can write term papers about. So let's rewind a bit and see where this thematically rich drama goes now.

(THE TEACHER *clicks to rewind and clicks again to resume.*)

THE GOOD SAMARITAN: Because life is worth living!

THE JUMPER: Mine isn't!

THE GOOD SAMARITAN: Gosh. Tell me all about it.

(THE TEACHER *clicks.*)

THE TEACHER: Some expositional subtlety, please.

(THE TEACHER *clicks again.*)

THE GOOD SAMARITAN: Because life is worth living!

THE JUMPER: Mine isn't!

THE GOOD SAMARITAN: Are you sure?

(THE TEACHER *clicks.*)

THE TEACHER: Better.

(THE TEACHER *clicks again*.)

THE JUMPER: Yes, I'm sure. I'm broke, I have no friends, and I see no reason to continue.

THE GOOD SAMARITAN: Look, so you're broke and friendless. All experiences are transient. Detach, as the Buddha once did.

(THE TEACHER *clicks*.)

THE TEACHER: Of all the world's great religions, Buddhism is the least entertaining. Let's try again.

(THE TEACHER *clicks again*.)

THE GOOD SAMARITAN: So you're broke and you're friendless. Why not try Prozac?

(THE TEACHER *clicks*.)

THE TEACHER: The popularity and effectiveness of modern anti-depressants is one of the great challenges of contemporary dramaturgy. We no more want Willy Loman to solve his problems with Prozac than we want Stanley and Stella Kowalski to get air-conditioning. How can today's playwright deal with today's medicinal deus ex machinas? Let's see.

(THE TEACHER *clicks again*.)

THE JUMPER: I tried Prozac once, and it made my mouth really dry.

(THE TEACHER *clicks*.)

THE TEACHER: Not great, but we'll let it slide.

(THE TEACHER *clicks again*.)

THE GOOD SAMARITAN: Let me help you.

THE JUMPER: It's too late.

THE GOOD SAMARITAN: No, it's not.

THE JUMPER: You don't understand. I haven't told you the worst.

(THE TEACHER *clicks.*)

THE TEACHER: Fictional characters are rarely straightforward.

(THE TEACHER *clicks again.*)

THE JUMPER: You see, until a few weeks ago, I was in love. Deep love. True love. I was involved with two of the most wonderful gals in the world. One was sexy, rich, generous and caring. The other was streetwise, daring and even sexier. Between the two of them, I had everything. Then they found out about each other, and they both dumped me. Not just one, but both.

(THE TEACHER *clicks.*)

THE TEACHER: Excellent playwriting. Here's a heartbreaking situation with which we can all identify. Maybe not in the specifics, but in the universal experience of rejection.

(THE TEACHER *clicks again.*)

THE GOOD SAMARITAN: At least you've had two exciting affairs. I haven't gotten laid in a year.

(THE TEACHER *clicks.*)

THE TEACHER: A superb response. Another situation with which, um, well, we've all had friends who've had that problem.

(THE TEACHER *clicks again.*)

THE JUMPER: So what are you telling me? That life can get *worse*? That's supposed to get me off this ledge?

THE GOOD SAMARITAN: Hey, I'm just trying to help!

THE JUMPER: Well, you're doing a lousy job.

THE GOOD SAMARITAN: At least I've got some money in the bank!

THE JUMPER: You've also got rocks in your head!

(THE TEACHER *clicks.*)

THE TEACHER: A common beginner's mistake. Two characters in
    hostile disagreement isn't conflict, it's just bickering. We don't
    go to the theatre to hear petty, puerile antagonism; that's why
    we have families. Let's hope this goes somewhere interesting,
    or I'll have to rewind.

(THE TEACHER *clicks again.*)

THE JUMPER: You've only got money in the bank because you're
    cheap.

THE GOOD SAMARITAN: I am not.

THE JUMPER: Well, you certainly dress like you are.

THE TEACHER: Now this is really degenerating.

(THE TEACHER *clicks, but the action continues.*)

THE GOOD SAMARITAN: Listen, you stupid twerp—

THE JUMPER: At least I'm a twerp with a decent sex life.

THE GOOD SAMARITAN: And if it was decent for *them,* maybe
    you'd still have a sex life.

(THE TEACHER *continues to click, but the action continues.*)

THE TEACHER: (*as the action continues*) Now stop it . . . Stop it! . . .
    Stop it!! (*Etc.*)

(*Shouting above* THE TEACHER*'s "Stop it"s, which they ignore:*)

THE JUMPER: Loser!

THE GOOD SAMARITAN: Pervert!

THE JUMPER: Cheapskate!

THE GOOD SAMARITAN: Cretin!

THE JUMPER: Asshole!

THE GOOD SAMARITAN: Imbecile!

THE JUMPER: Shithead!

THE TEACHER: (*clicking in vain*) *Stop it!!!!*

(THE GOOD SAMARITAN *takes out a clicker and freezes* THE TEACHER.)

THE GOOD SAMARITAN: Notice how organically the teacher's frustration has increased. What began as a minor irritation became unbearable when the human desire to control was thwarted.

(THE GOOD SAMARITAN *clicks again.*)

THE TEACHER: What are you doing?! I hold the clicker around here. How dare—

(THE GOOD SAMARITAN *clicks.* THE TEACHER *freezes.*)

THE GOOD SAMARITAN: See how frustration becomes "anger"? Although the real life stakes are minor, the character's emotional investment is intense. That's good playwriting.

(THE GOOD SAMARITAN *clicks again.*)

THE TEACHER: Stop that. What do you think this is, a Pirandello play?

THE GOOD SAMARITAN: Well, how do you think *we* feel? We can't say more than two lines without being interrupted by your self-important pronouncements. How'd you like it if I did that to you?

THE TEACHER: You have no dra— (THE GOOD SAMARITAN *clicks and stops/starts* THE TEACHER *during the following:*) matically vi—able rea—son to inter—rupt me. Damn it, will you get back in the play?

THE GOOD SAMARITAN: No, and you can't make me!

(THE GOOD SAMARITAN *clicks at* THE TEACHER, *who dodges the clicker.*)

THE TEACHER: Aha, missed. You superficial stereotype!

(THE TEACHER *clicks at* THE GOOD SAMARITAN *and vice versa during the following, both successfully dodging the other.*)

THE GOOD SAMARITAN: Control freak!

THE TEACHER: Cliché!

THE GOOD SAMARITAN: Semi-intellectual!

THE TEACHER: Contrivance!

THE GOOD SAMARITAN: Academic tapeworm!

THE TEACHER: First draft mistake!

(THE JUMPER, *who has been watching this, takes out a gun and shoots it into the air.*)

THE JUMPER: *Hey!!!* I'm the one with the problem. This play's supposed to be about me.

THE GOOD SAMARITAN: Tough. The well-made play died with Ibsen.

THE TEACHER: (*to* THE GOOD SAMARITAN) Damn it, get back into the play!

THE GOOD SAMARITAN: Don't tell me what to do. Ever since I was a kid, everyone's told me how I'm supposed to behave. When I was five, my mom sent me to my room (THE TEACHER *starts clicking manically at* THE GOOD SAMARITAN.) four thousand times because I wouldn't be the kid she wanted me—

THE TEACHER: This monologue is not justified!

THE GOOD SAMARITAN: Tough shit, it's my life!

THE TEACHER: It's bad drama!

THE GOOD SAMARITAN: I'll show you bad drama!

(THE GOOD SAMARITAN *and* THE TEACHER *begin to fight.*)

THE JUMPER: Stop it! Come on, stop it, you're pulling focus.

THE TEACHER: Butt out!

(THE JUMPER *tries to break up the fight.*)

THE JUMPER: Come on, guys, cool it!

THE GOOD SAMARITAN: Get away from us!

THE JUMPER: Just stop it!

THE GOOD SAMARITAN: Leave us alone!

(*The three of them are in a tight cluster. We hear a gunshot.* THE TEACHER *pulls away. There's blood on* THE TEACHER*'s chest.*)

THE TEACHER: I just got tenure.

(THE TEACHER *collapses.*)

THE GOOD SAMARITAN: Oh my God.

THE JUMPER: He's dead.

(THE GOOD SAMARITAN *looks at* THE JUMPER.)

THE GOOD SAMARITAN: How horrible. Is that good playwriting or bad playwriting?

THE JUMPER: I, I don't know. It just happened.

(THE GOOD SAMARITAN *and* THE JUMPER *look at* THE TEACHER.)

THE JUMPER AND THE GOOD SAMARITAN: (*simultaneously*)
    Hmmmmmmmm.

(THE GOOD SAMARITAN *and* THE JUMPER *begin to exit.*)

THE GOOD SAMARITAN: Gee, you could've hurt yourself.

THE JUMPER: Gosh, you're right.

THE GOOD SAMARITAN: Want to grab a brew?

THE JUMPER: Sure.

(THE TEACHER *comes to life for a moment, clicks into the air and: Black-out.*)

ROSIE IN THE
SHADOW OF THE MELROSE

Craig Fols

Rosie in the Shadow of the Melrose was first performed July 7, 1994, at the Currican Theatre, New York, as part of an evening of short plays and dances entitled Identical Houses. Kim Hughes directed the following cast:

FRANCES	Andrea Burrows
BOY	Jeff Huguet

(*A train platform in a suburban New Jersey commuter rail station. Night.*)

(*A bench stage center, like the platform constructed in blunt, clean concrete. A* GIRL *sits on the bench, waiting. She's about eighteen, very heavy, with long, dark hair. She wears an ugly blouse and pants. There is something about her which suggests another era: it's probably nothing more than the fact that she seems strangely out of place in this one, which is summer, 1980.*)

(*Crickets can be heard chirping in the fields behind the station.*)

(*A* BOY *enters. He's seventeen or eighteen, tall, thin, and pretty. He wears tight-fitting designer jeans and carries a small satchel. He notices the* GIRL *waiting. He checks out the scene in all directions: peers down the tracks for a train, reads all signs, looks out at the cornfields and condos beyond the platform. He seems nervous. He opens his satchel, gets out a commuter schedule, checks his watch.*)

FRANCES: We just missed one.

BOY: I'm sorry?

FRANCES: It says in there they run every fifteen minutes but they don't know. It don't mean nothin'. They don't know what they're talkin' about. It might take thirty, forty-five, even an hour, maybe.

BOY: Oh.

FRANCES: Yeah. I know cause I take this train all the time. (*Pause.*) My sister, she lives out here. (*Pause.*) You live out here?

BOY: No.

FRANCES: You live in Philly?

BOY: What?

FRANCES: I said, you live in Philly?

BOY: Yes, I . . . do.

FRANCES: That's nice. I figured. Me too. Yeah. Me also. Me and
     my whole family also live in Philly. What part?

BOY: What?

FRANCES: I says, what part of Philly do you live in?

BOY: Germantown.

FRANCES: We live in South Philly.

BOY: Oh. Why?

FRANCES: Huh?

BOY: I mean, why do you ask?

FRANCES: Just wondrin'. I got an aunt lives in Germantown. My
     Aunt Louise. Her husband, he died. Recently.

BOY: That's too bad.

FRANCES: Not really. He wasn't much, as my mother would say.
     Which she did. Often. Frances, she'd say, face it, the man's a
     bum. I don't think he even had a job. Not a real job. Not a
     good job, anyway. Not ever. Not that I heard about. Maybe
     she's better off.

(*The* BOY *says nothing and the conversation goes no further. He again
checks his watch, looks down the train tracks, moving away from the* GIRL
as he does.)

   You got a date or somethin'?

BOY: I beg your pardon?

FRANCES: You must gotta be somewhere, the way you keep checkin' your watch, and antsy, and all. I bet you got some hot date, huh?

BOY: No, I haven't got a date.

FRANCES: That's too bad. (BOY *reaches down and removes a paperback novel from his satchel. He opens it, stands reading.* FRANCES *watches him.*) You're cute. Did anybody ever tell you that? Real cute. (BOY *looks at her, says nothing.*) Oh, don't go get carried away 'cause I say that or nothin'. I don't mean nothin' by it, except to say it. I say things. That's my nature. My mother says I should change it but I say, that's stupid. How can you change your nature? But hey, it's okay, 'cause I'm all bark and no bite. That's what my friend Rosie says anyway and she should know. I never even kissed a boy til last year and that wasn't much, I can tell you. Now her, on the other hand, Rosie, that is, is a different story. You might say she was no bark at all and biting all the time, if you know what I mean. And I feel confident that you do. Yeah. Me and her is opposites. Total opposites. But, like in our case what they say is true that opposites attract. That's why we're such good friends. You ever had a friend like that? I bet you have. Somebody so different that you just gotta be near that person 'cause like by bein' near them you get to be more like yourself? Maybe I ain't sayin' it right. Like you can be added to by knowing them. And also, at the same time, be more than just yourself? Rosie's beautiful. Okay, she's got long blonde hair that hangs straight down her back. And she's real tall, and thin, but not too thin, she's got a nice shape on her, 'cause I do think it's possible for a girl to be too thin. But Rosie's not. She's beautiful. I think my mother wishes I was more like her. 'Cause Rosie bein' my friend is of course over the house all the time and sometimes I look at my mother sometimes and I can see her thinking why can't my own daughter Frances be more like that Rosie? But I think, I'm not Mom, I'm just not. And really, if my mother knew what was going on behind those beautiful blue eyes of Rosie's half the time she wouldn't wish that at all.

BOY: Where do you live?

FRANCES: In Philly. Philly. I live in South Philly. Right on Fifteenth and Snyder in the shadow of the Melrose Diner. You ever been to the Melrose?

BOY: No.

FRANCES: Lots of people have. It's a famous diner.

BOY: Oh.

FRANCES: Anyway, that's where I live. You live in Germantown. I remember I asked.

BOY: Right.

FRANCES: Funny. You don't seem like a Germantown boy.

BOY: Well . . . I haven't lived there very long.

FRANCES: Where'd you live before? (*Pause.*) You're from out here, aren't you?

BOY: Yes. Although . . .

FRANCES: Though I wouldn'ta picked you for a Jersey boy, neither.

BOY: You just did.

FRANCES: I woulda thought you were from England or someplace. The way you talk. Fancy like.

BOY: Well . . .

FRANCES: I haven't met many boys in New Jersey like you.

BOY: Originally I'm from upstate New York.

FRANCES: Maybe that explains it.

BOY: (*getting suddenly nervous*) I wish this train would come.

FRANCES: You got a girlfriend? I'm just asking. Being such a big mouth, I'm just curious. Rosie says sometimes, will you shut the fuck up for Christsake's Frances, why do you have to stick your fat face in everything all the time? But secretly I think she likes it. 'Cause that's like another quality we don't have in common. She's shy. That is, unless she don't want to be. Hoo Boy! So do you? I'm just asking. You don't have to answer or nothin', if you don't want to.

BOY: No, I don't. Have a girlfriend.

FRANCES: That's a shame.

BOY: Not really.

FRANCES: It comes as a surprise. A cute guy like you. (*Incredulous.*) What, did you just break up with somebody?

BOY: I'd really rather not talk about it.

FRANCES: Okay, I'm sorry. I didn't mean to pry. (*Pause.*) Was I . . . being a little bit too forward there, just for a minute?

BOY: Why don't we just drop it?

FRANCES: That's like a problem I have sometimes. Everybody tells me. I don't know when to stop.

BOY: Let's forget about it.

FRANCES: Really?

BOY: Yes! I mean, yes. It doesn't matter.

FRANCES: Hey. Okay. (*Pause.*) Are you sure? Are you sure it doesn't bother you, my prying?

BOY: Yes, I'm sure! Now can we please not talk about it anymore!

FRANCES: Because like I only mean the best. (*Pause.*) Rosie says that about me sometimes. She says Frances, sometimes you may be a pain the ass, but you got a heart as good as gold. (*Pause.*

For a moment neither says anything.) So what are you doin' all alone in New Jersey on a Saturday night?

(*He looks at her.*)

BOY: I'm going home. I'm on my way home.

FRANCES: To Germantown, right? (*Pause.*) Like, when you get off this train, do you transfer to the Broad Street, or the El, or the trolley, or what? (*Pause.*) I'm only asking because I want to know everything about you.

BOY: Why? I mean . . . why do you want to know?

FRANCES: No reason. Just curious. Hey, don't get all defensive or nothin'. I don't mean nothin' by it. I'm not out to get you. (*Pause.*) You seem nice is all. I'm interested. Is that a crime?

BOY: No, of course not. I'm sorry. It's been a long evening.

FRANCES: So? What train are you going to take?

BOY: Well, I would usually take the train from Reading Terminal. (*Pause.*) But tonight I'm staying with a friend. In Center City.

FRANCES: Oh. That's nice. Center City. Is it, like a boy friend or a girl friend? Listen to me, I sound like my mother. Stop me if I start to pry.

BOY: It's a man friend.

FRANCES: My mother would be relieved!

BOY: I don't think so.

FRANCES: Waddya mean? (*Pause. The* BOY *doesn't answer.*) Is this like, a really good friend?

BOY: Yes.

FRANCES: That's nice. It's nice to have a really good friend.

BOY: We're very close. Of course, he's a lot older than me but somehow that doesn't matter so much. Sometimes it even seems that I'm older than him sometimes. Do you know what I mean?

FRANCES: No. (*Pause.*) Yeah. Rosie sometimes bawls me out for my bad behavior. Sometimes we're walkin' down the street and she says to me, "Frannie," that's what she calls me when we're really gettin' along, "Frannie," she says, "You don't give a boy a chance. You're always chasin' after 'em. After 'em all the time, they don't want you like that. They want to be like chasin' after you." What I don't say is that sure, they want to be chasin' after you, Rosie, I mean, she weighs about a hundred pounds and looks like somethin' on a TV screen, but me, I've always been an exception and I've got a personality to prove it, you know what I mean? So forgive me if sometimes I start to feel that I should take the front seat in my life here, okay? (*Pause.*) What were you doing in Jersey?

(*There is a pause. The* BOY *drags his feet on the concrete platform, unsure and nervous about whether to go on. He seems like he knows that if he goes on, he won't be able to stop. Finally he takes a breath and goes on.*)

BOY: I went to see my parents.

FRANCES: Yeah?

BOY: They live here. I say my parents although it's really just my mother and my sister I went to see. My father, he lives in Florida.

FRANCES: Oh, Florida! That's nice! You ever go down and visit him there?

BOY: No. (*Pause.*) So I went to see my mother and sister. (*Pause.*) I had something to tell them. (*Pause.*) Although I don't want to tell you what it was.

FRANCES: Sure. No problem.

BOY: My mother started crying before I'd even gotten to the point. Before I'd even told her. I guess she could kinda tell what I was going to say before I said it. So she went out on the porch, and when I followed her out there she begged me not to say what I was going to say and then she said I would be killing her if I told her. Then when she saw she wasn't going to stop me she went back inside, I think so the neighbors couldn't hear. And I told her. Then she cried. And then my sister came in and she cried. Then my mother accused me of . . . well, it doesn't matter. Then I cried. And then I called a taxi . . . and I came here. (*The* BOY *sits on his haunches and covers his face with his hands.*) I'm sorry.

FRANCES: What are you sorry for? It don't matter.

BOY: I don't even know you.

FRANCES: So? So what's that matter?

BOY: Sometimes I also don't know when to stop.

FRANCES: Listen. You gotta do what you gotta do. I know that.

BOY: Sometimes . . . I just don't know what the right thing to do is.

(*Pause.*)

FRANCES: My mother is a jerk, that's one thing I know. She acts like she knows what the right thing to do is all the time and she don't. Times I do what she tells me, it only makes things worse. Then other times I do like I want, and that don't work out, neither. (*Pause.*) You oughta try tellin' somethin' like that to my mother. It'd be worse. Much worse. (*Pause.*) You wanna know what I think?

BOY: What?

FRANCES: I think we oughta band together. You and I. Make the world, I don't know, like . . . better. Make it safe for democracy or something. What do you think?

BOY: Sure. Maybe. I don't know.

FRANCES: Rosie's good like that. She always knows what to say.

BOY: What you said was okay, I guess.

FRANCES: All right then. (*Pause. After a moment,* FRANCES *begins humming, quietly singing to herself a tune. She looks at the* BOY, *who is still sitting on his haunches, kneeling a few feet away from her.*) Would you, like, touch me? In some way, some simple way, no sex or nothin', just . . . hold my hand or somethin'. Just to make me feel . . . better?

(BOY, *staying crouched over on his haunches, moves closer to the* GIRL. *He looks at her for a moment. Then he lays his head down on her knee, his face turned toward the audience.* FRANCES *lays her hand on his head as lights fade.*)

A RUSTLE OF WINGS

Linda Eisenstein

A Rustle of Wings was originally produced at the Vanguard Theatre Ensemble, Fullerton, California, in April 1999, where it was the second-place winner of the Sixth Annual West Coast Ten-Minute Play Contest (Jill Forbath, Artistic Director). It was directed by Sandy Silver. The cast was as follows:

MIRA	Sharon Case
JEWELL	Della Lisi
SHRAINE	Leslie Williams
FRANKIE	Jon Taylor Carter

CHARACTERS

MIRA: She wants it. Bad. If she only knew what it was.
JEWELL: A mystery in shades. She wears a black leather jacket with wings attached to its back.
SHRAINE: Mira's friend.
FRANKIE: Mira's friend (female or male).

(*At rise: A bar. Smoky. Very noir. A melting riff of saxophone music.*)

(MIRA *in a pool of light.*)

MIRA: Ever dreamed of flying? Sure you have. Everybody's had that dream—skimming above the sidewalk, the earth tilting below. Soaring, never even needing to touch down.

The more you plod along in real life, the more your dreaming self yearns for the air. Hungers for the rustle of wings. For the faint brush of feathers against your face.

Everybody thinks they want to fly. Until they actually meet somebody with wings, that is. That's when it gets . . . complicated.

I knew that the first time I saw Jewell.

(*Sax music. A smoky blue light on* JEWELL. *She is wearing shades and a black leather jacket. She poses, languid. Checking out the scene.*)

(MIRA *is on a bar stool. She sees* JEWELL. *Can't take her eyes off her.*)

She was something. Something else.

(JEWELL *catches her eyes, smiles, and glides over toward* MIRA.)

And oh my God. She is actually coming over here.

(*As* JEWELL *turns, we see that there are small wings attached to the back of her jacket. Note: These should be very noticeably fake—i.e., plastic, papier mâché, or aluminum foil and wire.*)

JEWELL: Hey.

MIRA: Hey. (*Beat.*) I, um, like your wings.

JEWELL: Thanks.

MIRA: Quite the conversation piece.

JEWELL: Only if you notice them. Most people don't.

MIRA: Funny. I can't believe that. They're so cool. Where'd you get them?

JEWELL: The usual place. (*Indicating "up" with her eyes.*)

MIRA: Well. I've never seen anyone who had them.

JEWELL: You just haven't looked hard enough. (*Beat.*) Do you want to touch them?

MIRA: How did you know?

JEWELL: (*Smiles.*) Be my guest.

(MIRA *strokes them tentatively with a finger.*)

MIRA: Wow. That's . . . they feel so silky. I wouldn't have expected . . . Yipes!

(MIRA *gives a little shudder—leaps back.*)

JEWELL: What?

MIRA: How'd you do that?

JEWELL: Do what?

MIRA: They moved! At least it felt like they did.

JEWELL: Interesting reaction.

MIRA: Sorry. I know that sounds too weird.

JEWELL: Not at all. It's one of the signs.

MIRA: Signs?

JEWELL: Signs. Portents. Small but significant. In a series of recognitions. It means . . . you're one of us.

MIRA: Ah. I'm, oh boy, feeling a little dizzy.

JEWELL: Didn't you know?

MIRA: All of a sudden.

JEWELL: Or at least suspect? That you weren't like the others.

MIRA: (*gathering up her purse to flee*) Excuse me.

JEWELL: Can I touch yours?

MIRA: (*Freezes.*) What?

JEWELL: Your wings.

MIRA: My, ah—

JEWELL: Can I touch your wings?

MIRA: I don't, uh, I don't have, uh, wings, oh my God, I have to go now, sorry.

JEWELL: But you do, Mira. You do. You have the kind of wings nobody sees.

(*A beat. Lights down on* JEWELL, *immediately up on* SHRAINE *and* FRANKIE—*who enter, continuing the conversation.*)

SHRAINE: Whoa. Now that is one great pickup line.

FRANKIE: Awesome.

SHRAINE: Wings, huh? On her jacket, like a biker? That's hot.

MIRA: No.

FRANKIE: Maybe she was a pilot! Everything you have heard about stewardesses? Goes double for pilots.

MIRA: It wasn't a logo, Frankie. These were real wings. Attached, to, to her back. I think.

SHRAINE: Like, what, a bird? This girl had bird wings?

MIRA: N . . . no . . .

SHRAINE: Angel wings?

FRANKIE: Oooh, oooh, no, Mira met a real live fairy. (SHRAINE *and* FRANKIE *laugh*.)

MIRA: Come on, you guys.

FRANKIE: Uh-oh, Mira's got it ba-ad.

MIRA: She was shimmering! It was incredible. Radiating off her, like heat on pavement.

SHRAINE: Wow. Like a mirage.

MIRA: Maybe she was. A mirage. Jeez, she'd have to be. Otherwise, how come nobody else noticed her? Why wasn't everybody in the place following her around like crazed bloodhounds?

SHRAINE: Mira, honey, everybody does not have the same taste as you.

FRANKIE: I'll say.

MIRA: No, no, no! This isn't "you like blondes, I like brunettes," Shraine. This was objectively measurable charisma. Of rock star proportions. Like, if you were holding a Geiger counter next to her, you'd be deafened by the clicking.

FRANKIE: Wow.

SHRAINE: So then what? Did you get her number?

MIRA: No, I . . .

FRANKIE: Oh, Mira, not again. You let her get out of there without . . . oh girlfriend.

SHRAINE: You are hopeless!

FRANKIE: Hopeless.

SHRAINE: You do this every time.

MIRA: I didn't know what to say!

SHRAINE: She's giving you this major voodoo, and

FRANKIE: Mira tanks. Again.

MIRA: (*distraught*) It wasn't like that!

FRANKIE: Well, go on, then!

(*Lights back up on* JEWELL. *They all look over at* JEWELL, *expectantly. Saxophone music restarts.*)

MIRA: I didn't run. Not because I didn't want to. More like I couldn't, because when she looked at me it was like my feet were nailed to the floor.

JEWELL: But you do, Mira. You have the kind of wings nobody sees.

(MIRA *laughs nervously.*)

MIRA: Ohhh, like a bird? Not me. Oh, no. Unless it's, um, a wren, maybe. Something brown and gray, hops around mostly, picks up straw and stuff, God I'm babbling, am I saying this out loud, or is this just rushing through my head while I stare at her gape-mouthed?

JEWELL: You don't have to say anything.

MIRA: Oh, thank God, she can't hear what I'm thinking.

JEWELL: I know what you're thinking.

MIRA: Noooo!

JEWELL: That you can't even feel them yet. But that's all right. To make them move, you have to practice. Here.

(JEWELL *touches* MIRA *in the center of her back.*)

MIRA: Oh!! (MIRA *goes up on her tiptoes, sways, like she's going to topple over.*)

JEWELL: See. (*Smiles.*) I know you can feel that.

MIRA: Feel it? My heart is fluttering, racing, faster than I can count.

JEWELL: Six hundred beats a minute, actually. Like a bird.

MIRA: And I think, oh, I get it, that's why birds have such short life spans. That's the price of flight. Their heart outruns their life, outruns their good sense. You can't live with that kind of heart-pounding excitement, and last.

JEWELL: Now: try to move them. You know you can.

MIRA: Move them? I can't feel anything except this pounding, this shuddering, in my head and my chest and my knees and . . . (*She stops.*) Except suddenly, I could.

JEWELL: Yes.

MIRA: There was this itching, this intense feeling crawling up my spine. And I could hear the beating of thousands of pairs of wings, like a humming. It started to fill the back of my throat with something sweet, something I'd never tasted. It got me so dizzy, I had to hold onto the table, or I knew I'd topple over. I was afraid to let go, and afraid to look at her. So, I ducked my head, and looked at the ashtray for a really really long time, until my head stopped spinning. And when I looked up again? She was gone.

(*Lights down on* JEWELL, *lights up on* SHRAINE *and* FRANKIE. *They all sigh.*)

FRANKIE: That. Is. Mira, what can I say.

SHRAINE: One of those moments. Major.

FRANKIE: Defining moments.

SHRAINE: I can't believe you . . .

FRANKIE AND SHRAINE: You looked at the ashtray??

MIRA: Yeah. I know. (*A beat.*) It doesn't seem fair. Somehow. That you don't get another chance.

SHRAINE: No, no. That's how it works. A story like that? It's like the myths, or the fairy tales. You seize the moment, or else . . . poof.

FRANKIE: The moment passes. That's how it works.

SHRAINE: You can never step into the same river twice.

MIRA: You sound like a fortune cookie.

SHRAINE: But it's true. She might show up again. But the second chance is never the same as the first one. It'll be different.

MIRA: Maybe I'm not interested in living a story where you don't get a second chance. I mean, what kind of angel or guardian or guide is that? Who is only interested in the people who'd jump into the flames the first time.

FRANKIE: Jump into the flames? Mira, all you had to do was buy her a ginger ale. Keep her from leaving. That's hardly incendiary.

MIRA: You weren't there. If you'd seen her, you'd know. The waiter would've needed asbestos gloves.

SHRAINE: And what's this about angels? It was a come-on. A unique one, I'll admit.

MIRA: A chimera, maybe. One of those impossible creatures.

SHRAINE: "It means you are one of us." Sounds dubious to me.

FRANKIE: Like a cult. "Klaatu barata nictu: We come from the sky, and rule over your sorry asses."

SHRAINE: And so can you, for only forty thousand dollars, six-to-eight years of reprogramming, and colon cleansers.

MIRA: You weren't there! You didn't experience it. It's hard to describe, an epiphany. They mostly happen inside your head. There isn't much to look at. You, you're in another dimension. Your own thoughts are going eight hundred miles per hour, you're mutating from longing to confusion to shyness to lust to guilt to hope and back again, and it doesn't look like . . . anything. Somebody watching you only sees you blink.

SHRAINE: Okay, okay. We'll take it on faith.

FRANKIE: Yeah. She's a knockout, a killer. You see her, boom!, your pulse does the mambo,

SHRAINE: you get the shakes—

FRANKIE AND SHRAINE: The usual!

(*They laugh. Lights down on* FRANKIE *and* SHRAINE. *They exit.*)

MIRA: Not for me. This was . . . she was . . . (*Lights up on* JEWELL. *Smiling, engimatic.*) I was always attracted to women who could fly.

JEWELL: Move them. Come on.

MIRA: I always wanted to feel the rustle of feathers against my face.

JEWELL: I can always see it on somebody. Potential. It's my gift.

MIRA: So I looked in the mirror. To see what she had possibly seen, in me. To tell the truth, it didn't much look like somebody who could fly. But if I squinted my eyes, just the right way, I could almost see them. Catch a glimpse of them. Shimmering. She was right, though. I definitely needed to practice.

JEWELL: Otherwise wings won't do much for you. Except make you stand out.

MIRA: They do do that. Because even though she'd gone—when I looked around a corner, I thought I recognized another one. He was just standing there, but . . . something. Maybe there were more of them than I thought.

JEWELL: More of us.

MIRA: So I kept trying, trying to feel them, feel the buds?—but they must have been in that place on your back that you can't quite touch yourself. Where the itch always is.

JEWELL: That spot that only someone else can reach—the one that's hard to find on your own.

MIRA: And I looked in the mirror, again—hoping to see something really different. Like one of those other creatures, turning into themselves. Not really. And yet—if I stood the way I'd seen her stand . . . and breathed a particular way . . .

JEWELL: Almost . . .

MIRA: Almost! I could almost feel the stirrings. Hear the rustling of something opening. (*She stretches. There is a sound. Something.*) Ah . . . (*A crackling? A humming?*) Practice.

SINNERY OF A SUNDAY

OR, THE QUEEN OF EIDERDOWN

Honour Kane

CHARACTERS

RASHER HOWLIN: The young leading man.
DOLLY THE MOTT: The ingenue.

SETTING: Rural Ireland. During World War II. Rasher and Dolly the Mott are members of a tribe of traveling actors. Tonight they are staying in the Widow Twankey's digs. This is a rundown room-to-let which can be as slovenly or as sparse as the set designer wishes.

(*In the Widow Twankey's digs.*)

(*A greasy iron bed, creaky and screeky, battered and worn.*)

(RASHER HOWLIN—*all a gangle in the doorway—with a sugar sack slung over his shoulder.*)

(*In the twatterlight, he's watching* DOLLY THE MOTT—*seated on the bed.*)

(*She wears a huge fur coat and is rolling silk, black-market stockings up her legs.*)

RASHER: Tormenting Jayz. Her-legs her-legs her-legs. Her-legs and-legs and-LEGS. (*To* DOLLY) What're you selling, my-damn-morsel?

DOLLY THE MOTT: Stop groaking at me with your goo–goo googeldies. Get into me drab room and have a fag.

RASHER: Hardly drab, for aren't YOU in it? Tricked out in your fine toggery.

(DOLLY *tosses him a packet of cigs, he pockets it.*)

DOLLY THE MOTT: HUP, said the ONE fag, not the whole packet.

(RASHER *puts a ciggy behind his ear.*)

RASHER: For later.

DOLLY THE MOTT: Light's going so. Strike up me cangles. And would you ever hand me over that cuppa cha . . . And me biscuit tin.

(*As* RASHER *lights her candles,* DOLLY *slips lipstick onto her smile.* RASHER *tosses the biscuit tin on her bed. When he hands* DOLLY *a teacup and saucer, he brushes her sleeve.*)

RASHER: Did that used to move?

DOLLY THE MOTT: What, this dead animal?

RASHER: Well, did it?

DOLLY THE MOTT: Mister, this used to hop.

(*Pinky out,* DOLLY *delicately sips her tea.*)

RASHER: I do like the style of you. You are a born hacktoress, did you know.

DOLLY THE MOTT: Thanks very much I'll tell her. Help yourself to a can of tea, Rash.

RASHER: Ahhh, she knows me name.

DOLLY THE MOTT: Bikkies?

(DOLLY *offers the open biscuit tin to* RASHER, *but he's busy taking a sip from the tea can.* RASHER *splutters tea all over.*)

RASHER: What to hell is that?

DOLLY THE MOTT: The Lap Sang Soo Chong.

RASHER: Oro, what does Lap Song Chew when she's home?

DOLLY THE MOTT: Don't be slaggering me Chinese tea.

RASHER: Has the desperate taste of a chimbley.

DOLLY THE MOTT: What're you after slummerboy?

RASHER: Tell me, have you seen sign of our wages?

DOLLY THE MOTT: You know yourself like, with that hellbag Basher Anarchy. He runs this company like a whoor to ride—

RASHER: (*over*) When's paynight? I need me thirty-five bob.

DOLLY THE MOTT: Double dog shag that twaggler Anarchy. Only offered me twenty-three. ME. Not that you'll see one sixpence. It's shift for yourself, boy. Shift for yourself.

RASHER: You alus seem to have a shilling, need a houseboy?

DOLLY THE MOTT: Have you no ready money?

RASHER: Living foot to mouth. It's the days of bread and tea.

DOLLY THE MOTT: Whyncha ask the proprietresssss. Old Widow Twankey for a bob-a-job?

RASHER: Tusky oul slapper pitched me this sugar sack. Said, "you can sleep in me cowstall if you muck out the toilet."

DOLLY THE MOTT: There's room going in my bed.

RASHER: No.

DOLLY THE MOTT: If you like.

RASHER: Woo-woo.

(RASHER *does an Injun wardance, whooping and twirling the sugar sack.*)

DOLLY THE MOTT: Cowboys and Injuns, Lads.

(RASHER *tosses the sugar sack offstage and launches himself onto the bed, laughing.*)

RASHER: WAIT. What'll we tell the Twankey oul cow?

DOLLY THE MOTT: That you're me brother. (*Silence.*) Name me your wishes.

RASHER: I wish. I wish.

DOLLY THE MOTT: Wish what?

RASHER: I wish for you.

DOLLY THE MOTT: Yeah?

RASHER: Yeah you. You allover me. I want your mouth.

(*A kiss—a* really *good one.* DOLLY *brushes* RASHER's *lap.*)

DOLLY THE MOTT: The joy, oh the joy Inish Mouth and Inish Trousers. For that is the biggest and best article I have EVERY felt.

RASHER: Really?

DOLLY THE MOTT: Would I lie?

RASHER: Hope not.

DOLLY THE MOTT: Do you not know?

RASHER: Know what?

DOLLY THE MOTT: You've a mickey long as me ar–um.

RASHER: So?

DOLLY THE MOTT: Oh rat me, you're not even a nearly-man.

RASHER: Am I now.

(RASHER *peels off the fur coat . . . a slinky slip.*)

DOLLY THE MOTT: You're miles too young.

RASHER: Give me your mouth.

DOLLY THE MOTT: Don't snatch after me.

RASHER: Give me your–all, your–all. I want your all.

DOLLY THE MOTT: Don't mess me about.

RASHER: Your boo-kakas are gorgia.

(RASHER *reaches one finger towards* DOLLY.)

DOLLY THE MOTT: What, these lickle boo-kakas? They aren't the real.

(DOLLY *takes two tangerines from her bra.*)

RASHER: Where'd you get the little oranges?

DOLLY THE MOTT: Galway. (DOLLY *climbs under the quilt, and roots around*.) I've sardines, crackers, a Five Boys chocolate bar.

RASHER: What would you be needing Five Boys for, when you've got me?

DOLLY THE MOTT: Would you eat this?

RASHER: I don't eat that.

DOLLY THE MOTT: What?

RASHER: Sugar. What else have you under?

DOLLY THE MOTT: I'd have the world, it you'd give it me. Get in, get under.

(RASHER *climbs in under*.)

RASHER: My own. My queenie. You. Are a queen. You're my Queen of Eiderdown.

DOLLY THE MOTT: Oh this is esplanade. (*There's a bit of rollicking here.*) Down a little bit so again Rash. Downlie. Downlier.

(RASHER *rolls on a book*.)

RASHER: Ow, what's this?

DOLLY THE MOTT: That's me book. Ah it's a grand play, let's read it.

(DOLLY *pops up and opens the book*.)

RASHER: No.

DOLLY THE MOTT: *My One Husband or The Constant Nymph*.

(DOLLY *sits up to read*. RASHER *pulls her back down*.)

RASHER: No-no-no.

DOLLY THE MOTT: (*over*) You NO-NO-NO.

RASHER: Back to your boo-kakas and your underdown.

DOLLY THE MOTT: We're reading it. I'm Tessa. And you're Gangly.

RASHER: Oh, am I?

DOLLY THE MOTT: No, the *part*. YOU will play Gangly. Love the end, oh I love the end when I die. Tragick-ully. Of consumption or something. And you say . . . Well here it is, have a go. (DOLLY *pushes the book into* RASHER's *hand*.)

(*Acting*.) I am going to live. (DOLLY *dies tragick-ully*. RASHER *looks and looks at the book in his hands*.)

Gewan stupid.

RASHER: Can't. I can't.

(RASHER *cries*. DOLLY *pulls him into her lap*.)

DOLLY THE MOTT: Ah love. Ah love. I'll learn you. And soon you'll be running out pens and filling up copybooks.

Here you go, listen. The last lines is, "Tessa's got away. She's safe. She's dead." Isn't it only beautiful.

First I'll teach you Farquhar. Then I'll teach you to farquhar. Give me your mouth.

RASHER: Dolly my Dolly.

DOLLY THE MOTT: Not yours.

RASHER: Mine mine mine.

DOLLY THE MOTT: I said NOT yours you beasting DubSlummer.

RASHER: Mind your mouth or I'll mind it for you.

DOLLY THE MOTT: That I wouldn't mind. (*A kiss*. RASHER *climbs into her mouth*.) More. The more. (RASHER *can't breathe*.)

RASHER: I lost my breath.

DOLLY THE MOTT: Well, FIND it.

RASHER: Let me let me . . . Catch me . . . Me breath.

(*Something's wrong*. "*Is he sick*," DOLLY *wonders*.)

DOLLY THE MOTT: You smell.

RASHER: What, rotten?

DOLLY THE MOTT: Sour. Your heart's a kettledrum. What's going on at all at all?

RASHER: Touch of the catarrh. And. The excitement.

Me being a nearly-man and all.

And you? You, a symphony of skin, freckles, and hair. And hair. The long throat of you.

DOLLY THE MOTT: None of your flipping tongue.

RASHER: More of yours, girleen.

(RASHER *climbs up her body.* DOLLY *draws the boy down.*)

DOLLY THE MOTT: Find me. Come on.

RASHER: Let me in.

DOLLY THE MOTT: Come into me, now.

RASHER: The tight of you.

DOLLY THE MOTT: Press in. Press on. Press up.

RASHER: Your legs your legs your legs. Letting me in. Letting me up your sleeky-legged lane.

DOLLY THE MOTT: You brute beastial. You're too many for me. Blow out me cangle, Rash. RIP RIDE ME.

(RASHER *takes her down, thrashing.*)

RASHER: Gloria Patri, Dolly. GLORIA PATRI.

THE SNIPER

Anthony David
and *Elaine Romero*

CHARACTERS

ᴢᴀᴋ ᴇʟᴏɴɪ: Twenty-three years old. A sniper. Lives in Tel Aviv.
ɪʀɪᴛ ʏᴇʀᴜsᴀʟᴍɪ: A Morrocan Jew. A journalist.

TIME: The present.

PLACE: Tel Aviv. A hip microbrewery.

SETTING: The bar.

(ZAK, *a twenty-three-old Israeli, sits at the bar drinking. He wears a khaki green military uniform. An ashtray full of cigarettes, a couple of empty glasses of Guinness, and a worn newspaper sit next to him on the bar. He drinks and smokes. Eerie techno-pop music plays in the background. He opens the newspaper and begins reading it, then sets it down. He can't seem to resist picking it up again. Something about the newspaper seems to increase his drinking and smoking.* IRIT *enters.* ZAK *doesn't notice her at first. She sits on the stool next to him.*)

IRIT: They didn't tell me they were going to print that.

ZAK: I can't believe you'd dare come in here after this.

IRIT: Look, my editor hacked my computer; I'm the victim here, too.

ZAK: You didn't tell me you were a journalist.

IRIT: I told you I was a writer.

ZAK: Yeah, but . . .

IRIT: You knew you were talking to a writer.

ZAK: I thought, I don't know. I didn't know you had a real job.

IRIT: People in my neighborhood do have jobs.

ZAK: I don't care if you're Moroccan.

IRIT: (*flirtatious*) That's what I thought.

ZAK: But you used me. I thought we liked each other.

IRIT: It was a good story. You don't understand. A story like
that—a story like that—you just don't understand.

ZAK: We made love.

IRIT: I made the front page.

ZAK: (*sarcastically*) Your editor hacked your computer. And I'm in
it up to here. Do you know what they'll do to me?

IRIT: Happens all the time. We put a name to it.

ZAK: But I'm the name here. And my commander is pissed. There's
talk of a court-martial.

IRIT: They've never court-martialed anyone for shooting an
Arab kid.

ZAK: (*a loud whisper*) It's supposed to be—an accident. You make
me out to be a cold-blooded killer.

IRIT: Shooting kids from behind a concrete barrier two hundred
feet away makes you a cold-blooded killer. And no one cares
anyway.

ZAK: Do you?

(*She picks up the paper.*)

IRIT: It made the front page. You don't know where I come
from. You don't know what it's like to be a Moroccan Jew in
this country. (*Short beat.*) Do you—care?

ZAK: What do you want from me? It's my fucking job. They give
me orders. If I were a bus driver, I'd drive people from Jeru-
salem to Haifa.

IRIT: It wouldn't require two years of training. You're the member of an elite unit. You, Zak, are not a bus driver.

ZAK: Sometimes I wish I were, but I'm damn good at what I do.

IRIT: Killing kids? (ZAK *shrugs.*) If you're so proud of your job,
why are you mad at me?

ZAK: It's just the way it reads. I keep reading it over and over. And, I just don't like the way it sounds. I mean, I didn't say that. You weren't taking notes. You didn't have a tape recorder.

IRIT: Are you denying the fact that last week you picked off a thirteen-year-old?

ZAK: He was fourteen.

IRIT: Do those Palestinian kids have their ages tattooed on their foreheads?

ZAK: That's not fair. My grandfather is a survivor.

(IRIT *gets quiet.*)

IRIT: What does he think about this?

ZAK: He wasn't supposed to know. And tonight, when I get home, you know what he's going to have in his hand. This newspaper. And there's no chance he's not going to have it, because he's meticulous. He reads that paper cover to cover every day—has for fifty years. He'll be ashamed. He just thought I was a member of an elite unit.

IRIT: You are a member of an elite unit.

ZAK: I was.

IRIT: If there's a court-martial, now that'll make the front page. But it's not gonna happen. Besides, what's the difference between killing a kid from thirty thousand feet or two hundred feet?

ZAK: I still see them. (*Beat.*) The kids.

IRIT: What kids?

ZAK: I have to look at them to shoot them. And I remember. (*Under his breath.*) I'm not a cold-blooded killer. I don't want to be a cold-blooded killer.

(*She rubs against him.*)

IRIT: I don't think you're a cold-blooded killer. It's a complex thing. You can't blame yourself. (*He pulls away.* IRIT *starts to rub his shoulders.*) Last night was amazing.

ZAK: Pretty amazing.

IRIT: Wanna dance? (*They do, soft and close. They start kissing.*) Let's go back to my place.

ZAK: Why not?

IRIT: (*referring to the newspaper*) Zak, don't worry about this stuff. Tomorrow the paper will be about somebody else's news. Grandpa can wait until tomorrow to chew you out . . . if he can remember. (*He pulls away. He gets up to leave.*)

ZAK: I'd better go face him.

IRIT: I really don't understand why you care about what he thinks.

ZAK: I love him. And I know how he feels about people who do this. And now that he knows that I do this—I did this—I don't know if he's going to survive that. His heart's gonna break. And I'm gonna know I did it.

IRIT: I did it. I wrote the article.

ZAK: I did it. I've gotta accept responsibility.

IRIT: Are we going to fight over who's guilty here?

(*She laughs.* ZAK *does not respond initially.*)

ZAK: I don't know what I'm going to say to him.

IRIT: Wanna practice?

ZAK: What do you mean?

IRIT: Simple, I'm your grandfather. I'm sitting in the living room waiting for you to come home. You come in and I confront you with it.

ZAK: That's a stupid idea.

IRIT: It's not a stupid idea. Let's try it. (*She breaks into the character of Grandfather. She picks up the newspaper in her hand.*) What is this? What is a grandson of mine doing something like this?

ZAK: Oh, come on, Irit.

IRIT: What's a grandson of mine doing something like this?

ZAK: Granddad, they picked me. They selected me into this unit. It's an honor. (IRIT *huffs.*) Hear me out.

IRIT: Do you know how the Germans justified what they did?

ZAK: How could you make such a comparison?

IRIT: They were innocent children.

ZAK: Innocent children grow up to be not so innocent adults.

IRIT: And you ask me how I can make such a comparison? (IRIT *now threatens him with the newspaper in his face.*)

ZAK: Put that down. I love you.

IRIT: Don't you think those kids had parents—and grandparents who loved them?

ZAK: I'm protecting you, so you can sit in your garden and read your books, and your daily newspaper. And if I have to do what I do to do that, that's the price for your freedom.

IRIT: Rubbish. You tell yourself that. You tell yourself that so you can do what you do. Your father and I didn't raise you that way. You're from an educated family. We respect human life. We want peace with the Arabs. We have ethics.

ZAK: What good did all your books and humanist ideals do for you in Europe? Did Goethe stop your mother and father from dying in the gas chambers?

IRIT: How dare you bring them into this. Who do you think you are?

ZAK: Irit, I don't wanna do this anymore.

IRIT: You didn't answer my question.

ZAK: C'mon, Irit. That's enough.

IRIT: I did not bring my son to Israel only for him to give birth to an assassin.

ZAK: And yet, Irit, you don't think there's anything wrong with killing a kid, do you?

IRIT: I abhor the murder of children.

ZAK: Irit thinks it's okay to shoot young Palestinians.

IRIT: Well, who's Irit?

ZAK: The woman who wrote the article.

IRIT: Are you mixed up with her?

ZAK: Yeah, sort of.

IRIT: This girl of yours, is she pretty?

ZAK: Beautiful.

IRIT: Were you intimate with her?

ZAK: Kind of. (IRIT *reads the name of the journalist off the paper.*)

IRIT: (*Reads aloud.*) Irit Yerushalmi. What kind of a name is Yerushalmi?

ZAK: Moroccan.

IRIT: Did this Moroccan of yours put you up to this?

ZAK: My grandfather is not a racist.

IRIT: (*Keeps going.*) They hate the Arabs. (*Beat.*) Is it because of this Moroccan that you justify the murder of children?

ZAK: You know all the people in my unit are white. I'm sure you've read that in your newspaper.

IRIT: Tell me about this Irit.

ZAK: Well, she's beautiful. And she's smart.

IRIT: Do you want to have a family with her?

ZAK: I don't know.

IRIT: Why don't you know?

ZAK: Well, there are some things that bother me.

IRIT: Like?

ZAK: Like, I wonder if she thought it was a good thing to write that article—if she considers my job the right thing. Did she write that article to brag about some hero? I'm no hero.

IRIT: (*Breaks character.*) Let's go back to my place and make love.

ZAK: Grandfather, this thing is killing me.

IRIT: Do you want me or not?

ZAK: How could I be with someone like that?

IRIT: Someone like you?

ZAK: Would she raise our children to kill children?

IRIT: (*Gathers her things.*) I'm leaving.

ZAK: Are you ashamed of me, Granddad? This isn't how you taught me to live. I should be sitting next to you reading in your garden instead of fighting in a bar with a woman who preys on the pain of others, and prints it in the paper for everyone to read. How could I love a woman like that?

IRIT: Look, all I did was show you the truth. If you don't like it, that's your problem.

ZAK: I'm going to ask for a court-martial.

IRIT: You're out of your mind.

ZAK: And at the trial, I hope that you will tell the truth. (*Beat.*) You will, won't you?

IRIT: Or we could just make love.

ZAK: I could face my grandfather again.

IRIT: I can't believe this is happening. You're gonna dump me because of him.

ZAK: (*beat*) I should be grateful to you.

IRIT: For what?

ZAK: What you wrote. It was a good article. Told the truth. Made people think.

IRIT: Zak.

ZAK: It made me think. So, thanks.

(ZAK *reaches to shake* IRIT*'s hand, but* IRIT *will not take it. She turns and exits.* ZAK *watches her walk away. He tucks the newspaper in his back pocket and exits. Blackout.*)

SPACE

Donald Margulies

Space was commissioned and first presented by New Writers at the Westside, in New York City, in June, 1986. It was directed by Chris Silva. The cast was as follows:

MAN (A)   Dennis Boutsikaris
MAN (B)   John Griesemer

(*Two men, A and B, in their mid-thirties. Late at night, after eating, drinking, and smoking dope. B's apartment.*)

A: (*Speaks very slowly.*) You're out there. In the middle of the desert. At night. And you turn off the headlights. And you're. The darkness. Like you're floating. In space. Like you're in space. You *feel* it. You *feel*. The nothingness. The, the. The *huge*ness. The utter. Vastness. Of space. And you'd think it should be quiet. Because it's so black. Because of all the nothingness. But, no. Then your ears. The motor is off. You turn off the motor and you hear. This buzz. This, this *symphony*. Of life. Of living things, you know? (*Pause.*)

B: We never went to the desert, me and Nan.

A: Oh, it's elemental. It's. There's so much life like you're not even aware of out there. All that emptiness. All that seemingly empty space. (*Pause.*)

B: I *wanted* to. She wasn't interested.

A: 'Cause the thing is. What makes it so elemental, the desert. Are the contradictions. You know what I mean?

B: Uh huh.

A: The contradictions. Like the temperature. You're sweaty *and* cold. At the same time. What do you call it?

B: What.

A: At the same time.

B: Simultaneously?

A: Yes, but that's not the word.

B: Um . . .

A: That's not what I'm thinking of. (*Pause.*)

B: Concurrently?

A: No . . .

B: Happening at the same time?

A: I can't think.

B: Anyway . . .

A: Anyway, the temperature. Paradoxes? Do I mean paradoxes?

B: Paradoxes?, yes.

A: Maybe. Maybe that's what I mean. Something and yet something else?, something that seemingly. Contradicts. The first thing?

B: Yeah . . .

A: Days. It could go above. The temperature could *surpass* a hundred, hundred and *ten* sometimes. At night. The temperature. Could drop sixty degrees easy. Plummet. The temperature plummets. The mercury. Way down.

B: I should've just taken off and gone by myself.

A: Wait: so, you're out there. In all this space. And this buzzing?

B: (*Preoccupied, then testily.*) What?

A: (*After a beat.*) Are you mad at me or something?

B: No.

A: I'm painting a picture for you. What it was like.

B: Go ahead.

A: (*After a beat, meaning, "What's the matter?"*) What.

B: Nothing. Tell me. Paint.

A: (*After a beat, proceeding cautiously.*) There's this buzzing. This music. I mean it. It *is* like a symphony or something. These creatures. Crickets and insects. And. Creatures. Sounds. Coming. Emanating. Coming out of the air, almost. Yeah, it seems to come out of the air. Or up through the earth. Like the sand is, is. The earth's skin. And this sound. This electricity. Yeah, it's an *electrical* sound. This sound seeps out of the earth's pores. And you feel yourself hum with it. You feel the buzz of your own aura. Like your lifeforce has a sound, too. Just like the lizards and the crickets and the creatures and stuff. You know?

B: Yeah . . .

A: And the next thing that happens. The next thing you're *aware* of. And the thing is, we weren't even stoned yet. That's right, we weren't. On purpose. We wanted to be straight. At least in the beginning. So we could experience it, you know, unadulterated. So we could come to our own conclusions, you know?

B: Uh huh.

A: Without drugs.

B: That's good.

A: You know? With*out* drugs. *Later* we got stoned. But in the beginning . . .

B: You were straight.

A: We were straight. That was a choice. A conscious decision. And I'm glad.

B: Uh huh?

A: I'm very glad. (*A beat.*) So what was I saying? (*Pause.*)

B: The—

A: Oh! So, the next thing you notice. After the buzz. Your eyes. They adjust to the darkness. And you know what?

B: What?

A: It isn't dark at all. It's like almost blindingly lit up. The desert is. Illuminated. By the moon! I'm talking just like seconds into it. Once you adjust. A) the buzz. B) the brightness. You can see everything in sight! Mountains and bushes and cactuses. Cacti. And like lizards 'tween your toes. And clouds! You can see a couple of clouds! And the moon! It's true! The moon is like a silver hole in the sky lighting up everything in sight! And stars twinkle like they're special effects or something. It's unreal. It is unreal. And we take off our clothes. It's like me and Katie, we're Adam and Eve. And the desert is our garden. And then we did it.

B: Uh huh.

A: Unbelievable.

B: I bet.

A: No, the feeling. This feeling of, of. Of nature. Of being a part of the cosmic buzz, you know? God. Amazing. (*Pause. Sadly.*) We had such a great time out west. (*Pause.*)

B: You want to sleep on the couch?

A: No, no.

B: It's no hassle. You *can*.

A: No, I'll go. I'll go home.

B: 'Cause I have to get up early.

A: I understand.

B: I'm temping.

A: I understand.

B: I've got to shlep all the way out to Long Island City.

A: I understand, really.

B: Some *furni*ture place.

A: I'll get out of your way.

B: 'Cause you're welcome to . . .

A: (*Not budging.*) I'll go home.

B: I mean it. (A *nods, "I know." Pause.*) Well, here we are. (*A beat.*) Did you ever think we'd end up like this, you and me? (A *shakes his head.*) Me neither. I thought I'd've been a father by now. Nan was making good money, we could've had a kid.

A: What is it with these women? (B *continues shaking his head. After a beat.*) I don't understand it. This trip out west. Things were never better.

B: I know, pal.

A: Everything had seemed to come together. But. At the same time. Everything was falling apart.

B: I know.

A: It's a paradox.

B: I'm really sorry. I really am.

A: Let's analyze this. (B*'s heart sinks.*) *I* felt we were never closer. *She* felt closed-in. That's what she told me. We were watching the sun rise and it's like she went cold on me. Like she shut off the juice.

B: You're gonna drive yourself nuts, you know that?

A: I should've known. I should've seen it coming. (*He smacks his own forehead.*)

B: Hey!

A: (*After a beat.*) We were. You know. While we were doing it? Katie was on top. Bouncing. Her hair blowing in the stars. Both of us breathing hard. Buzzing along with everything else. Sand crunching my back. The sweat and the goose-bumps. Everything, in other words. Everything. I was watching Katie go. Bouncing. Her eyes closed. I was watching Katie. And over by her ear. In the sky. I saw it. We went to the desert to see Halley's comet. And there it was. Katie wearing it like an earring. I didn't tell her. I didn't want to ruin it. Halley's comet. I'm sure it was. This smudge. This nothing little white smudge. Halley's comet. (*He shakes his head in disappointment. A beat.*)

B: I'm getting you a pillow. You're sleeping on the couch. (*He goes.* A *continues to shake his head. Blackout.*)

STUCK

Claire Reeve

CHARACTERS

SARA: Beautiful twenty-five-year-old woman on her way up.
SAL: The voice that dreams are made of.

TIME: Early morning.

PLACE: Elevator of New York City office building.

(*Woman is looking at image in handheld compact when she notices elevator is not moving.*)

SARA: Oh, no! (*Starts pressing buttons on elevator . . . bangs on door.*) No God, please . . . no . . . oh God! (*Presses emergency button.*) Hello, hello, help! I'm stuck. Please somebody . . . anybody . . . I'm stuck!

SAL: (*Male voice comes over the intercom.*) I know. Miss, could you take your finger off the emergency button please. I know you're stuck.

SARA: I'm stuck.

SAL: Yes, miss. Miss, your finger. (*Beat.*) Miss, you're still pressing.

SARA: Oh. (*Takes finger off button.*) Please . . . I . . . I have a job interview—that's why I'm here. When . . . when am I going to be unstuck?

SAL: Soon miss.

SARA: How soon?

SAL: We're experiencing some power difficulties which we're investigating now.

SARA: Power?

SAL: Yes.

SARA: That doesn't sound good. Alone and powerless.

SAL: Are you all right?

SARA: Stuck.

SAL: Stay calm.

SARA: Calm.

SAL: Are you breathing?

SARA: I think so. What . . . what about oxygen?

SAL: Oxygen?

SARA: (*Removes her coat.*) It's getting a little warm in here. You can tell me, how, how much oxygen do I have left?

SAL: The elevators aren't airtight.

SARA: Air.

SAL: Yes, you have plenty but it may be a little warm in there because the fans aren't working.

SARA: Fans not working.

SAL: Keep breathing. Deeply, deeply. Do you feel any better?

SARA: I feel faint.

SAL: Put your head between your legs.

SARA: What?!

SAL: It helps. (SARA *bends over and puts head between legs.*) Are you feeling any better?

SARA: Now I feel nauseous. (*Stands up and takes blouse off.*) It's so hot in here.

SAL: What's your name?

SARA: My name?

SAL: Yes.

SARA: Sara . . . Sara Ann Porter.

SAL: Sara, that's a pretty name. My name's Sal.

SARA: Sal. Italian?

SAL: Yes.

SARA: I love Italian food. Think I'll live to have another plate of pasta Sal?

SAL: (*Laughs.*) Of course. My treat.

SARA: It's a date. It's hotter than hell in here. (*Takes skirt off.*)

SAL: Are you breathing?

SARA: Sal . . . Sal, I'm not doing well. (*Takes off slip.*)

SAL: You're doing fine.

SARA: Fine? I'm stuck in an elevator hyperventilating in my panties and bra, sweating like a pig, needing to take a pee and (*Starts to cry.* SARA *takes stockings off. Pause . . . She starts to panic.*) Sal, Sal are you still there?

SAL: I'm here Sara, I'm here.

SARA: It's hot Sal.

SAL: Is it?

SARA: Yes. I'm very . . . very . . . hot.

SAL: Try and stay calm and still, don't use up all your energy.

SARA: Why? What will I need it for? (*Beat.*) Sal . . . what . . . what are you keeping from me? DISASTER! Has there been a disaster? TERRORISM. Is it terrorism?

SAL: No Sara. We're just waiting for the electrical problem to be fixed.

SARA: If it's just electrical, how come the lights are on?

SAL: Different generator.

SARA: (*to herself*) Got to stay calm. Keep breathing. You want to hear something funny, Sal? This morning I was reading the paper and looked at my horoscope. You know what it said . . . it said I was going to reach new heights today. New heights . . . funny and here I am STUCK! STUCK! (*Pause.*)

SAL: People get stuck on elevators all the time Sara and they go on to live full, productive lives.

SARA: All the time?

SAL: Yes. Think of it like being stuck in a traffic jam. You've been stuck in traffic jams haven't you?

SARA: Yes.

SAL: And you know that eventually the traffic starts moving again right?

SARA: Right.

SAL: What do you do when you are sitting in your car waiting for traffic to move?

SARA: I listen to music.

SAL: What kind of music do you like Sara?

SARA: I don't know . . . anything . . . PLAY ANYTHING!

SAL: Well I don't have a radio—

SARA: Then sing to me Sal, SING TO ME! (SAL *begins to sing in a slow, steady voice.*) East coast girls are hip I really dig the styles they wear (SARA *starts to sing.*) I wish they all could be California (SARA *and* SAL *together.*) I wish they all could be California / I wish they all could be California girls!

SARA: What's that?

SAL: Nothing.

SARA: I'm falling, I'm falling . . . THIS IS IT!

SAL: These elevators don't fall . . . well, not all the way. You may drop a floor or two.

SARA: DROP! What should I do?

SAL: Stay calm.

SARA: I heard that if you're in a falling elevator you should jump up and down and pray you're up when it crashes . . . (SARA *starts jumping.*)

SAL: Sara, it's okay stop . . . stop jumping.

(*Phone rings.*)

SARA: Now what?

SAL: Do you have a cell phone?

SARA: Yes, yes, my cell . . . oh my God, it's working. Hello, hello, Mom, I'm stuck! No, no really stuck. That's where I am in the elevator. What's that? that's good. (*To* SAL.) My mother is watching CNN and says there's no disaster. No, I didn't interview . . . I was on my way there . . . what? The powder blue suit with the shoes I got in Lord & Taylor. They don't clash. Mom . . . Mom . . . Mom! These could be the last words you have with your only daughter, your only hope of having a grandchild may be slipping away and you want to discuss fashion tips! You want to know what I'm wearing . . . DO YOU REALLY WANT TO KNOW? I'm standing here practically bare ass naked in my Victoria Secret Wonder Bra and panties wondering why I ever came on this god-damn interview for a job I don't even want!

SAL: Easy Sara, easy.

SARA: I'm breathing Sal, I'm breathing. Mom . . . what? Sal is my new friend. He's the barrier between me and total insanity and you know what Mom, he sang to me . . . that's right, sang to me. I don't know . . . Sal, my mother wants to know if you're gay?

SAL: Straight.

SARA: Mom, Mom . . . hello, hello! Dead.

SAL: Your mother?

SARA: The phone.

SAL: Sara, Sara, I thought you looked beautiful in your blue suit.

SARA: You did? Thanks Sal. (*Pause.*) Sal.

SAL: Yes.

SARA: You can see me?

SAL: Yes. You're a beautiful woman Sara, even more so out of the suit.

SARA: I go to the gym four times a week.

SAL: It shows.

SARA: Where's the camera?

SAL: To your left.

(SARA *blows* SAL *a kiss.*)

SARA: You'll get a real one when we meet.

SAL: We've got a date for pasta remember?

SARA: I'm getting hungry. . . . Sal, what's that?

SAL: The rescue team is here. You're caught between floors. They're trying to get your elevator to a floor so they can get you out.

SARA: Rescued? I need to be rescued. Sal!

SAL: It won't be long now Sara . . . hang in there.

SARA: I'm still breathing Sal.

SAL: Good girl. (*Pause.*) Sara.

SARA: WHAT?

SAL: They may have to rescue you from above.

SARA: Above, below, sideways, who cares just GET ME OUT OF HERE!

SAL: Listen to me Sara . . . they have to turn the generator that feeds the lights and intercom off in order to get to you.

SARA: I'll be in the dark?

SAL: Only for a short time.

SARA: And . . . and I'll lose you?

SAL: Never. Sing Sara, sing. I'm coming to get you.

(*Lights go out.* SARA *is in total darkness.*)

SARA: Oh God, no . . . Okay, Sal, okay. (SARA *starts to sing.*) I-I-I-wish they all-could be California—(*Hear noise, trapdoor on elevator ceiling opens . . . see a flash of light. Ladder drops down, hand reaches out to* SARA.) Sal!

SAL: COME SARA, COME.

(SARA *starts to climb out of elevator.* SARA *grabs* SAL*'s hand.*) I've got you Sara, I've got you!

(*Fade.*)

TABLE 5 AT EMPIRE SZECHWAN

FIVE SCENES OF DINNER

Alexander Woo

Table 5 at Empire Szechwan premiered February 15, 2000, at the Sacred Fools Theater in Los Angeles, California, directed by David Holcomb, produced by Gerald McClanahan. The cast was as follows:

ALEX	Martin Yu
WAITER	Ho–Kwan
MARION	Laurie Searle
ERICA	Jessie Thompson
HOLLY	Lizzie Peet
CHENG PI	Jennifer Avelyn Wu
SARAH	Ryann Davis

ONE

(*Table 5. The* WAITER *hands menus to a white woman,* MARION, *and an Asian man,* ALEX.)

WAITER: And our special tonight is attitude.

MARION: Attitude.

WAITER: Yes, fresh attitude.

MARION: How is it—

WAITER: It's served cold.

(WAITER *exits.*)

MARION: Well, I don't need any of that. (*Looking at the menu.*) Oh!

(ALEX *looks up.*)

No, nothing. (*Pause.*) The awkward tension sounds good for starters, don't you think?

(ALEX *smiles.*)

I know, I can never resist it myself. Oh, this sounds unusual—sexual disappointment—(*She looks at him.*) Oh, did you just have that for lunch?

(ALEX *looks away.*)

Mmm, okay. (*Pause.*) Well, what are you getting? Wait—let me guess . . . the spicy memories of ex-girlfriend, with bitter aftertaste?

(ALEX *makes an uncertain gesture.*)

No? Hmm . . . how 'bout the simmered insecurity smothered in possessiveness?

(ALEX *makes another uncertain gesture.*)

Oh, I know—the self-esteem, filleted, skewered, then seared over hot coals.

(ALEX *acknowledges.*)

I knew it. You've had it before, I see.

(ALEX *looks away.*)

Hmm, well I usually get the mindless, irresponsible inter-course. It's not very filling, but it does the job. (*They look at each other.*) But with you, I think I'll have something differ-ent. I think I'll have the strained, unconsummated teasing followed by the frosty, unreturned phone calls and finally the blanched look of recognition when I'm out with some-one else.

(ALEX *smiles weakly.*)

Oh, and I'd love to have the cream fellatio for dessert. (*They look at each other for a moment. She looks back at the menu.*) Oh, I'm sorry, you can't afford it. (*Pause.*) You know what's funny, I've had all of this before! I mean, I'd never gone for Chinese before, I thought the menu would be totally different, but it's not. (*Pause.*) It's a little disappointing, actually. (*Pause.*) I like getting to choose from the columns, though. (*Pause. She calls.*) Waiter?

WAITER: (*entering*) Yes?

MARION: We'd like some bread, please. What kind is it?

WAITER: Date nut bread.

MARION: Perfect.

TABLE 5 AT EMPIRE SZECHWAN 347

TWO

(*The* WAITER *leads another white woman,* ERICA, *and* ALEX *in.*)

WAITER: (*to* ERICA) Enjoy. (*To* ALEX.) Nice to see you. Again. (*The* WAITER *exits.*)

ERICA: Are you a regular here?

(ALEX *gives a half-acknowledging nod.*)

Oh, I like this place. It's very authentic. It reminds me of Kowloon. Have you been to Hong Kong?

(ALEX *shakes his head.*)

You *have* to go. Especially during the dragon boat festival. The nightlife in Lan Kwai Fong is sooo wonderful. I was there last summer with my ex, Marty. We had the *best* time. I bought the most adorable hapi coat there—I should have worn it tonight, it would have added to the experience, don't you think?

(ALEX *shrugs.*)

And look—oh my God, real ebony chopsticks! (*Pause.*) I haven't seen ebony chopsticks since I was in Japan three years ago. We went to this amazing kaiseki place in Roppongi with the lacquer bowls and the tatami mats and the most beautiful ebony chopsticks, just like these. Have you been to Japan?

(ALEX *shakes his head.*)

You really should. It's so important to experience other cultures. Yoshi showed me all over Japan—and the little village his family's from. Did you know they lived there for over three hundred generations? I was going to move back there with him, but he started losing his teeth and we broke up.

(*The* WAITER *appears with hot towels, which he hands to* ERICA *and* ALEX *with a pair of tongs.*)

WAITER: Towels?

ERICA: (*taking one*) Oh, yes, thank you! *Um goy nai.* ["Thank you."]

WAITER: (*to* ERICA) *Um sai.* ["No problem."]

(ALEX *takes a towel.*)

(*To* ALEX.) Thanks. (*The* WAITER *exits.*)

ERICA: This is just like the banquet halls on Orchard Road in Singapore. They always give you a little towel to wipe your hands with before your meal. I had the most wonderful time there five years ago. That's where I met Nap Chong. He's Thai, but that's the beautiful thing about Singapore—people from all different cultures living together in the same place— Thai, Malay, Indonesian, Japanese, Chinese, Indian, everything. Not like here, where everyone's *American.* Ugh. (*Pause.*) Have you been to Singapore?

(ALEX *shakes his head.*)

Of course not. You're missing out. I guess I'm just an adventurous kind of person. All the guys I've dated have been from really different backgrounds. Let's see—I've gone out with guys from India . . . Japan . . . Thailand . . . Hong Kong . . . Korea . . . Vietnam . . . Laos . . . Myanmar . . . Cambodia . . . Papua New Guinea . . . all over. I mean, Marty used to always say to me—*Yang yang du you see ha la.* ["You gotta try everything."]

(*The* WAITER *enters.*)

ERICA: *Ah! Gum yut yuw mut yeh ho sik ah?* ["What's good today?"]

WAITER: *Oh, dee bow yee ho sang seen.* ["The abalone is very fresh."]

ERICA: *Bow yee?* ["The abalone?"]

WAITER: *Hai.* ["Yep."]

ERICA: *Ho la.* ["Okey-doke."]

TABLE 5 AT EMPIRE SZECHWAN 349

(*The* WAITER *exits. Long pause as* ERICA *turns back to* ALEX.)

Ah, ngaw hai Hong Kong mai jaw nee tiew quon- ho laing ah! Ngow bai nai tai ha jung um jum lee la- ho ma? Na- hai nee do ah. ["I bought the loveliest dress in Hong Kong. I'll show you—see if you like it, okay? It's right here."] (ERICA *removes her dress to reveal a long Chinese cheongsam underneath. She continues to speak as she puts her hair up, holding it in place with the chopsticks.*) *Hai um hai ah? Ho laing ah. Jak gun nee tiew quongnow sang chang go* . . . ["Didn't I tell you? Gorgeous! This dress makes me feel like singing . . ."]

(*Chinese opera music starts in. Lights change.* ERICA *lip-syncs as she begins to perform an elaborate scene from the opera. Pause.* ALEX *signals to the* WAITER *for the check.*)

THREE

(ALEX *and another white woman,* HOLLY, *at the table.*)

HOLLY: You know, I could kill you with my bare hands. (*Pause.*) I'm not saying I will. I could. (*Pause.*) All I need is one free limb, and right now I've got four. (*Pause.*) Just watch it is all I'm saying. (*Pause.*) You don't talk much, do you? (*Pause. Silence.*) Oh, you're a winner. (*Calling.*) WAITER! (*Pause.*) Where the hell is he?

(*The* WAITER *enters.*)

Do you speak English? (*Pause.*)

WAITER: Yes.

HOLLY: (*Pause.*) Good for you. I have no idea what your friend here speaks. I have no idea *if* he speaks.

(ALEX *begins to say something, then stops.*)

WAITER: How did you two meet?

HOLLY: You ask too many questions. Just take my order. Do you
    know how to do that?

WAITER: Yes.

HOLLY: Good. We'll start with a couple of hot dog things.

WAITER: (*writing*) Pork buns.

HOLLY: Gimme that extra-crispy fried chicken—

WAITER: (*writing*) Peking duck—

HOLLY: And a burrito.

WAITER: (*writing*) Egg roll.

HOLLY: Whatever.

WAITER: Fine. And a fork as well?

HOLLY: (*pause*) Do I look like a cripple?

WAITER: (*to* ALEX) At least she can use chopsticks.

(*The* WAITER *exits. Pause.*)

HOLLY: Do you only come here with white women?

FOUR

(ALEX *at the table with a Chinese woman,* CHENG PI. *They sit in silence
for several moments.*)

(CHENG PI *starts to say something then stops.*)

(ALEX *gives a questioning look.*)

(CHENG PI *shakes her head.*)

(*They eat for several moments.*)

(CHENG PI *gestures toward the Happy Family* [*chef's special recommen-
dation #5*].)

TABLE 5 AT EMPIRE SZECHWAN   351

(ALEX *hands it to her.*)

(CHENG PI *smiles at* ALEX.)

(ALEX *gives a weak smile.*)

(*They eat for several moments.*)

(ALEX *begins to try to say something, but must finish chewing.*)

(CHENG PI *continues to watch* ALEX *patiently.*)

(ALEX *keeps trying to finish chewing. He chews for several moments.*)

(ALEX *feels something stuck in his throat.*)

(CHENG PI *gestures for the* WAITER.)

(*The* WAITER *enters. Seeing* ALEX, *he quickly goes to give him the Heimlich maneuver.*)

(*After several moments,* ALEX *spits out a microcasette, like those used in answering machines.*)

(*The* WAITER *picks it up. He wipes it dry with a napkin.*)

(*The* WAITER *places the microcasette into a handheld player.*)

(*The* WAITER *plays the tape. We hear:*)

CHENG PI: (*on tape*) Thanks for bringing me here tonight. I'm really enjoying myself.

ALEX: (*on tape*) I'm having a wonderful time too. You look very beautiful tonight.

CHENG PI: (*on tape*) Oh, thank you. You're so sweet.

ALEX: (*on tape*) I hope I can take you out again sometime.

CHENG PI: (*on tape*) I'd like that.

(*The* WAITER *stops the tape.* ALEX *and* CHENG PI *look embarrassed.*)

(*The* WAITER *begins to say something, then stops.*)

(ALEX *and* CHENG PI *give the* WAITER *a questioning look.*)

(*The* WAITER *shakes his head as if it weren't important, then exits.*)

(*They eat for several moments.*)

(*They look at each other.*)

(*They continue to eat.*)

FIVE

(*The* WAITER, *now a patron, sitting at dinner with another white woman,* SARAH.)

SARAH: (*rapt*) Oh my God, no!

WAITER: Yes.

SARAH: No!

WAITER: Really.

SARAH: Get out!

WAITER: It's true.

SARAH: I don't believe it!

WAITER: And you know what else?

SARAH: No, what?

(*The* WAITER *opens his mouth and makes a long, neutral noise for several moments.*)

　　　(*Pause.*) No, you're kidding me!

WAITER: It's true.

SARAH: I can't believe that!

WAITER: Honest.

SARAH: How can that be possible?

WAITER: I'm just an interesting guy.

TABLE 5 AT EMPIRE SZECHWAN   353

SARAH: You're so interesting!

WAITER: I'm really interesting.

SARAH: We have so much to talk about!

WAITER: So much to talk about!

(*They make neutral noises to each other for several moments, as though in conversation.*)

SARAH: Wow.

WAITER: Yeah.

SARAH: Yeah.

WAITER: Wow.

(*They continue to make neutral noises to each other. As they converse,* ALEX *enters, dressed as a waiter. He crosses to them to take their order. He begins to speak, but seeing them in conversation, thinks the better of it, and decides to leave.*)

TWENTY DOLLAR DRINKS

Joe Pintauro

Twenty Dollar Drinks was first presented in What I Did for Love, an evening of short plays about "life upon the wicked stage," at the John Drew Theatre at Guild Hall, East Hampton, New York, in July 2002. It was produced by Josh Gladstone, with original music by Margaret Pine; the cellist was Jason Dobranski. The costume design was by Gail Cooper-Hecht; lighting design was by Holger; casting was by Irene Stockton, CSA. Robert Kalfin directed the cast, which included Larry Pine, Stephan Wolfert, as well as Catherine Curtin and Patricia Randell, who starred in *Twenty Dollar Drinks*.

CHARACTERS

STAR
BETTY

(A drinks table at the Russian Tea Room.)

STAR: Someone handed me this golden statue, this naked man with no penis and remember how Larry used to get us up in class and make us do our Academy Award speeches, which was cruel but there I was for real and it felt like the Academy Awards must have been crap all along because there I was, crap on toast, getting the thing? And like all of a sudden it was less than pedestrian. I was in hell. . . . doing all in my power to act like I was an Academy Award–winning star, you know? Which I was. But who can really believe that? So I pretended I was my mother who is an accomplished actor and then I thought but she never won an Academy Award. I was like suddenly above her? And it made me this sort of dissociative experience to be like above her? So I pretended I was Jean Harlow just to like act that big and not crawl under the podium and at one point, don't ask me but I was doing Joan Crawford and that, wow, so freaked me. And afterwards before the press? I was in the skin of every star I could think of, Vivien Leigh, Catherine Da Vue. How do you say it?

BETTY: Deneuve.

STAR: And they were buying it but it was out of body for me. I'm possessed by some crazed imposter and my real self was in some sewer in Queens because I had to act like some star. But that's what I've become, a star, not for those eleven minutes there but forever, like suddenly I'm the Oracle of Delphi.

BETTY: You're no oracle of anything.

STAR: . . . and **real** movie stars are coming up to kiss me like they know me. Jack Nicholson and Nicolas Cage both at once like two large billboards falling on my face and suddenly it's like I went to high school in Australia with Nicole Kidman or something while the sweat is Niagara Falls between my butt cheeks down to my shoes. I loved it.

BETTY: The only stars I care about are the stars on my kid's report card.

STAR: Oh. How is he . . . uh . . . ?

BETTY: You forgot his name.

STAR: Jonathan.

BETTY: Try again.

STAR: Jesse?

BETTY: Yes, but you forgot before you remembered. Just the way you saw me the other night at Cynthia's and ham that you are you so badly pretended not to see me.

STAR: I saw you at Cynthia's?

BETTY: You pretended not to but so badly, as if you never read a word of Jerzy Grotowski.

STAR: Who's Jerry Zakowski? I was surrounded by twenty syco-phantic moving mouths.

BETTY: Congratulations! Congratulations! But meantime we waited on your leash for you to say hi.

STAR: I had to go to another party, I was late. I waved but you cut out in front of me. Betty talk about your son. If I remember correctly, that calms you.

BETTY: Thanks. He got into Trinity.

STAR: A church?

BETTY: A school.

STAR: So that's some kind of big deal?

BETTY: In my world it is.

STAR: Well, that's nice, isn't it?

BETTY: Till my money runs out. And don't you interpret that as I got you here to ask for a handout.

STAR: What? Well, here's to Jesse.

BETTY: That I'll drink to.

STAR: The drinks here are twenty bucks? What's the world coming to?

BETTY: Me, invite a star to a no-class joint?

STAR: Let me pick up the check.

BETTY: Well thank you.

STAR: Is Buchwald getting you any voice-overs? Are they any good?

BETTY: I booked a denture spot.

STAR: You didn't.

BETTY: Old people are getting younger every day.

STAR: One of the papers said you were up for a Pinter play?

BETTY: Didn't get it.

STAR: Is that why you look tired?

BETTY: No. I am pissed and when pissed I apparently look tired.

STAR: Pissed at Harold Pinter? Well I mean, at what?

BETTY: My parents for dying, the dying was bad enough but leaving me shit . . . My husband for being a drunk . . .

STAR: Oh dear. What time is it?

BETTY: Don't say you've got to go.

STAR: No, go on . . . your husband?

BETTY: I went and fell in love with an actor who hates himself, what else is new, except this one's a drunk so I go ahead and have his kid.

STAR: You're talkin' about . . . Whatsizname Jesse.

BETTY: A terrific kid, knock wood.

STAR: Does he see his dad?

BETTY: From a cab a couple weeks ago we saw him in rotted jogging shoes with glassy eyes, walking his dog.

STAR: He's not got that soap anymore?

BETTY: I don't watch for fear I'll see him.

STAR: So he could help with Jesse.

BETTY: He sends money.

STAR: I'm so relieved. Look, Betty, I hate to say this, but I've got a stupid meeting at William Morris. So . . . what is it? I showed up. What do you have to tell me?

BETTY: What do I have to tell you?

STAR: You said on the phone you had to tell me something.

BETTY: Oh. I'm not jealous of you.

STAR: You're not?

BETTY: Before we drift apart, as we will and you decide you don't know me at all anymore, I want it in the record that I'll never envy you no matter what you accumulate, acquire . . .

STAR: You've got too much on the ball to envy anybody for Crissakes Betty.

BETTY: True.

STAR: Don't blame me if the world hasn't acknowledged it. It's a crap shoot.

BETTY: Forget "the world." Let's keep it about you and me shall we? I am proud, not ashamed, to look you in the eye and show you my hurt.

STAR: What in the hell have I done to hurt you?

BETTY: Are you kidding? You walk around this town like you never knew a lot of your old friends.

STAR: Oh, Jesus.

BETTY: Get real for Chrissakes.

STAR: Oh I got real all right. I have to hit the streets in baseball caps and dark glasses every day. I'm asked for money which I don't have yet. I hear from relatives I haven't met yet. I'm a freak even to you. Listen to you. So have a good day.

BETTY: Sit down. You sit down. (STAR *sits.*) We acted in the same company for ten years. We ate more dinners, spent more rotten hours together. I paid for more coffees. We slept together more nights. . . .

STAR: You're not going around claiming that.

BETTY: You dog. I meant I had to put you to sleep, you drunk, on my couch a half dozen times. I'm not claiming to be your lost cousin or some high-school jerk. You always were using everyone, everything. And it worked. What are you complaining about? So here's to your fucking obese ego, your obscene Oscar and your fame.

(STAR *pushes her drink away.*)

STAR: You know what fame is? Multiply all the people you don't wanna know by two hundred million. That's fame. Fame is diarrhea. It's the drink that comes to your table from a dark corner of a restaurant and it could be from a deranged stalker or your future lover. Either way if you don't drink the shit they'll hate you till they die. There is nothing spiritual about fame. Fame is prostitution without body contact. It is no fun. It is hard on a person.

BETTY: Well I must say you looked like you had it in you.

STAR: Like I had what in me? Oh God tell me. You watched. You saw me up there?

BETTY: You said the perfect thing for exactly the right amount of time. I was surprised.

STAR: Katie and Bill didn't watch. It's amazing how many didn't bother.

BETTY: I can't believe Katie didn't watch it.

STAR: They had a gallery opening.

BETTY: She saw it on the news, didn't she?

STAR: They saw nothing.

BETTY: She didn't see the freaking *paper?*

STAR: She said it wasn't delivered that day.

BETTY: Maybe they were afraid to see you lose. I was.

STAR: Well, nobody expected I'd get it, least of all me.

BETTY: *I* didn't expect you to *get* it. You were up there with ancient deities, for heaven's sake.

STAR: So like I didn't deserve it?

BETTY: It's not for me to judge this stuff. So what if you didn't deserve it?

STAR: I didn't say I didn't deserve it. You hate me.

BETTY: I just hate your going off into the sunset like some Wagnerian myth.

STAR: You're a better actress than I. I know that.

BETTY: Just not as lucky as you. Is that the message?

STAR: It wasn't luck. You know you never were my best friend, for cryin' out loud. It was years ago.

BETTY: You want me to buy that you don't know me at all? Ask me. I'll pretend we never met. Oh, you should be punished. God . . .

STAR: Oh, c'mon. Hey.

BETTY: It's like watching a ship sailing away forever.

STAR: For me it's like being *on* the ship.

BETTY: I never had so close a friend win one of those horrid things.

STAR: You consider me a close friend?

BETTY: Yes.

STAR: So why don't you act like a close friend and tell me to my face that you in fact *are* profoundly jealous of me?

BETTY: I would despise myself if I felt one ounce . . . of . . . of jealousy of you of all people. I was a damned good actress, better than most of the clowns out there.

STAR: Including me. This you made clear.

BETTY: You said it yourself. And I'd hate myself if I stooped to . . . to . . . jealousy . . . or . . .

STAR: Then you hate yourself.

BETTY: I don't hate myself for having my son, for . . . for . . .

STAR: Your son has nothing to do with this.

BETTY: I couldn't drag my ass around La-La Land with that kid.

STAR: I didn't make it in L.A. I made it here on the same stage, in the same company as you.

BETTY: I waited on tables. You've been subsidized since you were born.

STAR: I worked my ass off.

BETTY: You're still not good enough. You don't even know who the hell Jerzy Grotowski is.

STAR: It's pronounced Yerzy. So why don't you throw your drink in my face? You've been dying to since you walked in here.

BETTY: That's where you're at.

STAR: Your hand's been shaking. You can hardly hold it back. Go ahead. Someone may take a picture. You'll get in the papers. People will gossip about it. You'll be welded to me for life. Maybe it'll get you a part in something.

BETTY: You weirdo.

STAR: Oh, cut the shit. You're just as fucking hard-hearted an entrepreneur as I am. For a month you've been trying to provoke this argument. I showed up. So go prove to the world you're intimate with a star . . .

BETTY: You know what a star is? You crock of shit?

STAR: Lower your . . .

BETTY: A star is one of those gorgeous glittering things in the heavens that mankind has been staring at for millions of years. It's a fucking *sun*, a giant, burning miracle that makes life possible, something all your Hollywood fatheads couldn't imagine, much less originate. The star you are is the paper kind, with glue on the back, the kind you buy by the hundreds in a little box for a buck.

STAR: Cut the monologue and throw the drink in my face.

(BETTY *stands in horror.*)

BETTY: I wouldn't stoop to that cliché.

STAR: You are a cliché, the same predatory thing you were from the day I met you. You got me here, for what, your cut of the pie? So humiliate me. Let them take a picture. Get into the action. What else do you have left?

(BETTY *lifts her drink and flings it into* STAR's *face. The two continue to look at one another.* BETTY *starts to leave.*)

STAR: Come back. Sit for Crissake.

(BETTY, *reluctantly, returns and sits slowly. The two women stare blankly at their separate futures.*)

BETTY: I've lived so long without money . . . that was never what it was about for me. I don't want any cut of your pie. I'm not even an actress any more. I . . . I just hate the way people suddenly go to some glittery Valhalla that you think is so cool but to me . . . It's like you all died and you're in some vault having a Hollywood virtual reality experience called success, and because of all this shit, I lose you. I knew it the minute you walked in, in those clothes. You'll never be the same to me nor I to you, the light around you will be too bright, too busy. I'll be some woman in a bad coat and a bad haircut who you'll be too guilty not to talk to and you'll hate me for showing up like some anchor on your velocity and it'll be that way till we both are too old to care. . . . So, I'm forced to disappear. . . . into the proletarian hordes of . . . those who claim they knew you. And that reduces me.

STAR: That's ridiculous.

BETTY: It hurts my existence. Can't you come over to understand that? What you've done to me?

STAR: What have I done?

BETTY: You're dangerous. You're dangerous to my life. You're dangerous to my spirit, to my self-esteem and I can't know you anymore or even remember you.

(*By now* STAR *has been brought to tears.*)

STAR: God.

BETTY: It's not easy for me. You gonna be all right?

STAR: No. Are you?

BETTY: No.

STAR: You just scared the hell out of me.

BETTY: I know. I know.

STAR: I don't know what to do.

BETTY: Either do I. Gotta go.

STAR: No.

BETTY: Let me go.

STAR: Not this way.

(STAR *grabs* BETTY's *hand, puts it to her cheek and kisses it.* BETTY *pulls away and exits. Music crawls in.*)

21

Sigrid Heath

21, by Sigrid Heath, premiered at Actors & Writers on June 1, 2002. The play was directed by the author. The cast was as follows:

BRYN	Nicole Quinn
BOO	Sarah Chodoff
THE WAITER	David Smilow

CHARACTERS

BRYN: Forties, an alpha creature.
BOO: Thirties, very beautiful, soft.
THE WAITER: Thirties to fifties, dignified.

(BRYN *and* BOO *are sitting at a table at 21 in Manhattan. They're both dressed and accessorized expensively;* BOO *in black,* BRYN *in red.* BOO*'s just arrived. She is crying copiously, and for a couple of beats* BRYN *simply waits.* BOO *doesn't stop crying.* BRYN *can no longer tolerate it.*)

BRYN: That's enough. (BOO *continues to cry.*)

BRYN: What's the matter with you! (BOO *looks at her, incredulous; cries harder.*)

BRYN: The schmuck is dead long live the schmuck. You're late. Did the funeral run over? (BOO *wails.* BRYN *studies her.*)

BRYN: You're off your meds, aren't you. (*Reaching into her large designer bag, she spreads the goods on the table in front of* BOO.) Prozac, Paxil, Zoloft . . . What do you need? Valium. Xanax. Heroin. Vitamin C? Vitamin E! I've suspected a vitamin deficiency. Kava. Rescue Remedy. No, none of that new age crap. Big Pharma! That's what you need. Go on! Help yourself! (BOO *sorts through the offerings, pops one or two.*)

BRYN: The drink! Your display diverted me. You'll feel better after our drink. WAITER! (*He enters. Impassive.*) Two stingers. Quickly. As you can see, we're in need. (THE WAITER *acknowledges the order and leaves.*) Now, go to the loo. Your face is a horror. *He* is due and he'll be on time. He's a Republican.

BOO: Why are they always Republicans?

BRYN: They have all the money.

BOO: I wasn't ready, Bryn.

BRYN: What do you mean you weren't ready?

BOO: I wasn't ready to be . . . without him.

BRYN: "Without *him*"? *Him, he, they.* Get in control of your pronouns. You're beyond *him*. *He's* coming through the door any minute. *They* are all alike and good for one thing only.

BOO: You don't understand. . . .

BRYN: Yes, I do. I knew your sentimentality was a potential liability. But I calculated that your appreciation for Fendi and Manolo, Prada and Harry Winston would eclipse it. And you've always proved me right. I like being right, Boo. (THE WAITER *delivers the drinks. Hovers near* BOO.)

BRYN: Thank you. (*He doesn't move.*) THANK YOU! (THE WAITER *looks at* BOO. *She smiles, releasing him. He nods and departs, with dignity.*)

BOO: I loved him.

BRYN: Yes. That's what you do. That's your talent.

BOO: No, Bryn. I *loved* him.

BRYN: Don't poeticize; it gives me gastric reflux.

BOO: I LOVED HIM!

BRYN: Describe his death to me. Improve my mood.

BOO: It was his birthday. I'd given him a six-pack of Viagra and that new translation of the Kama Sutra. It's odd how many people die on their birthdays.

BRYN: What about The Cocktail?

BOO: We were trying a particularly athletic position. I'd suggested something more within his comfort level, but he seemed inspired. He was scaling the sacred mount when his face turned magenta, then he paled to a poignant gray. But, Bryn, he looked as if he'd seen a light!

BRYN: No doubt. What about . . .

BOO: I can't believe he's gone.

BRYN: *What about The Cocktail?* I assume you gave him The Cocktail. You mixed it, watched him drink it, and you can't believe he's gone. Are you unwell? (*She signals.* THE WAITER *reappears.*) Two more of the same.

BOO: Make mine tea, please. Earl Grey.

BRYN: You *are* unwell. (*As* THE WAITER *turns to go, he offers* BOO *a handkerchief with which she dabs at her nose.*)

BOO: I didn't give him The Cocktail.

BRYN: WHAT?

BOO: I decided last year *on his birthday* not to give him The Cocktail. Ever.

BRYN: You . . . developed an alternative strategy without calling a meeting?

BOO: There was no alternative strategy.

BRYN: *No Plan?*

BOO: No Plan. At first he was just like the others. Besotted with himself; a god at his office and at all our restaurants. At home, he left the seat up, dribbled pee down the toilet, you know, the usual. And, of course, his cock was . . .

BOO AND BRYN: . . . his voice, his fist, his brain . . .

BOO: . . . *until it wasn't any longer.* He was terrified. He thought that's who he was! But I knew different. Anyone who'd seen him with his dog . . . HIS DOG! I'm keeping the dog.

BRYN: We never keep the dogs.

BOO: I'M KEEPING THE DOG! I loved the dog, too. They both had the same sweet, wrinkly muzzle.

BRYN: Insulin. Hold on, I've got this little pen thing, delivers a dose right in the thigh, easy, fast . . . (*She injects herself.*) Ah. That's better. And, now, I've heard enough of this nonsense. (THE WAITER *returns with tea for* BOO.)

BOO: Oh! Cookies with my tea. That's so *thoughtful*.

BRYN: My Stinger? (THE WAITER *gives her a look.*) Never mind. Thank you. THANK YOU! (THE WAITER *stands guard by* BOO.) THANK YOU, ASSHOLE, YOU MAY LEAVE NOW! (BOO *nods and he leaves reluctantly.*) There's something about this I don't like.

BOO: Why, Bryn?

BRYN: Why what?

BOO: I never asked, and now I'm asking. Why?

BRYN: Eros and Kratos, Boo. Kratos must win. Otherwise . . . *le deluge.* Chaos. We take what we've got—our assets, our capabilities—we maximize, leverage, cram, ram, dope, demand, cajole, we turn it to gold. We make it all—*them all!*—serve *us.* Why? Because I'm not interested in having it the other way around.

But there's something else at stake, here and now. We had an arrangement. A contract! I will consider this an aberration. But Boo. Never, never go off your mins and meds again. COMPLIANCE: That's your role.

And now, pull yourself together. Deep breath. Sit up tall, let's see that swan's neck. Lick your lips . . . (BOO *complies: slowly lengthening her neck, lifting her elegant head, composing her features. Then, suddenly, she stops, considers, hides her face in her hands, sobs once, and when she reemerges she's a new woman.*)

BOO: No.

BRYN: *"No"*?!

BOO: I'm done. I loved him. I loved.

BRYN: STOP SAYING THAT! I'm getting a vicious headache. One more, Boo. The Plan was four. This was only number three. One more and the world is yours. Or whatever you think you want. Be a fucking zen nun, I don't care. But your last assignment is on his way, Boo, a marvel in Armani; his aorta patched with PVC. High level investor: Enron and . . . Never mind, you never care about their portfolios. You never *need* to care.

BOO: No. Never again. Excuse me? May I have the check? Please?

BRYN: WHAT? (*To* THE WAITER *who has come to* BOO's *side.*) NOT YET! GO! (*He moves closer to* BOO.) You do not exist. (*She zeros in on* BOO.) *WHAT'S HAPPENED TO YOU!*

BOO: He was faithful.

BRYN: He was half dead!

BOO: Faithful in his mind!

BRYN: Senile dementia!

BOO: He *changed* me!

BRYN: (*controlling herself with great effort*) Now, Boo. You got a little tired. Lost your way in the woods. Watching bunnies and birdies, you thought, for a bizarre moment, you were one of *them.*

BOO: That's what he called me! Bunny!

BRYN: I think I've got some crack in here. . . .

BOO: *Why can't I be Bunny?*

BRYN: The logarithm of survival: You are either an eater or you're eaten and that's the way it is.

BOO: No. I'm done. (THE WAITER *is at her side. They look at one another. They look at* BRYN.)

BRYN: (*her eyes suddenly drawn to the door*) Wonderful. *He's* here. Do you hear the pronoun? The tense of the verb? HE IS HERE. NOW! Walking in the door. The Plan, the Plan . . . (THE WAITER *offers* BOO *his hand. She takes it. She stands.*)

BOO: (*looking toward the door*) Good high color. Hypertension? A little blue around the lips. Congestive heart disease? You've done well, as usual, Bryn. Good-bye.

BRYN: WAIT! What am *I* supposed to do with him?

BOO: Marry him.

(BOO *and* THE WAITER *waltz off.*)

VIRGINIA STREET

Toni Press-Coffman

Virginia Street was originally produced by Upstairs Theatre Company (Anthony Runfola, Artistic Director) in Tucson, Arizona, in April 1997, directed by Adam Burke. The cast was as follows:

ABIGAIL	Amy Christensen
MARTIN	Jonathan Ingbretson
HENRY	R. Gabriel Nagy
JENNIFER	Jennie Mahalick

CHARACTERS

ABIGAIL: A woman in her late twenties/early thirties, who lives on Virginia Street.

MARTIN: A boy, seventeen, who visits Virginia Street.

HENRY: A twenty-year-old Latino, who visits Virginia Street in his wheelchair.

JENNIFER: A young woman, eighteen, who lives on Virginia Street.

Virginia Street should be multiculturally cast. It may be presented entirely in English, in Spanish, or in a mix of English and Spanish.

SETTING: A residential city street in late summer. This particular street has a park and neighborhood center on it. At different points in the play, we hear many kinds of noises coming from the park. We constantly hear cars drive by. We see the porch of a house painted bright yellow and the sidewalk in front of it.

This play is dedicated to Sue Berman and Pete Richter,
whose home on Virginia Street afforded me time to contemplate and to write,
thus restoring my quickly fading sanity.

ONE

(*The sun is about to go down. We hear people in the park, particularly teenagers.* ABIGAIL *walks onto the porch from her house, wearing exercise clothes, exercise bag over her shoulder. Just as she steps out her front door, a beer bottle thrown into the street breaks noisily. Startled, she jumps back with a quick intake of breath. After a beat, she walks into the street, picks up shards of glass there. A car honks at her.*)

ABIGAIL: Sorry. (*Another car honks at her, from the other direction, then another.*) Sorry, Sorry. (*Another honk.*) HEY! I'm hurrying.

TWO

(*The sun has set. Norteno music blasts, in Spanish.* ABIGAIL *walks toward the porch, carrying her exercise bag, two bags of groceries, a rented movie. She stops to get the mail and, when she opens the mailbox, she drops something. When she bends down to pick it up, she drops something else. She lets everything in her hands fall to the ground. She follows suit.* MARTIN *enters, walking backwards.*)

HENRY: (*off*) Then fuck you, Marty.

MARTIN: Shut up, you know?

HENRY: (*off*) It don't matter to me you know. I don't care.

MARTIN: (*stopping in front of* ABIGAIL'*s porch*) Then why don't you shut the fuck up?

HENRY: (*off*) Then be pussy whipped. Be pussy whipped. I don't care about that shit.

MARTIN: (*Sees* ABIGAIL, *steps toward her.*) Hey, lady, that's your house, right?

ABIGAIL: Is there something you need from me?

MARTIN: Do I need something from you? Like what?

ABIGAIL: (*looking toward* HENRY, *intrigued*) Who's that?

MARTIN: Like what could I possibly need from you?

ABIGAIL: Who's that telling you you're pussy whipped?

MARTIN: I been meaning to tell you about this yellow thing you did to your house?

HENRY: (*off*) Who you talking to?

(ABIGAIL *stands up.* MARTIN *takes several steps toward her.*)

ABIGAIL: (*distracted by looking at* HENRY) It was white four and a half years. I needed a change.

MARTIN: You're all sweaty. You lookin' good, all sweaty like that.

HENRY: (*off*) Who the hell you talking to, Marty?

MARTIN: People 'cross the street at the pool or whatever, playing basketball or whatever, we got to look at that house.

ABIGAIL: Or you could hang out someplace else. (*She walks off the porch, onto the street, referring to* HENRY.) What happened to him?

MARTIN: What do you mean?

ABIGAIL: Your friend's in a wheelchair.

MARTIN: He is? I did not realize that.

ABIGAIL: What happened?

MARTIN: I don't know.

ABIGAIL: How long's he been in the wheelchair?

MARTIN: Long time. (*Beat.*) Maybe he got shot or something.

ABIGAIL: (*still looking at* HENRY, *off*) Is he Italian?

MARTIN: No, he ain't Italian, what you talking about, Italian?

ABIGAIL: (*gathering up her things*) I nearly got killed picking up the pieces of your broken beer bottle.

MARTIN: You gotta be pretty stupid, go in the street and pick up the trash.

ABIGAIL: It is not nice to litter. Didn't your mother teach you that?

MARTIN: It is not nice to litter? Are you for real?

JENNIFER: (*off, overlap*) Martin, what is keeping you?

MARTIN: No way he's Italian.

(MARTIN *runs off in the direction of* JENNIFER'*s voice.* HENRY, *about twenty, rolls by in a wheelchair.* ABIGAIL *watches him as he follows* MARTIN *off.*)

THREE

(ABIGAIL *sits in the morning sun on her porch, wearing shorts and a brief top, no shoes. Now there are children in the park; we hear them making kid noises.* ABIGAIL *looks sharply across the street, stands up. After a couple beats, she steps onto the street, waves. She doesn't see* HENRY *enter. He stops the wheelchair on the sidewalk in front of her house. She backs into him, falls on him.*)

ABIGAIL: (*getting off him*) God Almighty. Sorry.

HENRY: No problem.

ABIGAIL: What's your friend doing over there?

HENRY: He got community service.

ABIGAIL: What'd he do?

HENRY: Why you want to know?

ABIGAIL: He's hanging out across the street from my house. What'd he do?

HENRY: He robbed a store's all. He didn't even have a piece. He pretended. Now he gotta work at the day care center.

ABIGAIL: He robbed a store, now he's working with three-year-olds?

HENRY: He volunteered for it—uh, what's your name?

ABIGAIL: Abigail.

HENRY: (*holding out his hand; she takes it*) Henry. So Martin wanted the day care and (*kidding*) those judges are so overworked, you know, that poor judge must not have been thinking straight. I'm sure he did his best with that sentencing.

ABIGAIL: So what are you doing here? You have community service too?

HENRY: Nah, I just like to help him out over here sometime. What can I say? I love children.

ABIGAIL: Did you get shot?

HENRY: What's it look like?

ABIGAIL: Looks like you might have been in a skiing accident.

HENRY: Yeah. That's right. I was in a skiing accident. (*Calling.*) HEY, MARTY. (*Back to* ABIGAIL.) Yeah, when I was on the Olympics. It was tragic. I was gonna get the gold medal, you know? But then I had this terrible accident. It was a fucking tragedy.

(MARTIN *enters.*)

HENRY: (*to* MARTIN) How's the brats?

MARTIN: They're kids. They can't help it. (*To* ABIGAIL.) You better put on your shoes. People around here's mamas don't
teach 'em nothin', broken glass all over the place.

FOUR

(*After midnight, porch light on. An occasional car drives by. Noise of
shouting, punching—someone is getting beaten up. After several seconds,*
ABIGAIL *steps out onto the porch in her robe.*)

ABIGAIL: Shit. (*Shouting toward the noise.*) I'm going to call the
police, so you better get the hell out of here.

(*She turns to go back into the house, but stops when she hears sirens. She
steps back out onto the porch and watches as the sirens get closer and
closer. Then we see the lights of a police car.*)

FIVE

(*Afternoon.* ABIGAIL *enters from her house, sees* MARTIN *crossing the street.*)

ABIGAIL: How long's your sentence?

MARTIN: Hundred hours.

ABIGAIL: Nothing tacked on for last night? (*Silence.*) That was you
I saw with those other brave boys, beating up on— (*somebody*).

MARTIN: You know, you just a bitch with nothing to say. Business
is business.

ABIGAIL: My mistake. (*Beat.*) Poor kid.

MARTIN: What poor kid? Hector ain't no poor kid.

ABIGAIL: I meant you.

MARTIN: Yeah right. Poor pitiful me. I am a piece of work. Huh? Aren't I?

(JENNIFER *enters. She is pregnant.*)

JENNIFER: (*glaring at* ABIGAIL) I'm waitin' on you, Marty.

ABIGAIL: I'm Abigail.

JENNIFER: So?

HENRY: (*off*) MARTY.

(HENRY *enters.*)

JENNIFER: Would you just crawl off someplace and die, Henry?

HENRY: (*entering*) You here again? Why don't you lay off this guy?

JENNIFER: And who are you to be telling me to lay off anybody? You are nothing but a fucking cripple.

HENRY: (*overlap*) You already gone and got yourself pregnant, he already says he's gonna do the right thing, so why don't you make yourself scarce sometime?

JENNIFER: Faggot.

(HENRY *lunges at her with his wheelchair.* MARTIN *stands between them.*)

MARTIN: (*to* JENNIFER) Shut your mouth. (*To* ABIGAIL.) A man gets a beating sometime. So what? He deserves it, he gets it. He takes it like a man. (*Back to* JENNIFER.) Stop with him, all right? (*Beat, he touches her stomach.*) You all right?

(MARTIN *puts his arms around* JENNIFER, *she leans into him.*)

MARTIN: What's the matter? Huh?

JENNIFER: I'm still bleeding.

MARTIN: (*to* HENRY) Man, we got to go to the clinic. She's bleeding.

HENRY: Catch you later, bro.

(MARTIN *and* JENNIFER *exit. As they go,* JENNIFER *swats at* HENRY. HENRY *moves toward her, but she's out.* ABIGAIL *moves toward her car.*)

HENRY: Where you goin'?

ABIGAIL: To work. You should try it.

HENRY: I work.

ABIGAIL: At what?

HENRY: I'm a speech writer for the president. (*She laughs.*) What's so funny? I write speeches for the president and what I can do, I can write speeches for any president, for any political party, it don't matter, they're all after me. You know, Hank, write for me, he's just a sucky liberal. Nah, Hank, don't write for him, he's a nazi, write for me, bro. How about you?

ABIGAIL: I'm a trainer.

HENRY: Like with dogs?

ABIGAIL: Like with athletes. (*She starts to leave.*) What happened to you, Hank? You get shot? (*She looks at him for several beats. He says nothing. She leaves.*)

HENRY: (*calling after her*) Hey, I'll catch you later.

SIX

(*Night, about eight P.M.* MARTIN *and* JENNIFER *sit on* ABIGAIL'*s porch,* HENRY *sits in his wheelchair; they're all drinking beer, listening to Ice Cube.* ABIGAIL *enters, again carrying a lot of things, wearing her exercise clothes.*)

HENRY: (*seeing her*) Hey, you're home.

MARTIN: Mama, you sure look— (*fine*).

JENNIFER: Shut up. (*To* ABIGAIL.) You're practically naked out here in the street, why don't you get dressed or something, stop sticking your tits in everybody's face.

ABIGAIL: What was the bleeding? (JENNIFER *shrugs.*) When are you due, shouldn't you be in the hospital if you're bleeding?

MARTIN: They don't know what it is. Fucking doctors.

JENNIFER: (*overlap*) We ain't got the money for the hospital and even if we did, I don't want to go to no hospital. I'm havin' the baby at home. (*Beat.*) It's due October.

HENRY: Halloween. Perfect. I'm sure the little guy's gonna look just like you.

ABIGAIL: (*putting her packages down*) Did the bleeding stop?

JENNIFER: Yeah, it stopped. Don't worry yourself, all right? You ain't my mother.

MARTIN: (*overlap*) I'm gonna take care of her, all right?

ABIGAIL: She shouldn't be drinking beer.

JENNIFER: You standing out here with no clothes on, who you telling not to drink beer?

ABIGAIL: (*overlap, matter-of-fact*) It's not good for your baby. And you're sitting on my porch.

(JENNIFER *gets up.*)

JENNIFER: No I'm not. (JENNIFER *starts to exit.*) You comin', Marty? (*To* ABIGAIL.) Good thing it's nighttime. This house the fucking ugliest color I ever saw.

MARTIN: (*to* ABIGAIL) What did I tell you? Huh?

(MARTIN *and* JENNIFER *exit, taking Ice Cube with them.* ABIGAIL *sits down on the porch, looks after them. Now Caribbean dance music can be heard, faintly.*)

HENRY: (*imitating* JENNIFER) You comin', Marty? He's pussy whipped. She tricked him, getting pregnant. Women always wanting to trick us, right?

ABIGAIL: I knew immediately you were an expert on women.

HENRY: Yeah. I'm a psychologist, did I forget to tell you? (*She smiles. A beat.*) I'd help you with your packages, but, you know, here I am, stuck in this— *(wheelchair).*

ABIGAIL: God, that smells good. You smell that? Juan next door, he barbeques a couple times a week in the summer. Sometimes I sit out here and try to look so tired and hungry he'll take pity on me and offer me some. He always does beef, you know, and sometimes he does corn too and then his whole family sits on his porch and eats.

HENRY: So I see. But what the hell kind of music is that?

ABIGAIL: (*Shrugs.*) It's music from Juan's native country, except he's lived next door so long, I can't remember where that is. (*Beat.*) You have nice eyes, Hank. I've been meaning to tell you that.

HENRY: I'm named after Hank Aaron. Henry Aaron. My old man's favorite ballplayer. (*He touches her arm.*) I like you callin' me Hank. (*Beat.*) You got nice eyes too. What color are they anyway?

ABIGAIL: Gray.

HENRY: Yeah, but—. They change, right?

ABIGAIL: So I've been told.

HENRY: (*referring to her packages*) You got anything you need to put in the refrigerator?

ABIGAIL: What? (*Realizes he's referring to her packages.*) No.

(*She touches his face. He kisses her hand. Lights fade to very dim as they kiss. We see them, kissing passionately and* ABIGAIL *climbing up onto* HENRY's *lap.*)

SEVEN

(*A gunshot. Lights up full—fast.* ABIGAIL *jumps off* HENRY'S *lap.*)

ABIGAIL: Oh, my God. (*Beat.*) What was that?

(HENRY *pulls her back onto his lap, kisses her, then rubs her back. A few beats.*)

ABIGAIL: What happened to you?

HENRY: (*rubbing her back*) It was a mistake, that's all. I was drunk, I was sittin' in the street with friends from work. I work. At one of those places where they sell used office furniture. Now they got me doing inventory and shit, but I used to be able to move things around.

ABIGAIL: (*referring to his rubbing her back*) You're distracting me.

HENRY: (*Stops rubbing.*) Oh. (*Beat.*) So we were all out in the street and here they come, the boys from two different crews. It was like the gunfight at the OK Corral, man, they walking down the street at each other, you think you're about to see holsters slung across their hips or something. I'm polluted. I get up and yell HEY. Don't ask me why, I don't know. Marty thinks I did it to warn him, but how am I gonna warn him, he's walking with the others, they headed straight for each other. Nah, I was just drunk. (*Beat.*) Just drunk. Just fucking stupid and drunk.

ABIGAIL: (*after a pause*) How about that time? Did he have a gun that time?

HENRY: Nah. Martin don't own a gun.

ABIGAIL: He's in a gang without a gun?

HENRY: He's not in a gang exactly. What are you—writing a story for *People* magazine? (*Beat.*) I was an investigative reporter myself once upon a time, but I didn't do this sociology bullshit. I liked to do features—like on Madonna and other famous celebrities of her ilk.

(*She puts a finger on his mouth to stop him talking. A couple beats.*)

ABIGAIL: I lift weights, you know.

HENRY: (*running his hand down her arm*) Yeah?

ABIGAIL: I could get this chair up on that porch and into my house. You want to see my house?

HENRY: What, now?

ABIGAIL: We could practice now. Then you could come for real, and we could be in my house in case there's shooting at night. Then in the morning we could sit out on the porch in the sunshine. Then maybe you could leave Martin and Jennifer alone. Why are you so jealous about that?

HENRY: I am not jealous, what the fuck do you mean, jealous? A kid, this girl following him everywhere, it's a dead end that's all.

ABIGAIL: Walking down the street facing off the other—"crew"— is what? A golden opportunity?

HENRY: That's the reality. You go where your posse goes.

ABIGAIL: He loves the girl, he's working at a day care center learning how to be a good father, leave them alone.

HENRY: (*Comes in on "good father."*) You're full of shit, that's court ordered.

ABIGAIL: (*after a beat*) You go where your posse goes? Or are you retired?

HENRY: (*looking at her intently*) Neither. I'm a rugged individual- ist. Like John Wayne.

(ABIGAIL *turns his wheelchair so it faces her house.*)

ABIGAIL: Okay, here we go, we're going to try it. (*A beat. She stops.*) What are they doing here?

HENRY: Excuse me, I didn't hear you right. What are they doing here?

ABIGAIL: The posse, the crew. Where'd they come from?

HENRY: Mars? (*Beat.*) They live here, what the hell do you think?

ABIGAIL: No, *I* live here.

HENRY: So do they.

ABIGAIL: Since when?

HENRY: They live *around* here, what, you never leave this block?

ABIGAIL: Yeah, I do.

HENRY: Yeah, sure.

ABIGAIL: In my car.

HENRY: Two blocks from here? They got a fresh fish market.

ABIGAIL: (*amused*) I know that.

HENRY: Yeah. (*Beat.*) So that's where I got shot. Right in front of the fishmonger. He came runnin' out. I bled all over his apron. A fluke he was there. It was nighttime, you know, so he must have been late with ordering or something. I don't know. (*Beat.*) He took me to the hospital. (*Beat.*) I took him for a beer when I got out. (*Pause.*) So, now Martin has the day care, his crew hangs out on your block. (*Beat.*) And you and me are gonna do what? We're gonna perform this amazing feat of getting my sorry wheelchair into your extremely yellow house? That's what you want to do?

ABIGAIL: It is. You're not allergic to cats are you? I have four cats. The number of cats roaming around this neighborhood—not fixed—starving—it's disgraceful.

HENRY: I'm not allergic to cats.

ABIGAIL: (*taking hold of the wheelchair*) Okay. We can do this. You ready?

HENRY: Ready for liftoff. This definitely reminds me of the time I was the first guy to walk in space. (*As* ABIGAIL *leans the wheelchair back and starts to bring it up the couple porch steps.*) I am ready.

(*The lights go down, and then out.*)

A WHOLE HOUSE FULL OF BABIES

Sean O'Connor

A Whole House Full of Babies was first produced at Cap 21 Stage in New York City, on April 21, 2002. Patricia Henritze directed the following cast:

SHEILA   Libby Pokel
RENO   Robin Barnier

CHARACTERS

SHEILA and RENO: Both sixteen-year-old girls.

SETTING: A somewhat secluded grassy area on the edge of a county fair. The lights of the rides twinkle in the background and the faint strains of carnival music and occasional faraway shouts of children filter in throughout the scene. A discarded crate sits on the ground.

TIME: A summer night. Present day.

(*At rise:* RENO *stands upstage left and watches her friend* SHEILA, *who is barefoot and a little drunk, weave her way downstage with a can of cheap beer.*)

RENO: You all right?

SHEILA: I had too much to drink. (SHEILA *sits down on the grass.*)

RENO: You gonna sit down on the grass? You gonna get your butt wet. You wanna get your butt wet?

SHEILA: Yeah. I wanna get my butt wet.

RENO: Come on, now. Let's get up. (SHEILA *shakes her head.*) All right. We'll just sit here and get our butts wet. (RENO *sits down next to* SHEILA. SHEILA *looks up at the stars.*)

SHEILA: The stars are all milky.

RENO: Well, that's the Milky Way.

SHEILA: They're wet.

RENO: Just like your butt?

SHEILA: Yeah. Just like my butt. (SHEILA *lies on the ground.*)

RENO: You ain't gonna last long out here like this. They're gonna find you on the ground and they're gonna toss you in the trash with the beer bottles and the candy-gum wrappers and the hot dog buns. They're gonna clean you up with the rest of the fair. They'll pack you up with the Ferris wheel and all the rides and animals. How'd you like that? To get packed away with the pigs?

SHEILA: I like pigs.

RENO: You like 'em? They stink.

SHEILA: They're cute. They're like little babies.

RENO: Don't start with that.

SHEILA: Little babies in their pens—no one to take care of them.

RENO: Your baby's got plenty of people to take care of him. He's got the doctor and the nurses—and pretty soon he'll have a nice young family with credentials—with a good job and brothers and sisters and a grandmother, probably. You can't take care of your baby.

SHEILA: I'm a tree. A tree without fruit.

RENO: Now, Sheila . . .

SHEILA: I have no fruit! (SHEILA *is standing up.*)

RENO: Sit down, Sheila. There's nothing you can do.

SHEILA: I'm gonna go get my baby back.

RENO: He's gone, Sheila. He's not yours, anymore.

SHEILA: Just 'cause I gave him away don't mean he's not mine! If I gave you my finger, it'd still be my finger, you'd just have it.

RENO: Your baby's not a finger.

SHEILA: It's unnatural.

RENO: People do it all the time.

SHEILA: I never had anything that was mine like that and I gave him away.

RENO: You couldn't handle him by yourself.

SHEILA: You could help me. You could help me raise him.

RENO: Sheila, you know that's impossible.

SHEILA: Why? Why is that impossible? We were always best friends way back since we was kids. I wish it was your baby, Reno. If that was possible.

RENO: Well, it's not.

SHEILA: But it could be like that. You could be like the man and I'll be like the woman. It was always kinda like that with me and you.

RENO: Honey, I'm sorry you had a baby you can't take care of. But I can't take care of a baby, neither. Besides, they won't let us take him back.

SHEILA: They'll let us—they will. If they see how much we love him.

RENO: You already signed the papers.

SHEILA: When they see our love—our love'll burn right through those papers. Those papers don't mean nothing but a bunch of words. They can't take away my love with a bunch of words.

RENO: It's not your love they care about. It's your word. And you gave your word that you didn't want your baby.

SHEILA: I changed my mind!

RENO: It's too late now.

SHEILA: No, it's not! (SHEILA *starts to walk away.*)

RENO: Where are you going?

SHEILA: I'm going to get my baby.

RENO: In your bare feet? (SHEILA *looks down at her feet.*)

SHEILA: What happened to my shoes?

RENO: You threw them off the Ferris wheel.

SHEILA: Well, we need to get them so I can get my baby.

RENO: Sheila—you can't even hold onto a pair of shoes. How are you gonna take care of a baby?

SHEILA: Well, I was mad.

RENO: I know. What happens when you're mad and you throw your baby out the window 'cause he won't stop crying?

SHEILA: I wouldn't throw my baby out the window.

RENO: How do you know that? What do you know about raising babies?

SHEILA: My momma raised me when she was only fourteen.

RENO: And look what happened. (*Beat.*)

SHEILA: You're not my friend.

RENO: Yes, I am.

SHEILA: No, you're not. If you were my friend, you'd drive me to the hospital right now and get my baby back. If it was your baby, I'd drive you to the hospital—if I could drive. But you're jealous 'cause I can have a baby and you can't. You can't get a boyfriend.

RENO: I don't want a boyfriend that gets me pregnant and leaves with the fair.

SHEILA: It's not his fault. He had to go.

RENO: Well, he didn't come back, did he?

SHEILA: He probably had another fair to go to. There's a lot of fairs around the country. Sometimes it's not the same fair that comes to town as it was the year before. Sometimes they don't have the same Ferris wheel. Sometimes they have the kind with the cages on it and sometimes they have the kind that are open and you can dangle your feet and lose your shoes and feel like you're flying or like you're falling.

Sometimes it's like you're falling and flying all at once and you can't tell the difference.

RENO: Especially when you have too much to drink.

SHEILA: Even without drinking. Even without losing your baby or your boyfriend or your best friend. Even when I'm not on the Ferris wheel, I feel like I'm floating in a box above the world—and all the lights are so far away I can't tell which one is home. They might as well be the stars in the sky for all the good they do me. They might as well just disappear like the stars in the morning, like the fair every year, like my baby. (*Pause.*)

RENO: You haven't lost your best friend, Sheila.

SHEILA: Would you have given up your baby? If it was yours?

RENO: I don't know, Sheila. Probably. (SHEILA *goes and sits on the ground by* RENO, *who has sat down on the crate.*) You wanna go home?

SHEILA: No.

RENO: You want me to take you to the hospital?

SHEILA: I don't think they'd give him back.

RENO: Probably not.

SHEILA: I can't raise a baby. Not in my house. My daddy would throw me out. I don't have anywhere else to go.

RENO: I know.

SHEILA: I can't live by myself, Reno. I'm not like you. I can't do it by myself.

RENO: I wouldn't, either.

SHEILA: But you could. If you wanted to. If I was like you, I'd raise a whole house full of babies by myself. But I'm not like you. I wish I was. I hope my baby gets someone like you. (SHEILA *rests her head on* RENO's *lap.* RENO *strokes* SHEILA's *hair as the lights fade.*)

CONTRIBUTORS

TAYLOR MAC BOWYER's plays include *The Hot Month* (Ensemble Studio Theatre's *Next-Step Fellowship*), *Red Tide Blooming*, *Blue Grotto*, *Dilating* (an evening of one-acts) and the solo play *Okay*. He has performed in venues such as Joe's Pub, FEZ, and the San Francisco Opera House. Acting credits include work with the Jean Cocteau Repertory, Circle East, and many regional theatres across the country.

LAURA SHAINE CUNNINGHAM is the author of *Sleeping Arrangements* and *A Place in the Country*, first published in *The New Yorker* magazine, and now in hardcover and paperback editions. Her plays have been produced at Steppenwolf Theatre, in New York and London. Her first play, *Beautiful Bodies*, appears in *Plays for Actresses* and is widely produced.

ANTHONY DAVID, who received his Ph.D. from the University of Chicago, is a historian who has spent most of his adult life in Germany and Israel. David has published a book on the German-Jewish scholar of the Kabbalah, Gershom Scholem (Harvard University Press, 2001). In 2003, Metropolitan Books published his book *The Patron*.

STEVEN DIETZ's twenty-plus plays and adaptations have been seen at over one hundred regional theatres, as well as off-Broadway. International productions of his work have been seen in England, France, Germany, Japan, Australia, Argentina, Peru, Singapore, Slovenia, and South Africa. He lives in Seattle, Washington.

CHRISTOPHER DURANG was born in Montclair, New Jersey. He is author of *A History of the American Film*, *Sister Mary Ignatius Explains It All for You*, *Beyond Therapy*, *Laughing Wild*, *The Marriage of Bette and Boo*, *Betty's Summer Vacation*, and *Durang Durang*. He is one third of the cabaret act "Chris Durang and Dawne."

LINDA EISENSTEIN's plays and musicals include *Three the Hard Way*, *Rehearsing Cyrano*, *Discordia*, *Star Wares: The Next Generation*, and twenty-four one-act plays. Her work has been produced in New York, regionally, and abroad. Awards include the Gilmore Creek Playwriting Competition, Sappho's Symposium Competition, and three Ohio Arts Council Fellowships. She is a member of the Cleveland Play House Playwrights' Unit.

SIMON FILL was born in Hong Kong. His full-length plays include *Post Punk Life* and *Naked Under Your Clothes*. *Night Visits* won the Heideman Award from Actors Theatre of Louisville. He was an A.S.K. exchange playwright with the Royal Court Theatre. His plays have been produced in New York City, regionally, and internationally.

CRAIG FOLS is an actor and playwright who has been working on new plays in New York for several years. As an actor, he has appeared notably in Lanie Robertson's *Nasty Little Secrets* at Primary Stages and in his own play *Buck Simple* at La Mama. He has received the Berrilla Kerr Playwriting Award and BMI's Harrington Award. His first play, *Buck Simple*, was published in *The Best American Short Plays 1994–95*.

SIGRID HEATH—actor, playwright, director, teacher, journalist—was a recipient of the Berrilla Kerr Playwriting Award in 2000. An active member of Actors & Writers, she contributes regularly to the annual short play festival. *Wingbone*, her one-woman play about aviatrix Beryl Markham, premiered at Actors & Writers and has seen several successful productions.

DAVID IVES is probably best known for his evenings of one-act comedies: *All In the Timing* (available from Vintage Books) and *Time Flies* (available from Grove). His young-adult novel *Monsieur Eek* is published by HarperCollins. His most recent play is the full-length comic fantasia *Polish Joke.*

CALEEN SINNETTE JENNINGS is professor of theatre and director of the theatre/music theatre program at American University in Washington, D.C. She teaches playwriting, acting, directing, and academic courses in theatre. She also directs for main stage. She is a recipient of a 1999 Kennedy Center Fund for New American Plays Award and a 2002 Heideman Award from the Actors Theatre of Louisville.

HONOUR KANE's plays have been produced by The Public Theatre New Works, Sydney's 1995 Mardi Gras Arts Festival, and Actors Theatre of Louisville. Her work has been developed by London's Royal Court Theatre, the Australian National Playwrights Conference, and Portland Center Stage. A member of New Dramatists, she holds an NEA fellowship, a Bunting Fellowship at Radcliffe/Harvard, and a Pew Fellowship in the Arts.

ERIC LANE's *Times of War* premiered at the Adirondack Theatre Festival and has won numerous honors including the Berrilla Kerr Playwriting Award. Plays include *Shellac, Dancing on Checkers' Grave*, and *Cater-Waiter.* He has written and produced two short films, *First Breath* and *Cater-Waiter*, which he also directed. Honors include a Writers Guild Award, the La Mama Playwright Development Award, and numerous Yaddo fellowships.

EDWARD BOK LEE was born in Fargo, North Dakota, and educated throughout the United States, Korea, Russia, and Central Asia. Performing venues of his plays include the Taipei Theatre, Trinity Repertory Company, Theater Mu, and the Guthrie Theater Lab. A two-time national Jerome Fellow at the Playwrights' Center in Minneapolis, he also writes poetry, spoken word, and fiction.

WARREN LEIGHT's *Side Man* won multiple awards, including the 1999 Tony Award for Best Play. His other recent plays include *Glimmer, Glimmer and Shine*; *No Foreigners Beyond This Point*; and *James and Annie*. Warren is the vice president of the Writers Guild of America, East council, a member of the Dramatists Guild council, and a writer/producer on *Law & Order: Criminal Intent*.

ROMULUS LINNEY is the author of three novels, many short stories, and about twenty short and twenty full-length plays, staged throughout the United States and abroad. They include *The Sorrows of Frederick*, *Holy Ghosts*, *Heathen Valley*, *Childe Byron*, and *2*. He is a member of the American Academies of Arts and Sciences and Arts and Letters.

DONALD MARGULIES received the 2000 Pulitzer Prize for his play *Dinner with Friends*. His plays include *Collected Stories, The Model Apartment*, *What's Wrong with This Picture?*, *The Loman Family Picnic*, and *Found a Peanut*. Honors include an Obie Award, grants from the Guggenheim Foundation, NYFA, and the NEA. Mr. Margulies is an instructor at Yale University and a council member of the Dramatists Guild.

SUSAN MILLER won the 2002 Susan Smith Blackburn Prize for her play *A Map of Doubt and Rescue*. She holds two Obie Awards for *Nasty Rumors and Final Remarks* and *My Left Breast*, which premiered in Louisville's Humana Festival. Other plays include *Flux* and *It's Our Town, Too*, and the indie film *Lady Beware*, starring Diane Lane. Miller is currently a consulting producer on the Showtime series, *Earthlings*. She is recipient of a 2003 John Simon Guggenheim fellowship in playwriting.

CHIORI MIYAGAWA's plays include *Nothing Forever*, published in *Positive/Negative Women*; *Jamaica Avenue*, published in *Tokens?*

The NYC Asian American Experience on Stage; *Woman Killer*, published in *Plays & Playwright 2001*; and *Yesterday's Window* published in *Take Ten*. She is a recipient of many grants and awards, including a 2002 Alfred Sloan/Ensemble Studio Theatre Commission.

ITAMAR MOSES's plays include *Outrage* (Bloomington Playwrights Project New Play Award) and *Bach at Leipzig* (Southwest Theatre Association New Play Award; Dallas Playwrights Theatre New Play Award; S. F. Playwrights Center New Play Award). He holds a B.A. from Yale University, an M.F.A. in Dramatic Writing from NYU's Tisch School of the Arts, and is an active member of the Dramatists Guild.

SEAN O'CONNOR is a writer, actor, and teacher. His plays have been performed at the Zipper Theatre, Ensemble Studio Theatre, The Neighborhood Playhouse, Cap 21 Stage, and New York Performance Works. He has an M.F.A. in Theatre from Sarah Lawrence College and lives in New York City.

MARK O'DONNELL's plays include *That's It, Folks!*, *Fables for Friends*, *Tots in Tinseltown*, and *Strangers on Earth*. He is the Tony Award–winning coauthor of the Broadway musical *Hairspray*. Among his books are *Vertigo Park*, *Getting Over Homer*, and *Let Nothing You Dismay*. His humor has appeared in *The New Yorker*, *Spy*, *McSweeney's*, *The Atlantic*, and *Esquire*.

DAEL ORLANDERSMITH was a finalist for the 2002 Pulitzer Prize in Drama for *Yellowman* and the 1999 Susan Smith Blackburn Award and is the recipient of a New York Foundation for the Arts Fellowship and the Helen Merrill Award for Emerging Playwrights. Her plays include *Liar, Liar*, *Beauty's Daughter* (Obie Award), *Monster*, and *The Gimmick*.

RICH ORLOFF is one of five playwrights to receive the 2003 Dramatists Guild playwriting fellowship. A prolific author of short plays, four of his one-act comedies have been published in the annual *Best American Short Plays* anthology series. More about Rich's plays, including his ten award-winning full-length comedies, can be found at his website, richorloff.com.

JOE PINTAURO is a playwright, poet, and fiction writer. His plays include *Snow Orchid*, *Raft of the Medusa*, *Men's Lives*, and *The Dead Boy*. He has written several award-winning books of poetry and the novels *State of Grace* and *Cold Hands*, which *The New York Times* named one of the best novels of the year. Pintauro was the recipient of the 2001 chair in Theatre, at Saint Mary's, Notre Dame.

CRAIG POSPISIL is the author of *Months on End* and *Somewhere in Between*, which are published by Dramatists Play Service and have been produced in New York, Los Angeles, and around the country. Other plays include *The Dunes*, *Catch as Catch Can*, and numerous short plays written for the stage and radio. He edited the collections *Outstanding Men's Monologues 2001–2002* and *Outstanding Women's Monologues 2001–2002*.

TONI PRESS-COFFMAN's plays have been performed at theatres throughout the country, including productions at Actors Theatre of Louisville's Humana Festival and Purple Rose Theatre. Plays include *Touch*, *Stand*, *Bodies and Hearts*, and *Trucker Rhapsody*. Honors include an NEA/TCG Playwright Residency, an Arizona Commission on the Arts grant, and the Brodkin Award. She lives in Tucson, Arizona.

CLAIRE REEVE was born and raised in New York City. *Stuck* is Ms. Reeve's first published play. Currently employed as a social worker, Ms. Reeve studies playwriting with Tina Howe.

ELAINE ROMERO's plays have appeared at Actors Theatre of Louisville, the Women's Project and Productions, Arizona Theatre Company, and The Working Theatre. She has been a guest artist at South Coast Repertory and the Mark Taper Forum.

The Pew Foundation and the NEA have supported her award-winning plays, which are published by Samuel French, Smith and Kraus, and UA Press.

SUSAN SANDLER's plays include *Crossing Delancey*, *The Moaner*, *The Renovation*, and *The Burial Society*. Her plays have been produced in New York City, at regional theatres across the country, and around the world. She is a playwright member of HB Playwrights' Theater and Ensemble Studio Theatre. Screenplays and teleplays for Warner Brothers, 20th Century Fox, Hallmark, and CBS include *Crossing Delancey* and *Friends at Last*.

NINA SHENGOLD won the ABC Playwright Award for *Homesteaders* and the Writers Guild Award for *Labor of Love*. Her ten-minute plays (including *Finger Food*, *Women and Shoes*, *Everything Must Go*, *Handyman Special*, *There Goes the Neighborhood*, *No Shoulder*, *Forty to Life*, and others) are widely performed. She has just completed her first novel, *Clearcut*.

DIANA SON is the author of *Boy*, *Fishes*, *R.A.W. ('Cause I'm a Woman)* and *Stop Kiss*. They have been produced at The Joseph Papp Public Theatre, LaJolla Playhouse, Actors Theatre of Louisville, Seattle Rep, Woolly Mammoth, and others. *Stop Kiss* was nominated for an Outer Critics Circle and a Drama League award. She is a member of New Dramatists and the Dramatists Guild.

ALISON WEISS is a native of Manhattan, where her plays have been workshopped and produced at Ensemble Studio Theatre and HERE Arts Center. As an actress she has appeared in New York theatre productions including *Spike Heels* (NYU) and *Boys' Life* at the Blue Heron Arts Center (Walter Carlson Players).

MARY LOUISE WILSON coauthored the play *Full Gallop*, which had a successful run off-Broadway and subsequently in London,

France, Italy, Australia, Brazil, and regional theatres in the United States. She has written articles for *The New York Times*, *American Theatre*, and *The New Yorker*. She is also a veteran actor of stage, television, and film.

GARTH WINGFIELD's other plays include *Are We There Yet?*, *Sunday Styles*, *Flight*, *Touching Howard There*, *Cha-Cha-Cha*, and *Adonis*. His work has been performed in New York, Los Angeles, and London. For television, he has written episodes for Showtime's *Queer As Folk* and was a staff writer on the ABC sitcom *Clueless*. He lives in New York City.

ALEXANDER WOO accepts responsibility for such plays as *Forbidden City Blues* (Pan Asian Repertory, New York, New York), *Debunked* (Triad Stage, Greensboro, North Carolina), *In the Sherman Family Wax Museum* (Circle X, Los Angeles, California), and *Post-Coitals, Pre-Nuptials* (S. F. Stage & Film, San Francisco, California). He is a graduate of Yale Drama and Princeton University.

ABOUT THE EDITORS

NINA SHENGOLD and ERIC LANE are editors of nine contemporary
  play collections. Anthologies for Vintage Books include *Take
  Ten: New Ten-Minute Plays*, *Plays for Actresses*, and *Leading
  Women: Plays for Actresses II*. For Viking Penguin, they edited
  The Actor's Book of Contemporary Stage Monologues, *The Actor's
  Book of Scenes from New Plays*, *Moving Parts: Monologues from
  Contemporary Plays*, *The Actor's Book of Gay & Lesbian Plays*
  (Lambda Literary Award Nomination), and *Telling Tales*.

NINA SHENGOLD received the ABC Playwright Award & the L.A.
  Weekly Award for *Homesteaders*, published by Samuel French.
  Her play *War at Home*, written with Nicole Quinn and the
  students of Rondout Valley High School, is forthcoming
  from Playscripts Inc. Ms. Shengold won the 1998 Writers
  Guild Award and a GLAAD Award nomination for her tele-
  play *Labor of Love*, starring Marcia Gay Harden, and the Shine
  Award for *Unwed Father*; other screenplays include *Blind Spot*,
  starring Joanne Woodward and Laura Linney, *Double Plat-
  inum*, and an adaptation of Jane Smiley's novella *Good Will*.
  She is artistic director of theatre company Actors & Writers,
  and has just completed her first novel, *Clearcut*.

ERIC LANE is an award-winning playwright and filmmaker. His
  play *Times of War* premiered at the Adirondack Theatre Festival and won grants from the Puffin Foundation, Pilgrim Project, and Jonathan Larson Foundation and was an O'Neill
  Center Finalist. Other plays include *Shellac*, *Cater-Waiter*, and

Dancing on Checkers' Grave, which starred Jennifer Aniston. Mr. Lane has written and produced two short films: *First Breath* and *Cater-Waiter*, which he also directed. For his work on TV's *Ryan's Hope*, he received a Writer's Guild Award. Honors include the Berrilla Kerr Playwriting Award, La Mama Playwright Development Award, numerous Yaddo fellowships, and a St. James Cavalier Center fellowship in Malta. Mr. Lane is an honors graduate of Brown University and is artistic director of Orange Thoughts, a not-for-profit theatre and film company in New York City.

INDEX

*F=Female, M=Male

PERMISSIONS ACKNOWLEDGMENTS

and of all countries covered by the Pan-American Copyright Convention, the Universal Copyright Convention, the Berne Convention and of all other countries with which the United States has reciprocal copyright relations. All rights, including professional/amateur stage rights, motion picture, recitation, lecturing, public reading, radio broadcasting, television, video or sound recording, all other forms of mechanical or electronic reproduction, such as CD-ROM, CD-I, information storage and retrieval systems and photocopying, and the rights of translation into foreign languages are strictly reserved. Particular emphasis is laid on the question of readings, permission for which must be secured from the author's agent in writing.

The stage performance rights in *Kitty the Waitress* (other than first-class rights) are controlled exclusively by Dramatists Play Service, 440 Park Avenue South, New York, NY 10016. No professional or non-professional performance of the Play (excluding first-class professional performance) may be given without obtaining in advance the written permission of Dramatists Play Service, and paying the requisite fee.

Inquiries concerning all other rights should be addressed to Helen Merrill Ltd., 295 Lafayette Street, Suite 915, New York, NY 10012.

Linda Eisenstein: *A Rustle of Wings* by Linda Eisenstein, copyright © 1998 by Linda Eisenstein. Reprinted by permission of the author.

Inquiries contact: Linda Eisenstein, 1378 W. 64th St., Cleveland, OH 44102, Tel. 216-961-5624, www.lindaeisenstein.com.

Simon Fill: *Night Visits* by Simon Fill, copyright © 2000 by Simon Fill. All rights reserved. Reprinted by permission of the author.

CAUTION: Professionals and amateurs are hereby notified that *Night Visits* is subject to a royalty. The play is fully protected under the copyright laws of the United States of America, and of all countries covered by the International Copyright Union (including the Dominion of Canada and the rest of the British Commonwealth), and of all countries covered by the Pan-American Copyright Convention and the Universal Copyright Convention, and of all other countries with which the United States has reciprocal copyright relations. All rights, including professional, amateur, motion picture, recitation, lecturing, public reading, radio broadcasting, television, video or sound taping, all other forms of mechanical or electronic reproduction, such as information storage and retrieval systems and photocopying, and all rights of translation into foreign languages, are strictly reserved. All inquiries should be addressed to Susan Schulman: A Literary Agency, 454 West 44th Street, New York, NY 10036, Attn: Susan Schulman. E-Mail: Schulman@aol.com. Tel. 212-713-1633; Fax. 212-581-8830.

"El Santo Americano" was originally commissioned by the Guthrie Theater (Joe Dowling, Artistic Director).

For all other rights contact: Edward Bok Lee, 246-1 West Naomi Dr., Naples, FL 34104, Tel. 612-722-9027.

Warren Leight: *Nine Ten* by Warren Leight, copyright © 2001 by Swingline Productions, Inc. Reprinted by permission of the author.

Inquiries contact: George Lane, The William Morris Agency, 1325 Avenue of the Americas, New York, NY 10019.

Romulus Linney: *The Cure* by Romulus Linney, copyright © 2002 (first published in *Bright Pages,* Yale University Press, 2002). Reprinted by permission of the author.

Inquiries contact: Peter Hagan, The Gersh Agency, 41 Madison Avenue, 33rd Floor, New York, NY 10010.

Donald Margulies: *Space* by Donald Margulies. Reprinted by permission of the author.

Susan Miller: *The Grand Design* by Susan Miller. Reprinted by permission of the author.

Inquiries contact: Carl Mulert, The Joyce Ketay Agency, 1501 Broadway, suite 1908, New York, NY 10036. E-mail: carl@joyceketay.com.

Chiori Miyagawa: *Antigone's Red* by Chiori Miyagawa, copyright © 2002 by Chiori Miyagawa. Reprinted by permission of the author.

Inquiries contact: Morgan Jenness, Helen Merrill Ltd., 295 Lafayette Street, New York, NY 10012, Tel. 212-226-5015.

Itamar Moses: *Men's Intuition* by Itamar Moses, copyright © 2003. Reprinted by permission of Mark Christian Subias, The William Morris Agency, Inc., on behalf of Itamar Moses.

Inquiries contact: Mark Christian Subias, The William Morris Agency, Inc., 3125 Avenue of the Americas, New York, NY 10019.

Sean O'Connor: *A Whole House Full of Babies* by Sean O'Connor, copyright © 2003 by Sean O'Connor. Reprinted by permission of the author.

Inquiries contact: Sean O'Connor, 101 Quaint Acres Dr., Silver Spring, MD 20904. E-mail: seanpolka@aol.com.

Mark O'Donnell: *Marred Bliss* by Mark O'Donnell, copyright © 1989 by Mark O'Donnell. Reprinted by permission of Mark O'Donnell. Commissioned and first produced by Actors Theatre of Louisville.

CAUTION: Professionals and amateurs are hereby warned that *Marred Bliss* is subject to a royalty. It is fully protected under the copyright laws of the United States of America, and of all countries covered by the Inter-

Inquiries contact: Peregrine Whittlesey, Agent, 345 E. 80th St., #31-F, New York, NY 10021, Tel. 212-737-0153.

Claire Reeve: *Stuck* by Claire Reeve, copyright © 2003. Reprinted by permission of the author.

Inquiries contact: Claire Reeve, 509 E. 78th St., Apt. #5-D, New York, NY 10021.

Susan Sandler: *The Find* by Susan Sandler, copyright © 2003. Reprinted by permission of the author.

Inquiries contact: Mitch Douglas, ICM, 40 West 57th St., New York, NY 10025.

Nina Shengold: *Emotional Baggage* by Nina Shengold. Reprinted by permission of the author.

Inquiries contact: Phyllis Wender, Rosenstone/Wender, 38 East 29th St., 10th Floor, New York, NY 10016, Tel. 212-725-9445.

Diana Son: *The Moon Please* by Diana Son, copyright © 2001 by Diana Son. Reprinted by permission of the author.

Inquiries concerning all rights should be addressed to Sarah Jane Leigh, ICM, 40 West 57th St., New York, NY 10019.

Alison Weiss: *Fight Dreams* by Alison Weiss, copyright © 2001 by Alison Weiss. All rights reserved. Reprinted by permission of the author.